FROM THIS DAY FORWARD

Esme Cromer

From This Day Forward

ESME CROMER

**Thomas Harmsworth
Publishing Company,
Stoke Abbott**

© 1991 Esme Cromer
First Published 1991

Cover photo: Photographer — Snowdon
Reproduced from British Vogue by kind permission of
© The Conde Nast Publications Ltd

British Library Cataloguing in Publication Data
Cromer, Esme, *1922-*
From this day forward
I. Title
327.2092

ISBN 0948807148

Printed and bound in Great Britain by
Bookcraft Ltd. Midsomer Norton, Nr Bath

PREFACE

Many years ago it fell to my lot to have the good fortune to dine alone with Nancy, Viscountess Astor at her home at Sandwich in Kent. On being admitted I met in the hall a harassed American lady who, not realising my acquaintance with Lady Astor was slight, implored me to try to persuade her to write her memoirs. I promised to do what I could, and broached the subject during dinner. Her response was emphatic: 'only great egoists and the self-centred wish to write about themselves, and I am not one of them.' I admired her then, as I do now, and indeed, perhaps she is right.

Esme Cromer

ARMY WIFE

1

SHOELESS IN FLEET STREET

Saturday, January 10th 1942 was our wedding day, and I left the Ritz Hotel on my father's arm to be married to a soldier: a soldier called Captain The Viscount Errington, only twenty-three years of age and young to hold the rank of Captain in the Grenadier Guards.

Outside, the streets were clean. Cleaner far than fifty years on. The broken glass which covered Piccadilly like a giant storm of hail, had long been swept away. The lull in the bombing had been a long one, people had resumed their ordinary life as they always did, when given the chance, and continued with their business as usual.

The day broke sunny and cold. A pale wintry light shone on grimy, pitted walls; cavities where the walls had dropped to reveal rooms partitioned like dolls houses, infinitely pathetic. The wall coverings of each room, from the cheap striped paper of the attic to the grander silk damask of the downstairs rooms, all obscenely exposed to the world. But these were noble battle scars which the beloved city wore with pride.

Gone were the great black iron railings that had protected the Royal Parks, the iron melted down for guns. Trenches slit through the green sward, with the double intention of preventing any aerial landings and providing some shelter. In Hyde Park batteries of anti-aircraft guns were manned, while barrage balloons shaped like miniature airships floated above. A far cry from the days when the Parks were full of grazing sheep and Nannie would scold when our white boots came home covered in dung. Sandbags were piled around the entrances to public buildings, most people wore uniform and the traffic was sparse.

Our engagement had been a short one, as was customary at that time, for there were few preparations to be made. No new home to refurbish or to furnish. No rooms in romantic places to be reserved for a honeymoon. No trousseau other than one new suit and dress due to clothing rationing and the need for coupons. No bridal retinue, no invitations to be written and no icing even for the wedding cake.

My wedding dress provided no problems, for lace and fine net were not rationed, and with these materials Victor Stiebel produced a pretty gown. My mother-in-law had kindly given me her family veil which, being made of fine net with a deep border of old Brussels lace, made a perfect match for the dress. There was, however, a sad set-back: neither the shop that had cleaned and rebacked the veil, nor my family, had pointed out that some means of attaching the veil to my head would be necessary. So on the morning of the wedding itself I removed the veil from its nest of tissue paper, to be confronted with this problem. Alone at the Ritz, with the help of a chambermaid, we contrived, at more or less at the last minute, to attach the veil with the aid of hairpins to my hair. The result looked decidedly homespun, and by no means could it be said to be safely secured. The slow procession up the aisle was somewhat disconcerting, as was the rest of the ceremony, for at any moment it was more than possible that the fairly heavy veil and I would be parted.

There were other problems to an otherwise happy day. Rowley had chosen a brother officer, Captain Richard Rasch, to be best man. It was an excellent choice and no-one could have performed his duties better, but he was a person of short stature, and I had always been very self-conscious of my height. With the vanity and unconcern-for-comfort of a nineteen-year-old, and in spite of the cold, I wore no shoes.

Rowley, in his turn, had called on the Vicar-General to obtain a special marriage licence, for at that time neither of us possessed a London address. When Rowley was asked the name of his prospective bride's father he had to confess that he was not certain, and that it might be Esmond Harmsworth. A slightly amused Vicar-General gently explained that perhaps it might be best to make sure by looking him up. To Rowley's surprise it was found to be Viscount Rothermere. This was not as strange as it might seem, for in wartime country seats and large London houses had been requisitioned, as had my father's. Instead, my father had rented a modest, pretty little house near Ascot for the Duration. His domestic staff had been reduced to two: his old cook and a kitchen maid. This had hardly given Rowley much idea of the circumstances of the family from which he had selected a wife.

The church that we had chosen was St Dunstan's-in-the-West. It was so described because it is west of the City. Its appeal to Rowley was the shortness of the aisle; to my father because it had connections with my family, being situated in Fleet Street. My great-uncle, Alfred Northcliffe, had been a supporter and his bust decorated the front wall of the church.

When Rowley and I visited the vicar to discuss dates, times and the service, he listened to us for some time before asking us when we expected the coffin to arrive. We had possibly been unclear, through shyness; also a wedding was almost unheard of in that particular church. We were both embarrassed and somewhat mortified. The clergyman who actually officiated at the service, however, was the Reverend W H Elliott, the Precentor of the Chapels Royal, who had prepared me for confirmation, and who arranged for the choir from the chapel to sing. This met with the approval of my mother-in-law, who used to listen to his broadcasts when he had been the Radio Parson, and who much admired him. She did not, however, take so kindly to the singing of the Ave Maria, which I had especially chosen without realising that it is more usually sung in Catholic churches. My mother, being a catholic, had made it familiar, but brought up by my father as a Protestant, I made no clear distinctions between the two. Not so my mother-in-law, who was a Presbyterian by upbringing, and she was, therefore, somewhat disconcerted.

My mother and her four sisters all chose to wear black, as did my mother-in-law which doubtless pleased the vicar and made him feel more at home as he assisted at the service. The Reception was held at the Savoy Hotel. The guests mingled, or kept to themselves, and there must have been some comic moments, since my father, instead of sending out invitations, had inserted a notice in *The Times* announcing that all friends would be welcome. With rationing, no doubt people arrived who were complete outsiders, and with scope for each family thinking, mistakenly, that they were members of the other, there must have been some rather funny encounters.

Our honeymoon was spent at my parents-in-law's small house on the edge of Exmoor. Never having visited it before, and the country being spectacularly beautiful, it was not a bad choice for our ten-day honeymoon. For Rowley too, because he was able to show me his childhood home, and introduce me to the village people who had known and loved him as a boy.

The day after our wedding the newspapers were full of photographs and descriptions. It was still the custom, even with the shortage of wartime newsprint, to cover important weddings in detail. No longer were there lists of wedding presents and who had given them, but still careful descriptions of the bridal attire and who had attended both church and reception. I looked anxiously the following morning, dreading what I might find, for the perilously-attached veil had no connecting small one that customarily covers the face, and I had only been told at the reception that only ladies of royal blood appeared at the church as a bride with an uncovered face. Happily, nothing of a critical nature was mentioned. In fact it was to the contrary. One reporter had been carried away to the extent of writing: 'like a fairy princess, she looked as if she had stepped out of some old-world picture by Reynolds or Whistler, and one corner of her veil was fastened to her head by a single silver cord'! I had got off lightly! *Swaffer's Press News* printed how glad they were that the Rothermere Press had dealt so modestly with Esme Harmsworth's wedding, unlike other newspaper proprietors over their own family happenings.

Before the war, daughters of the English leisure classes made up from aristocratic and wealthy mercantile families, were not considered to be destined for any other career than marriage. With few exceptions, schoolgirl daughters were intended for the Altar. This gave them no feeling of sacrifice. On the contrary, nothing else was considered to be an option, and the idea itself was wreathed in romance. Their fathers, who wished in the first place for sons, hoped that any daughters born would be pretty and therefore easily disposed of in marriage. The preparation for such a future was curious and presumably inspired by an earlier age. Education was sketchy, and not considered significant. If a brainy daughter should, by chance, enter the nest, she was well advised to minimise her intelligence. As a grown-up woman she would be expected at best to be pretty, witty, well-mannered and well-dressed; little else, if anything, was required. She was also, if pretty, expected to make a good match, and the sooner the better, and to be 'off father's hands' at an early age.

After a somewhat poor education at school or by a governess, she would be sent to be 'polished' at a finishing school. The appreciation of Art and Music, deportment, and a smattering of another language or two which might be hazily learned; if in Paris, a little chic might rub off. This was often the sole training for a future life: a life like their parents', in which they would be waited upon by a household of domestic servants for the rest of their lives. Earlier, in their childhood, riding was obligatory. Character was forged in the hunting field or on the playing fields at school, where to fall or be hurt was not treated with sympathy. Up and off again immediately,

7

unless severely injured, was the rule.

None of this preparation, with the exception of the last, was any help at all for the lives we were actually to lead. We would be totally unfitted for the challenges that would be encountered as wartime army wives.

It was not until the week before my wedding that the awesome thought entered my mind that I might be expected to cook a meal. At the various restaurants and nightclubs we had attended together Rowley had never once asked me whether I could cook. As it was, my culinary skills were nil. Housekeeping and housework, too, were a closed book. I did, however, know First Aid and Home Nursing, having been a member of the St John Nursing Brigade, and worked as a nurse at St Bartholomew's Hospital in the City up to the time of our wedding. Therefore I was at least conversant with bedpans and bandages, vomit bowls and hygiene, and most useful of all, knew how to make a bed better than most.

Rowley was a Staff Captain of the 33rd Guards Brigade in the defence of London, his headquarters, a substantial old house in the undistinguished suburb called Hatch End. He had, with some pride, found a furnished villa to rent, whose back yard gave on to the overgrown grounds of the HQ to which he was able to gain admittance over a broken fence. It was to this house that he took me after our honeymoon. I had not seen it before, which was just as well. The only furniture that we possessed was a new divan bed, a small table, some lamps, and a little good linen. A splendid satin eiderdown and a lace bedspread was an island of comfort in a desert of cheap, shoddy and ugly furniture. Still, it was our first home. Incredibly, I waited, wondering why dinner was so late appearing, before the dreadful realisation that there was no-one in the kitchen and we had no domestic staff.

Fortunately Rowley took astonishingly well the news that I could not cook, or even knew how to make a pot of tea: a ritual that sounded somewhat complicated when described in books. He had more domestic experience than I, being an Old

8

Etonian. He had, as a fag, learned the mystery of the teapot and, moreover, how to use the frying pan. I then invested in Mrs Beeton's *Complete Household Management* which, disappointingly, proved to be almost useless. It informed me that the first requisite for a cook was a stock pot. This, in a rather large quantity, I made from bones, scraps and vegetables. It took hours and resulted in a thin and tasteless brew which went bad before I could find any uses for it.

The only kitchen utensils that could be purchased were made of tin. Any better materials had gone into making bombs. They were flimsy and easily burned. Moreover, they went rusty unless quickly and carefully dried. The allowance of one elderly egg a month, two ounces of butter, four ounces of margarine and of sugar and the equivalent of two chops, four rashers of bacon and three ounces of cheese per person a week was hardly the basis for gourmet cooking. Sausages were unrationed, although their contents were rather suspect; glorious Spam a real treat. Sardines and golden syrup were obtainable on a system of points. Although undernourished, the people did not seem to suffer from salmonella, listeria or other contamination, although jaundice was prevalent.

Fortunately for me Rowley was able to live on a vague mixed fry-up for two weeks until I mastered some other dishes. If a dish was a failure it was a minor catastrophe, for to throw it away and start again with minute rations was impossible. Rowley took it all in good heart. He seemed to think that whatever I did was a marvel and I basked in his admiration.

The cold was unexpected. An icy February followed a chilly January. The little suburban house had no central heating. I could neither make a fire nor clean a grate, and fuel, in any case, was scarce. The rooms were glacial, and it took me some time, to my shame, to realise why it was so cold. Having taken central heating for granted, the lack of it came as an unwelcome surprise. The answer was to wear two or three thick sweaters at once, and sleep in them, too, until the next thaw.

My first attempts at catering were hilarious: 'half a pound

of potatoes, please' to an astonished greengrocer. Or a handful of fresh spinach, later cooked to vanishing point in a sauce-pan-ful of water. The most difficult achievement of all was to co-ordinate the various saucepans, for there was no place in the ancient gas cooker to keep anything warm.

Rowley, as Staff Captain, was allotted a Soldier Servant, whose duty it was to look after his uniform and see that he was immaculately turned out. In battle it was his duty also to dig a slit trench deep enough to sleep in. He occasionally condescended to help with the washing-up, which was greatly appreciated, particularly as there were no detergents (soap was rationed, and that left only household soda, which was very hard on the hands). To my relief, I discovered that this tall Guardsman not only knew how to make rice pudding, but was only too happy to cook one. As a child in Manchester it had been his steady diet in the Depression, and he knew how to make it to perfection. Never before or since has a rice pudding tasted as good, and we came to look forward to that humble dish as if it were the best Persian caviare.

We owned a small car, a Standard Eight, and drove around on an allowance of five gallons a month. This was not much, but better than none at all, which came later. After all, every pint was brought in at the risk of someone's life. There were no signposts, for all names of places, or indications of where they might be, had been removed. We navigated by means of Public Houses, especially in the maze of suburbs. 'Turn right at The Target and left at the Green Man' was the usual manner of giving directions.

Becoming the wife of a Guards Officer, even in wartime, had its pitfalls. There were words that should be uttered and others distinctly frowned upon. Possibly, every regiment had its 'in' words and phrases, and certainly every English public boys' school does. But a Guards officer's wife was expected to know, and woe betide her if she did not.

The most terrifying personage I was ever to meet was Rowley's then-commander, Brigadier Julian Jefferson: gruff when he was not silent. We were invited to dine with him and his even-more commanding wife. Intimidated by the brigadier's reputation as a stern martinet, the reality was worse. We sat mainly in an embarrassed silence, just the four of us, with no third party to ease the discomfort. Never was such an alarming evening to be experienced again. Also, I assumed that all senior army officers and their wives were equally blunt and forbidding, and decided to avoid them at all costs whenever possible in the future. This resolution was, however, shattered a year later after Rowley joined the Guards Armoured Division, and he told me that it was high time I met his new commander. 'But he is a general,' I protested. 'He will be even more frightening than the brigadier.' Rowley insisted and told me that now was as good a time as any, which seemed extraordinary, for walking towards us down a country lane was a slim, young-looking man with a kind face, who was gentle, charming, and unassuming as well. He was Sir Allan Adair, who proved to be a great commander, and successfully led the Guards Armoured Division through the invasion of France and the liberation of Belgium — a man for whom all who served under him would have died. Brigadier Jefferson was barely heard of again.

We had not been married more than three months when in the mail one morning a bombshell arrived in the shape of my call-up papers, commanding me to appear at the nearest branch of the Ministry of National Service as soon as possible. My customary daily garb was trousers and a pullover, and since the Ministry's branch was situated in a nearby suburb of no special merit or standing I saw no reason to dress in anything more formal. I therefore presented myself at the Ministry in my usual clothes, and carrying a shopping basket, for there was always a chance of finding something off the ration in a different place. Behind the counter a surly young female official proceeded to ask me questions in an officious and patronising manner. The fact that I was married and looking after my husband appeared to be of no consequence

11

whatsoever. 'What did you do before?' she asked. 'Nothing,' I nervously replied, naively thinking that only gainful employment was considered of any real account, and not yet having learned that in certain situations, particularly where jobs are concerned, it is always necessary to make the most of all small achievements. The official's reaction was one of anger, her voice rising as she told me I was a good-for-nothing and should be ashamed of myself. She ended triumphantly that, without a doubt, I would soon be called for service in the ATS (the women's army) which was short of recruits: a fate which filled me with the utmost horror. My pleadings were in vain, and I returned to Hatch End in utter despair and with deep forebodings. When Rowley heard my sorry tale he laughingly told me that I had not set about it in the right way. He sat down and composed a letter, which he addressed to the head of the same branch of the Ministry of National Service politely asking for an appointment in order to discuss my call-up.

My second appearance at the Ministry was very different from my earlier one. On the advice of Rowley I was attired in a formal coat, hat and gloves. The head of the branch proved to be a staid, old-fashioned and kindly lady who met us respectfully at the door and apologised for taking up our time. To my relief and astonishment she gently declared that I was obviously fully employed keeping house for a serving officer, so there was no reason to fear compulsory conscription at that particular time, although the threat did hang hazily in the future.

2

UP AND DOWN DALES

In December Rowley was promoted to the rank of major, as Deputy Assistant Adjutant and Quarter-Master General of his Brigade Group. At the same time my sister's husband, Neil Cooper-Key, who was some ten years older, became a captain. The timing of their promotions always tactlessly coincided. My father would laughingly tease Neil: 'What! Pipped again?'

In January 1943 Rowley was sent on an intensive training course at the Staff College in Camberley. This experience, if successful, would lead to further advancement in his military career. But the course was a formidable one, and known for the suicides that, tragically, took place — it was the pressure put on their mental abilities more than the test of physical endurance. Rowley had been considered a frail child, and highly strung as well, and at that time was very thin, but he came through it with flying colours, even enduring the added anxiety of a wife whose pregnancy was to be terminated in March by caesarian section, then considered a fairly major operation.

We took two rooms in a boarding house in Camberley where, on retiring for the night, various religious texts would reprove and caution us from the walls, and where we would wake in the morning to the sound of trains rattling past at the bottom of the small garden. The gas geyser in the bathroom was wont to blow up, and the neighbour's dog, after barking for four nights in succession, was eventually silenced by the local policeman after all appeals to the owner had failed.

Unfortunately, the timing of my caesarian coincided with the largest and, up to that time, most important military exercise mounted in Britain. Its code name was 'Spartan' and it was absolutely necessary for Rowley to take part in it. He was allowed compassionate leave on the actual day of the operation, but within an hour of the baby's delivery he left to return to the exercise.

The place of the birth was an old-fashioned nursing home in London, the choice of the surgeon who wished to do the matron a good turn. But the fact that it lacked a lift had escaped his notice. Walking up to the operating theatre on the top floor presented no difficulties. Coming down was a different matter. But since I was unconscious, it was not my problem.

The nursing home was situated in the centre of London, a position approved by all concerned, as being accessible to the surgeon who lived in Hertfordshire, and Rowley, wherever he might be at the time. The lull in the bombing continued, and it was just a little unfortunate that a sortie of enemy aeroplanes should chose the night of my operation to fly over the metropolis. Placed in a chair, I was carried awkwardly down a narrow staircase from the fourth floor to the basement by two stalwart nurses. No-one was sure at the time whether this might be a serious raid or not. In the cellar, patients were assembled in various stages of post-operative recovery or other indispositions, and hovering nurses took pulses and watched carefully for any signs of relapse. It brought to my notice for the first time the closeness of the giving and taking of life. Those who were very ill looked resigned; those with their new-born babies smiled at the incongruity of it all. It made me think that maybe all nursing homes and hospitals were like railway stations, with souls arriving and souls departing more or less at the same time.

It was not until ten days after the birth that Rowley was free and the arduous exercise was at last over. He rushed to London at the first opportunity and entered my carefully-sterilised room wearing battledress, to proudly and gently take his tiny first-born in his arms, the arms of a weather-beaten soldier, grimy with the dust and mud of the fields.

The following month Rowley was posted to the Guards Armoured Division as Deputy Assistant Adjutant-General especially in charge of personnel. At that time the Division sprawled over a particularly remote part of Norfolk. As a wartime army wife two choices were open: either to settle in one place and make occasional visits; or stay by one's husband's side in whatever place he might be sent. The first alternative was usually chosen by the longer-marrieds who had permanent homes and growing families. The young-marrieds, with no place of their own to keep up, opted for the second. I had engaged the formidable Nannie Brown to look after our baby daughter. She was not the sort of Nannie who took kindly to any makeshift accommodation, or anything less than the high standard she had been accustomed to before the war. Had I been aware of her starchy grandness I would never have engaged her. She was, however, totally reliable, and quite happy to devote herself to the baby without a day off, an annual holiday of three weeks being all she expected. This, at that time, suited us very well and I was able to leave her in sole charge, under either my father's or my mother's roof, to follow Rowley.

One never knew how long one would be in the same place, for at a moment's notice the army would move. The initial scramble for accommodation would be followed by a sudden abandonment. Those who had rented cottages were left with unexpired leases, for which there might be no demand, in places that had lost their appeal and which were remote as well. It was best to find something more adaptable, if possible.

Fortunately, Rowley's new Staff Captain, Michael Menzies, was occupying a flat with his wife (the former Kay Stammers) in an old manor house, and they kindly agreed to allow us to share it with them. As petrol was still strictly rationed none of us was able to bring a car; the small amount allowed would not have brought us as far as the Norfolk borders. So we depended on bicycles. Kay and I divided the household chores, and the venerable owners of the manor house would occasionally invite us to join them for lunch in their stately dining room. But like poor relations we hardly liked to invite them back to eat with us in what had been their old nursery wing. Besides, being country landowners of long duration, they knew where to find the odd pig or chicken. Our sojourn in Norfolk proved to be short, for the entire Division was ordered to Yorkshire.

For more than six years the people of Britain, other than those serving overseas, remained incarcerated in the Fortress Isle, for all travel was impossible. In compensation, the interior movement of the forces gave many people unique opportunities to see and to live in parts of the British countryside that otherwise might have remained unknown.

The new divisional location in Yorkshire was to be a large area between Scarborough and Malton, the headquarters staff to inhabit an imposing manor house in a village called Brompton-by-Sawdon, recently vacated by the local squire, Sir Kenhelm Cayley, who moved his family to a dower house close by.

The early scramble for accommodation was frenzied. Calls would be made on surrounding cottages or inns for any empty rooms, or even attics needing a little renovation. At first we put up at the local public house, the Cayley Arms. We ate pretty well, and even if our bedroom contained three double beds, it was not uncomfortable. There were other officers and their wives who lodged there too while looking for more permanent dwelling. The noise and pungent aroma of beer permeated the whole place, and sometimes we wives had to be very chary of the usually kindly publican who, after closing hours, would lurk behind a door and clutch at us as, unwary, we made for our bedrooms.

It was not long before Rowley found more permanent accommodation. It looked as if the Division would remain in

Yorkshire for some time. The sweeping Yorkshire Dales appeared to be most suitable for training for armoured warfare. As it turned out Sussex might have been better since, with its small hedge-bound fields and orchards, it was closer to the terrain of Normandy.

I had been on a visit south to see my baby at my mother's house in Dorset when Rowley telephoned with the exciting news that he had found a place; and, moreover, it was in the same village as the HQ — an enviable advantage for, being close to the seat of operations, it would be possible for him to have a direct army telephone installed, which would preclude his being called out during late or early hours when a problem arose which could just as easily be solved by telephone. In the keenness of his resolve to live as close to headquarters as possible he had, however, overlooked other important requirements.

He had taken two rooms in a small semi-detached cottage belonging to the squire and occupied by his butler's family. The butler had been called up. With three rooms upstairs and two down (one being the kitchen) the house was occupied by the butler's wife, their two sons and a land girl. It was not an old cottage, having been built shortly before the war. I entered the plain little house with some trepidation even though Rowley assured me that we were very lucky to have found it. 'The landlady says you may share her cooker and sink,' he rather doubtfully reassured me. I inspected our two rooms, one up and the other down, and the communal kitchen, with some reservation. A sneaking suspicion nagged at my mind, and I asked Rowley where the bathroom was supposed to be. 'Oh, that...' he replied. 'Well, there is a tiny cupboard in the kitchen which will make you laugh.' I cannot say that I did but, more important, when I asked him where the WC might be he told me that he had never thought of it. It was, to my dismay, situated in the garden, and had to be shared between six people. By that time there was really no other accommodation to be had and the thought of the proverbial cold

Yorkshire winters was hardly comforting.

It was, nevertheless, quite extraordinary how quickly we adapted ourselves to this rather primitive form of living. In those days there was no central heating: only one small fire lit in the evening, and a glass or two of port. And the fact that Lady Errington could be glimpsed on occasions groping her way down the garden at night with the aid of a small torch, and clothed in a nightdress, mink coat and gumboots, caused some merriment among the locals.

The old cottage dwellings of rural Yorkshire should have taught modern architects something about cosy family comfort. Their spacious kitchens were dominated by shiny black ranges with twinkling brass knobs. The room was warmed by a friendly fire, while a kettle gently hissed upon the hob, and in the side-ovens a savoury pie or brown stew bubbled peacefully to fill the room with a delicious aroma, mixed with the damp earthy smell of drying clothes and muddy boots. The weary farmer would doze in a comfortable chair while his wife knitted between occasional peeps at the cooking pots so close at hand. The one other downstairs room, the front parlour, smelled stale from lack of use, crammed with carefully-polished, uncomfortable furniture and old knick-knacks proudly-preserved, and was shown to visitors with quiet pride. The door was then firmly shut behind their backs and not opened again until the next caller.

In the village almost everyone's name was Mudd. They were the tenant farmers who had tilled the soil of the Cayleys' land for some hundreds of years. Humorous, loyal, rosy-cheeked people bursting with health. When I occasionally accompanied Lady Cayley on her regular rounds to see how they were, her opening remark was always the same: 'I do hope that you are feeling better, Mrs Mudd?' 'Oh, aye, but me back,' or sometimes it was 'me feet' or 'I've been real poorly, my lady.' I never once heard anyone admit to being in good health.

Once or twice a week the local bus took me the seven miles

into Scarborough for the foraging of food. I would scour the shops for some likely purchases, usually returning later, laden with a heavy basket. Sometimes, on Saturdays, Rowley would accompany me, but always it was made clear that under no circumstances could an officer in uniform be seen carrying a shopping basket. I could never understand the ethics of this principle and thought that it smacked of the Orient. Often we would argue about this trifling point, particularly when he sometimes passed me in his army car with driver. One day, as I was struggling along the narrow Scarborough pavements under the weight of two laden baskets, I came face to face with the General. 'Please allow me to help you,' he said, and overcoming my initial embarrassment and reluctance, he carried both my baskets all the way to the bus station, with his army car slowly following on behind. If only Rowley could see me now, I thought. And when, triumphantly, I recounted the incident to him, he replied: 'It does not mean that a junior officer can do what the General does.'

On other days I would take the bus and go in the opposite direction, to the small town of Pickering, where I found some voluntary work in the Food Office counting minute pieces of paper, known as points, which enabled people to obtain their ration of tinned food. The Food Office had been short-handed, and were delighted to discover a well of untapped and unpaid labour in the shape of the officers' wives, even if they did find it somewhat peculiar that none of us went by the title of Mrs. It was also unlikely that they had heard of Noel Coward's remark to commend us, 'that the war had revealed that it took one British peeress to do the work of twenty Indians.'

Next door to the Food Office a butcher, by the curious name of Mr Pickup, did a roaring trade in sausages which were home-made and exceedingly tasty. Mr Pickup was also oblig-ing, and liked to help the army and their families by supplying fresh eggs, an occasional ham or a bladder of lard. This benevolent gesture was, of course, a flagrant breach of the law, but one in which everyone took part who was fortunate enough to be trusted. After all, in the depths of rural Yorkshire ham and eggs were plentiful, and surely the food officials would never come to notice so tiny a gap in their supplies. However it had come to Mr Pickup's notice that some of his chosen customers were working at the Food Office next door, so after a few months of plenty we were back on our hard rations again, and wishing fervently that we had never volunteered at the Food Office.

During the late summer I travelled fairly frequently to London in order to organise, as chairman, a concert at the Albert Hall. This was to be in aid of the Newspaper Press Fund. I had been invited to do it, not by my family, but by Rowley's, for his aunt was married to Lord Astor of Hever who, at the time, was chief proprietor of *The Times* (having, in the first place, bought it from the estate of my great-uncle, Lord Northcliffe). The chief soloist was Moiseiwitsch and the conductor Sir Malcolm Sargent with Eva Turner as singer. It was not difficult to sell the tickets in spite of my total lack of musical appreciation, and the concert was considered a success. Travelling to and from Scarborough and London was somewhat arduous. One was certain of a seat to York where the main line trains were caught, but after that, unless it was a night journey, the only seat was one's suitcase, which after some hours could barely be said to be comfortable. The greater ordeal, however, was having to make speeches for the first time in my life. Many were the times when some poor Yorkshire cow would look startled by being practised upon from behind a farmyard gate.

Once again, in 1946, I became involved with music by presiding over a benefit organised by *The Evening News*, again at the Albert Hall: this time in the presence of Queen Mary. I was to receive her at the door and, in the interval, present the performers, none of whose names I had ever heard of, being ignorant of the more serious music at the time. Frightened, and only twenty-four, I turned to my mother-in-law for advice. 'Kiss her hand, dear,' she said, and that I did, which was my first embarrassment since I was wearing lipstick and the Queen white gloves. My mother-in-law, an impractical and ethereal lady, had advised me to wear my wedding dress at the first post-war Court when everyone else had on short frocks and hats. Fortunately, I did not take her advice, even though her husband had been the Lord Chamberlain for some twenty-five years.

For the Albert Hall in 1946 I had luckily studied photographs of the musicians, for in the interval it fell to my lot to present Ralph Vaughan Williams, Constant Lambert, Sir Arnold Bax, Guilhermina Suggia, Warwick Braithwaite and others to Her Majesty. Enormously relieved at having succeeded in getting the names right I followed the Queen as she turned back down the reception line. Queen Mary was wearing a green velvet dress with a train which unhappily matched the carpet. Half way down the line she stopped, anchored to the ground by my foot. Slowly she turned, with infinite dignity, and without a word; while I equally slowly realised my transgression, under the horrified gaze of these august masters of music. It was a nightmare never to be forgotten — fixed in the mind like a halted frame from a film.

On one of my visits to London from Yorkshire it occurred to me that it would be a very good time to buy a house, for property was going cheap due to the war. Wasting no time, and after seeing but two houses, I bought a tall narrow house on a ninety-year lease in St Petersburgh Place off Bayswater Road for one thousand six hundred pounds. With the savings from my pocket money and a loan from Coutts bank it was mine, my Blitz Bargain house. On returning to Yorkshire I told an astonished Rowley, for there had been no mention or talk about finding a permanent home or buying a house when I had left him but two days previously. It was a slightly risky buy, for no-one could possibly know what turn the war would take, or whether the bombardment of London recommence.

In London, as before the war, the sordid spectacle of

prostitutes could be seen walking their beats at twilight in almost every street. They were always clearly distinguishable by their gaudy clothes, heavy make-up and very high-heeled shoes. No doubt, they were courageous in braving the blackout and the air raids to ply their trade, made more lucrative by so many military visitors from overseas; but to the young, raw and unworldly characters pulled from their simple lives in the prairies and forests of North America by the demands of war the scene was, for them, somewhat confusing; and perhaps they can be forgiven for thinking, at first, that all english women were there for the taking.

On one of my visits to London to preside over a committee for the first concert in the Albert Hall, I had arranged to call upon my mother-in-law at her house north of the park for tea. It was dark when I left her and no taxi appeared to be obtainable, so I took the Underground, which entailed two changes to reach Knightsbridge, where I was staying with my mother and her then husband, Captain Thomas Hussey, RN. It was rush-hour and the Oxford Circus train was full. I barely noticed a young Canadian Air Force officer who stood next to me in the squash. It was hardly noteworthy that he changed to the same train as me at Piccadilly Circus, or that he entered the same carriage, since it was the first that we came to. When I disembarked at Knightsbridge, it did appear to be a slight coincidence that he rose to leave as well. On reaching the street and walking with care through the dense darkness of the blackout I heard, with increasing consternation, the steady crunch of a pair of boots behind me. I turned into Lowndes Square. So did the pair of boots. Far too frightened to look behind me, hastening, I gained the entrance to my mother's block of flats — with enormous relief. But as I entered the lift I found the airman just behind me. Not a word had been uttered. I pressed the button to my mother's floor thinking that, possibly, stranger coincidences had happened. At the door of the flat, still without a word being spoken, I pressed the bell and my mother opened the door. She seemed a little

22

surprised but thought the stranger must be a friend, although she said later that it struck her as odd since she knew I had been visiting my mother-in-law. Hospitably she offered him a drink, but I somehow, with a signal, managed to get her out of the room for a moment and describe what had occurred. It was a situation she knew exactly how to deal with and found it highly amusing. When she heard my step-father's key in the lock, and he had been put in the picture I spoke to the young man for the first time and asked him how long he had been in England. By this time he was becoming uncomfortable. 'Only a few weeks,' he stuttered. Then my step-father marched into the room and took the man firmly but politely by the arm, muttering something about the wrong address, and propelled the poor fellow out of the front door, as my mother collapsed with laughter into an armchair.

A small library of books had been donated to the Guards Armoured Division by Viscount Kemsley for the pleasure and delectation of the troops. Two volunteers were required to distribute the volumes by visiting each platoon in turn throughout the entire Division. A junior staff officer's wife, Lady Meyer, and I undertook this rather pleasant duty. Given a special supply of petrol and with a trailer to contain the books, we would drive for miles through enchanting Yorkshire villages and across bleak moors, supplying one third of the Division at a time. Occasionally we would be royally entertained by Brigadier Sir John Marriott to an excellent lunch or, on less happy occasions, become stuck fast in mud in a desolate spot and wait, hopefully, for a passing tank whose crew might stop and help us.

The books were hardly the sort of reading likely to be appreciated by the ordinary soldier, for the greater part were somewhat indigestible biographies, but here and there an adventure story could be found among the dusty pile. On arrival at each platoon we would be greeted by the plaintive cry: 'Got any westerns?' Unhappily, we had about two dozen, and each became more ragged in appearance with every loan.

Guardsmen are not chosen for their erudition or keenness on learning, but for their height. If our visits produced some disappointment, the sight of two young women cheered them up and, now and again, we succeeded in introducing a new element into the lives of a few by challenging them to read more weighty material than the rigours of the wild and woolly west.

That December Barbadee Meyer and I volunteered to help with the pre-Christmas rush at the Post Office in Scarborough. It gave us an important feeling of responsibility driving a Royal Mail van, and to unlock the scarlet letter boxes with one of a heavy bunch of keys. We would stuff our mail bags, return to the sorting office, and repeat the exercise again. Sometimes we would help with the sorting, and stand aghast at the mountain of parcels constantly arriving in an endless stream, to be thrown with force and not always caught. We discovered that any registered parcel was handled with careful respect, and made note that, in future, a registered packet was worth the extra expense. Although the wartime Post Office was undermanned and had many obstructions to counter, it gave a far better service than it does today. People, possibly, were more conscientious.

Among much else, Rowley's job concerned personnel, and the human problems that involved. There were never any cases of proven rape for which, by Courts Martial, the penalties were severe. Rape was occasionally alleged by a girl, and could, possibly, be used as an excuse, for at that time pregnancy, without the promise of marriage, was viewed with disfavour by the family and considered a disgrace. Rowley, at that time, always maintained that rape was impossible for a man to commit on a protesting kicking female. And at no time was it ever alleged that more than one man was ever present; nor that a girl had been terrorised by a knife or a gun. Yet the fifteen-thousand healthy men in the Division, deprived of their wives or girlfriends, and who kept rifles and bayonets at hand, and were well trained in the use of them, never took

24

advantage. Unlike today, rape was a crime seldom heard of, and only talked about with hilarity.

In January 1944, with the cold Yorkshire winter closing in and with Rowley's advice, i.e. that he would become more involved in military exercises and, therefore, be away much of the time, we gave thought as to what would be the best arrangement. Dorset was too far away; we had our London house; Nannie Brown was anxious to return to Hyde Park; and there had in fact been no bombing of London for a very long time. Therefore it seemed to us completely normal to make a home in our new house. With not a single warning nor a voice of dissent, we went ahead. But with the benefit of hindsight, our naive and pathetic plan was in reality quite mad.

Leaving Yorkshire brought to an end a happy interlude of companionship, of being part of a circle of others in the same circumstances. It was also the start of a rather frightening beginning.

3

SEEKING REFUGE

We equipped our narrow house in London with scraps of furniture, a few cheap pieces found in Westbourne Grove, some nursery furniture and old carpet sent from storage by my father and, at first, packing cases. The only kind of blackout material available came in green as well as black. Being so closely woven, it made good loose covers and passable curtains. Our china was utility white, for no colours were obtainable, and with Rowley's canteen of cutlery (bought for his time at Cambridge) we made do. Rowley was able to take some leave, and being a 'do-it-yourself' man made himself extremely useful hanging our few pictures, re-wiring, and other household jobs, which was a labour of joy and excitement since it was our first house.

Nannie Brown and the baby arrived from Dorset. The former delighted to be back in London again, although disappointed to find our house was the furthest corner from the place in the park she wished to be. And the latter, our baby girl, a great joy as it was the first time we had all been together under our own roof.

Our happiness lasted only a few days before Rowley's leave was up and he returned to Yorkshire to play his part in organising the massive movement of troops to the south coast of England.

Nannie Brown wasted no time in getting ready for the 'Dell' in Hyde Park. A huge new pram with a white silk cover was obtained. The baby, resplendent in a white satin coat edged

26

with fur, would be pushed at top speed the width and length of both Kensington Gardens and Hyde Park twice a day. This incongruous sight did not last long, for within a few days of Rowley's departure, and as I was settling down alone to sleep, the chilling sound of an air-raid siren was sounded. At first I took no notice. Then, hearing a loud 'crump' followed by more and closer ones, I decided I should collect Nannie and hasten her and the baby down to the cellar. This proved to be more difficult than I could have dreamed, for Nannie, at first, refused to budge. 'I will not allow *my* baby to be moved. She might wake up, and the cellar is anyway damp.' At that moment I heard a sinister whistle, and the sudden blast of a nearby bomb hurled me on to the floor. After that, Nannie lost her argument, but for the next few hours in the tiny coal cellar she scolded me for waking the baby and, for good measure, announced that it was far better to be killed by shrapnel than be buried alive. As I was at that time barely twenty-one years old, it was very difficult to stand up to her. The next morning did, however, shake her, for when she left the house as usual for the 'Dell,' outside was an enormous hole, and in the next block, where a substantial house had stood the day before, there was now nothing but a very large gap.

In spite of the devastation the sun shone brightly and the terrors of the night receded. But as the day wore on, uneasiness returned and with the dusk, fear. This air-raid had affected me quite differently from other experiences of bombing. Then, I had been relaxed and carefree, dancing and dining with a handsome young man. Now I was alone with a defenceless baby, a cross old woman and plenty of time to think. That night, no sooner had I put out my bedside light than the sinister undulating wail of the siren started again. No longer could the cellar be faced, so I climbed up to the nursery floor to be near my baby and watched from the window. This time the raid took a different form. Instead of high explosives, fire bombs rained down. This method of intimidation, although far less frightening, caused more damage to the buildings. With morbid fascination, Nannie and I watched as flames consumed the houses opposite. Then the door bell rang. It was our local air-raid warden, who strongly advised me to evacuate our house as the wind had risen and was blowing in our direction from the burning houses opposite.

We were rescued by an American colonel who was a friend of my mother and who, in an unguarded moment, volunteered to help her if she ever needed him. He was induced to save us in his army car somewhat reluctantly. As he later told me, the roads were either impassable because of the previous night's bombing, or closed for other reasons. In any case he considered it dangerous. In spite of his misgivings he did appear, and by the time he arrived we were ready with clothes packed. He told us that there was no time to lose and that we must hasten, but just as the driver let out the clutch there was a shout from Nannie Brown: 'Stop! I must get out and fetch something most important.' The redoubtable Nannie Brown had her way, and while she was gone the impatient colonel and I wondered what on earth could be so important that took precedence over our safety when, silhouetted in the doorway, lit by the roaring fires, stood Nannie holding the baby's potty. The colonel remarked with some force that he would never forget the sight for the rest of his life. He drove us to the other side of the park, which had escaped that night and the one-before's blitz, where we managed to get some sleep.

In spite of an angry Nannie, who still, despite it all, wished to remain close to her beloved Hyde Park, I insisted on going at once to the country. Our refuge proved to be Hever Castle, where Rowley's very kind aunt took us in. True, it was south of London and therefore on the route of enemy aircraft who were wont to unload any left-over bombs for their return flight home; but, unknowingly at the time, it had the great advantage of being within the vicinity of Rowley's last HQ in England and so he was able, if rarely, to pay us a visit.

Lady Astor of Hever, Rowley's Aunt Vi, possessed the rare

quality of understanding others and their present trials. She had been widowed in World War One, and her present husband had lost a leg.

In the last few days before the dreaded 'Happening,' which for so long had hung distantly in our all minds, Aunt Vi opened her house to many of us wives, and for the final weekend when our husbands were allowed to come and bid us farewell, she rightly treated it as being no different from any of her other House Parties. No word was spoken or reference made of the reason for our presence and, if a note of difference crept in, it was one of greater conviviality and warmth than was usual. If there had been any mention of the final departure in sympathetic or emotional terms, it would have been too much to bear.

For our soldier husbands it was a little different; they had been training and planning for the Invasion for years. Now it had come. They felt a bit like actors who, after prolonged rehearsals, looked forward to the opening night with excitement not unmixed with dread.

From the peace and beauty of Hever's Tudor gardens they left us to join the greatest Armada the world had ever seen. To fight, to liberate others and, above all, to preserve our freedom. Farewell scenes are best borne if brief; and, of course, a soldier's wife must not be seen to shed any tears. For me it was not so much a stiff upper lip, as trying to distance myself from reality. There was no other way.

After Rowley's departure there seemed no further point in remaining in Kent, nor stretching my kind host's hospitality. Early summer had begun, and Rowley's parents had offered us shelter in Somerset. So with our daughter and Nannie we booked in to the Paddington Hotel in London for one night en route for the West Country. Once more, lying in bed, I was to hear the Alert and the All Clear, this sequence continuing all night, which was puzzling. As we embarked on our train a loud explosion was heard. It was the beginning of the buzz-bomb — an unmanned device like an aeroplane which, with

29

the engine cut off, glided to the ground as a huge bomb. We were leaving them behind us.

Great importance was placed on ordinary mail by the military authorities and speed was of the essence with the post from France. It came as a pleasant surprise that letters arrived so soon from Normandy. In Rowley's first he wrote to say how the most glorious sunset he had ever seen lit up the skies as their ship churned its way across the English Channel. 'It must be a good omen.' As for the sea, well, it was distinctly choppy in spite of the weight of so many thousands of ships.

We wrote to each other every day, as did thousands of other couples. Rowley had little of substance to say for he was always the soul of discretion and refrained from even the sketchiest of descriptions in case his letters should fall into the wrong hands. Instead, he would write of the discomforts of sleeping in a slit trench. That under bombardment, at five feet deep, water would seep in and cover the bottom. Lying in a pool some eight inches deep meant lying face-up and soaking wet. In more tranquil places the trench would be far less deep and broad enough to contain a camp bed, but being near the surface he was at the mercy of hoards of ants and earwigs. But in spite of these primitive hardships Rowley always insisted that a telephone was installed.

My daily letters were even more empty of interesting events, the only excitement that summer being the arrival of two very mellow cheeses sent by Rowley from Normandy, the heart of the Camembert country. Their arrival was greeted with undisguised delight — the first fruits of victory; loot from the front; cheese such as we had not tasted for years. Britain had long since produced no other speciality than Mousetrap.

Living in Rowley's childhood home, the scene of our honeymoon, was a lonely experience. Rowley's parents had not involved themselves in local society so the people I met during the summer were the local villagers and shopkeepers, all of whom thought the world of Rowley. They told me how he had learned to drive the local train from Minehead to Taunton. How he had built with his own hands a garage for his parents; and of many other small achievements. He had been, apparently, a solitary boy. The youngest by seven years of his two elder sisters, and had seldom mixed with other children; at once shy and inquisitive, he had always found himself an occupation and been quite self-contained.

Maybe my letters telling him of humdrum days in his childhood home evoked pleasant memories and brought an unchanging and peaceful picture of a more secure scene than the blood, sweat and noise of the battlefield. If our letters lacked interest, the exchanging of them became the touchstone of our existence. Any delay in their arrival brought agonizing worry.

In September we moved from Somerset to Dorset, to my mother's home, Athelhampton, which being a large house had plenty of room for other members of the family and their children. It was more agreeable and less lonely. A map was hung on the nursery wall, and with each new advance by the army through France, little flags would be proudly pinned. The encirclement of the Falaise Gap, its shrinkage, and the subsequent tear-away to Brussels.

No soldier who took part in the liberation of Brussels ever forgot the cheering crowds gone mad with joy, the toasts and the kisses. No army received so rapturous a welcome; to the glory of being victors was added the adulation of being liberators. It was also necessary that the weary, if jubilant, soldiers should be paid, for the shops were full of merchandise not seen in England for many years. Besides, after the first day of rejoicing drinks were no longer handed out with the same free abandon; it was to Rowley, as Deputy-Assistant Adjutant General, that the problem fell.

Rowley summoned the Divisional field cashier to ascertain what provision had been made, and if any Belgian francs were available, for he knew that the Government had printed masses of occupation money against such a contingency. 'I am afraid, sir,' the field cashier said, 'it is still resting on the beaches of Normandy.' Rowley, left to his own initiative, fully realised the importance of this matter, especially for the soldiers' morale. He therefore ordered the field cashier to approach the nearest large bank and ask for ten million francs. The field cashier did what Rowley ordered, and at the first large bank, to his surprise, was greeted with much acclaim and shown immediately into the Directors' room where a celebration was in full swing. After many toasts, he timidly mentioned his mission without any expectation of success. 'But we would be delighted to provide you with the money. How will you take it?' they asked. 'In my three-ton lorry' was the reply. Rowley was therefore able to report that the money had been found and the Division was duly paid. However, instead of Rowley being congratulated for his resourcefulness, he found himself in trouble. The bureaucracy was outraged at such an example of free enterprise, and the Treasury assuredly spent several years working it out.

The winter 1944-1945 was a severe one and very hard on the fighting men. Nor was it without privation for those at home. At Athelhampton, heavy snow lay on the ground for some weeks, so fodder for those creatures in the wild was scarce. Even so, we were not prepared for the huge rats that emerged from the river to forage for food. There were no longer gardeners and gamekeepers to keep them down, and they had bred freely, and with audacity climbed the creepers to peer in windows. Crumbs put out for birds produced the ugly sight of swarms of rodents fighting each other for each morsel.

By the spring Rowley had left the Guards Armoured Division and been sent to the Headquarters of the Twenty-First Army Group. Promoted again, he was now the youngest Lieutenant-Colonel, at the age of twenty-six, in the Brigade of Guards. The strains and exertions, however, of the past years on a not-too-robust constitution had taken their toll, and he submitted to intermittent abdominal infections which kept him periodically in hospital in Germany and England for quite a long time.

Rowley was awarded a military MBE. His citation mentioned 'that he had been responsible for all planning as far as personnel were concerned, and that the success of the move of the Division overseas was largely due to his care of detail and powers of organisation.' This distinction was followed by a Mention in Despatches.

In June 1945 came the formal announcement on the radio of the end of hostilities with Germany. Curiously, I heard these welcome words in the same room at Athelhampton as the grim news of the Declaration of War six years previously. For me we had come full circle.

BANKER'S WIFE

4

TOASTS WERE NOT DRUNK

When the men came out of uniform they seemed somehow diminished, their civilian suits drab, unexciting and certainly unbecoming. The longed-for freedom felt more like an abandonment; for indeed, as the forces disbanded and the wartime soldiers went home, they were left to their own devices. The same pre-war jobs for some, and new ground to be tested for others. No longer now part of a huge company, alone they would find their way.

For Rowley it was no different. In March 1946 he was demobilised. His pay as a Lieutenant-Colonel ended and he possessed no private means nor expectations.

Before the war Rowley's predilection had been towards the film industry, not as an actor, but as a director. He had taken an active part in producing and lighting shows as a schoolboy at Eton, and this led him towards finding a job through John Maxwell (the-then chairman of Associated British Cinemas) who, in turn, gave him the sage advice to 'go into the City to learn about the management of money first, and then think about the cinema afterwards.' Rowley, therefore, started at Barings bank on the very lowest rung of the ladder, earning the far-from-princely salary of two pounds a week, and becoming less and less enchanted with the job as time went by. The time, however, had been short due to the outbreak of war, when he was immediately transformed into a soldier.

Now, once again, the decision as to which career to follow arose. Rowley still nursed feelings towards the film industry, but he realised the insecurity of that profession. During our short engagement, while lunching with my father at Swinley Golf Club, Sir Edward Peacock (the-then head of Barings) chanced to pass our table. He stopped, and addressing himself to me, he said, 'You are marrying our future star.' These words I did not forget. In spite of Rowley's disenchantment with his short experience at the bank he had, evidently, made an excellent impression. It therefore seemed a pity if he did not pursue what appeared to be a promising career. I therefore brought all the persuasion I could bear.

Our small family was ensconced in our blitz-bargain house which, fortunately, was placed near the Central Line, the trains of which ran directly to the City. So Rowley joined the rat race moderately comfortably and began working at Barings on April Fools Day 1946.

By the autumn our family had swelled with the addition of a baby son. The blitz-bargain house proved too small, therefore. Selling at a substantial profit, and with the aid of another bank loan, we moved into larger premises in Gloucester Square just in time to endure the worst winter within living memory, or to suffer since.

After the war Britain was virtually bankrupt. The shortage of food was acute and rationing severer still; fuel was still rationed and scarce. The Serpentine froze sufficiently solid for people to use it as a thoroughfare, not for days, but for weeks. We kept warm as best we could and stretched the rations even further. During this grim and gloomy winter Barings decided, much to Rowley's satisfaction, to send him to the United States in order to obtain some experience of the American banking system.

This American assignment provided treble reason for pleasure. A new country which Rowley had always longed to visit; an escape from the gloomy banking hall at Barings; and to leave behind the frustrating and suffocating constrictions of the Labour Government whose rallying call was Austerity.

The ambition of most of our generation to go to America

was brought about mainly by the-then influence of Hollywood, the films of which, infinitely superior to any others, portrayed a bewitching existence peopled by glamorous or amusing characters continually making wisecracks.

Exchange Control was strict due to Britain's hopeless financial situation, and the Bank of England was grudging in its allowance of ten thousand dollars. It was hoped that Rowley's stay in the USA would last a year, but with a family of four and a nannie, it became a simple matter of how long the money would last. Help came in the shape of one of my family business's newsprint salesmen, Colonel Frank Clarke, a Canadian, who generously lent us his flat in New York rent free. Also, Lord Perry, a friend of Rowley's father who was chairman of Ford UK, made available a brand-new American Ford car. This, we found, was not free; but at the time new cars were at a premium due to a waiting list of some three years, and we were able to sell it after a year's use for a profit. We were, indeed, lucky, and with careful husbandry of our resources, plus even more careful housekeeping, we did finally manage to last a year.

In April 1947 we sailed first-class in the *Queen Elizabeth* with our two young children, plus Nannie Brown who, happily, was paid in sterling, and could not change her job for an American one with a temptingly large salary due to the restrictions on foreign labour.

The *Queens* were, as ocean liners, incomparable. Huge and magnificent, they took four days to reach New York, weather permitting. Luxurious, with an excellent cuisine, a cinema and many other diversions, the crossings were a pleasurable treat as long as the ocean remained relatively calm. This voyage was a far cry for me from my earlier one. My first Atlantic crossing had been as a seventeen-year-old evacuee.

In 1940, just after Dunkirk, my parents had seen fit to send my brother Vere and me to the safety of North America. It was a reluctant departure and any feelings of excitement, or the spirit of adventure, were dispelled the moment the ship sailed and there was no turning back. I had been told by my mother that my presence in England would only constitute a burden. She reminded me that I had always left the room at children's parties before the crackers were pulled, and at shooting weekends hid in a cupboard. 'How will you face up to the noise of guns?' she asked me, and the question seemed unanswerable. We sailed in a CPR steamship accompanied by six hundred children. The journey of three weeks took a zig-zag course to avoid enemy submarines. There were no films or amusements other than those we contrived ourselves. The children were very sea-sick, and it could not have been described as an experience that anyone would want to repeat. Our ship had stalled for days in the face of a gigantic storm, during which my fourteen-year-old brother had broken his arm, and it was no comfort, either, that our ship was still within reach of German U-boats.

Looking back, this pointless voyage over a dangerous ocean to an uncertain future on the other side, can be seen as part of life's pattern. Without this private experience I would never have seen American life before my other roles there. In a curious way, it re-directed Rowley's life as well. For that experience gave me a complete certainty that, come what may, I could only live in England. When Rowley's first stay in America came to an end he decided that he wished to remain, and indeed to work for the rest of his life in the United States, but I was adamant and would not hear of it on any account.

New York was at that time a far less violent place than it is now, although in some quarters, such as Harlem and the Puerto Rican sector, the crime rate was notoriously high. Colonel Clarke's apartment, although distinguished by a Fifth Avenue address, proved to be in the last apartment block on the Avenue. Situated between 100th and 101st street it was in the Puerto Rican sector. With blissful ignorance we moved in, glad too for the children's sake that we overlooked Central Park. Each weekday Rowley caught the downtown subway from an insalubrious station behind our block, and fortunately never knew the risks he took until just before we finally left, when he read that the most dangerous street in New York was East 101st. Our children, dressed immaculately by Nannie Brown, who herself wore a uniform, would have been an easy target had she lingered in the park in the vicinity of our flat, but happily Nannie Brown was Nannie Snob. She discovered in a very short space of time that the smart part of the park, where other nannies congregated, was thirty blocks further down the Avenue. She therefore, as she had done in London, walked with speed and fervour twice a day to gain the hallowed Nannie spot, and thereby unknowingly avoided many a perilous encounter.

Quite soon after we had established ourselves in the Fifth Avenue apartment, Junius Morgan invited us for a weekend at his large house at Glen Cove on Long Island. The Morgan family had long been friends and associates of the Baring clan, and we immediately struck up a life-long friendship with his son, Jack, and daughter-in-law, Clare. Rowley started work at the bank of J P Morgan almost at once. His first task was to take messages round to other financial institutions in Wall Street. This was a chore given to newcomers and proved useful in both finding their way round, and meeting more senior bankers.

Being the month of May, the younger members of the bank were full of enquiries as to where Rowley would be sending his wife and children for the summer. It was the custom to send the wives and families away from the intense heat of the city. At the time, moreover, there was also a compelling and frightening reason: for New York was considered to be germ-ridden with the dreaded polio during the hot months, the vaccine for which was not yet available. On hearing this depressing and worrying news I was frantic, and looked hopelessly at the map to find some kind of refuge. Rowley's fellow workers were discouraging. 'You have left it far too late; people book up from year to year, and certainly months in advance. You could not possibly find anything now.' Rowley,

41

however, was not discouraged, and put on a calm expression to allay my fears.

The following weekend he drove down to the only place outside New York that he knew, namely Glen Cove. In the face of my hopeless scepticism, he entered an Estate Office and asked them if they had anything to rent for the summer. The assistant looked somewhat surprised, and to my astonishment and great relief answered that she had. Evidently an American lady had, only that morning, asked them to let a fully-furnished cottage on her husband's estate as they had only recently made their plans to leave for Europe. As she had only just finished re-decorating the cottage they wanted good tenants for a reasonable rent. It was an incredible stroke of good fortune. The empty estate was ours to wander in, a sea-water pool lay alongside, Rowley could commute from a nearby station, and even the gardener's wife was available to help with the housework. When Rowley returned to work on the Monday his colleagues were astounded, none more so than the Morgans whose house was just up the road.

On May 15th Rowley was amazed on arriving at the bank to find all the male staff wearing pyjamas. May 15th was the day on which they changed from winter suits to shapeless, striped, cotton seersuckers: loose, light and practical for the American summer, but not as yet seen in London.

Our cottage was not air-conditioned. With the beds placed under the windows, and the curtains left undrawn, we were not uncomfortable. The fireflies and the glowworms which lit the darkness at night, and the continual chorus of croaking frogs still linger in memory. It was a happy and uneventful summer. Once I tried to drive to New York for some shopping but the sight of the dark pall of steam rising from the hot, humid city turned me back in my tracks.

My father came to stay in our tightly-packed cottage of four small bedrooms, but it was not long before we moved on to rather better accommodation with an old girlfriend who had since married a billionaire. Betty Deering Howe was a good friend to us and entertained us frequently. She had, she told me, been cited by my mother in my parents divorce case. That did not worry her until she discovered that she was one of more than twenty. Fortunately she possessed a very good sense of humour and was more than kind to us. Her sister-in-law, Lorraine Shevlin, married secondly Senator John Sherman Cooper, both of whom we came to know very well later on.

Our social life was confined to weekends because of Rowley's work. There were not very many young people like ourselves in the neighbourhood, but enough to make life pleasant. Once we were invited to a dinner given by Madame Balsan, the former Duchess of Marlborough, who had been born a Vanderbilt, and whose daughter, Sarah, had been a schoolfriend. We arrived late as, hopelessly lost, her house was difficult to find. We were not more than forty minutes late, which with the long drinking hour or more before dinner in the USA might have passed muster, but Mme Jacques Balsan kept more to European times. Our embarrassment was evident and the grandeur of the evening more so, for behind each chair stood a liveried footman with powdered hair. The next time we received an invitation from another elderly lady, Mrs George Baker, who also possessed a reputation for grand living, we arrived on the dot, only to discover that in this case it would have been more polite to have arrived late, for our hostess had not yet gone upstairs to change. Social life, evidently, was full of pitfalls.

We returned to the apartment in New York by the end of September. Our ability to entertain there was limited; the flat was small and our funds meagre. The best we could offer was drinks for just a few. Housekeeping was made somewhat easier by the cheapness of chicken. These birds were a rare treat, for we had seldom eaten poultry in seven years, and were not long enough in America for the taste to become jaded. The difference in prices, too, for the same article was strange, for the war years had produced a sameness in cost. Up and down the Madison Avenue food shops I would wander, looking for the cheapest cuts and finding quite extraordinary bargains.

That autumn The Princess Elizabeth was married to Lieutenant Philip Mountbatten. Rowley was in Akron, Ohio, where he discovered that everyone had been up since 5.30 am listening to the marriage service on the radio. For myself, grabbing a quick snack for lunch at Woolworths on Fifth Avenue, I was astonished to find that all the shoppers had stopped buying goods and, with the shop assistants, were listening to a recording of the wedding on the store's loud-speakers. On hearing my english accent as I ordered a hot dog, a group of people immediately crowded around: 'Oh, you must be just thrilled,' they excitedly chanted.

The great blizzard which cut off New York from the outside world took place in December. For five days deep snow and ice covered the streets, the shape of cars could barely be discerned, just small humps of white in rows down the cavernous streets. This white seige lasted about a week and Rowley was amused to receive a letter from his mother suggesting that she should send him a food parcel. Earlier we were anticipating with curiosity and some pleasure an invitation to dine, accompanied by my father, with the Duke and Duchess of Windsor at their apartment in the Waldorf Towers. With the heavy fall of snow, and the complete stoppage of traffic, it looked as if we would have to cancel, which we were loathe to do.

Clad in furs and snow boots and holding the skirt of my long evening dress as high off the ground as I could, we incongruously caught a subway train from the perilous East 101st Street down Park Avenue. Our return later in the night would have been more hazardous if the appalling conditions had not kept any roaming footpad indoors. On emerging from the subway, opposite the Waldorf Towers, we were faced with the almost impossible problem of how to cross the street. This was solved by Rowley who gallantly decided to carry me across. Ice had made huge ruts and craters which, in turn, were covered with snow. About half way across Rowley slipped and fell. He dropped me with some force on a singularly hard slab of ice, where I lay in some pain before being able to pick my way to the other side of the street. We finally arrived, a sorry, sodden pair, to be made most welcome in a warm and friendly manner by our host and hostess.

The Duchess of Windsor gave the impression of being more feminine that her photographs suggested; animated and talkative but neither especially witty nor amusing in her conversation. It was a small dinner party, of no more than nine or ten people. Besides my father, it included Lord Dudley, his son Peter Ward, and Mrs Ogden Mills, a very wealthy American lady. All went merrily until we reached the dessert when Mrs Ogden Mills rose to her feet and, quite carried away, announced that we should drink to 'the greatest of all Englishmen, the Duke.' For a seeming eternity each one of us English sat and looked fixedly at our plates, each, independently, making a silent decision not to participate. The awkward silence was finally broken by the Duke himself who, with a sad smile, said 'we do not drink toasts at my table.' With that remark he adroitly defused an embarrassing situation, and gained our respect and even affection.

After dinner the Duchess took Rowley on one side and, in spite of his youth and unimportance, deplored the fact that her husband had no job, and implored him to help. Conceivably the Duke's lack of occupation weighed heavily and continually on her mind at that time. When we came to make our departure and to thank them both, I to curtsy to him, he followed us into the hall where, perforce, we had to change our evening shoes for snow boots. To my everlasting embarrassment the Duke insisted on kneeling on the floor and helping me on with my boots, which act, as my ex-King, was disconcerting, and somehow seemed infinitely pathetic.

In January we left New York with our family for a holiday in the Bahamas to stay with my father who had taken a house in Nassau. We enjoyed a very pleasant stay, but unfortunately Nannie Brown was not too careful over giving our small son the local unpasteurised milk, with the sad result that he became infected with tuberculosis of the glands, a disease that did not manifest itself until some months later.

We sailed from New York to England in March on the *Queen Elizabeth*, where a fellow passenger, Geoffrey Crowther, then editor of *The Economist* invited The Hon Evelyn Baring to a cocktail party after seeing his name on the passenger list, without realising that he was an infant aged two, our son.

Mission accomplished, by May we were once again installed in Gloucester Square.

5

COWS AND CORONETS

By April 1948 Rowley was back at Barings and promoted to being a managing director, and soon afterwards a junior partner. At first he settled down happily, but the restrictions imposed by the Labour government, and the lack of initiative, innovation or venture by the two senior partners, Evelyn Bingham Baring and Arthur Child-Villiers, was very discouraging, particularly after the vigour and dynamism of America. For ten years, sharing the Partners Room, these two hidebound, elderly men, poured cold water on all new ideas. Frustrating and enervating, their attitude quenched and lowered the spirits of the younger ones. I began to wonder if, after all, I had been wrong to insist on returning to England. And if banking was the right career for Rowley.

These years of office boredom were, however, mitigated by the need to leave London for the fresher air of the countryside to benefit our frail son, Evelyn. Our new home had to be within commuting distance and, preferably, without changing trains. Our scope was limited further by the strict regulations then in force: of spending no more than one hundred pounds on any improvements or decoration to a house. This meant that our choice of dwelling had to be of one suitable for immediate occupation. We could not purchase that which we would have preferred, but only that which was possible. After much frantic searching and inevitable disillusion, we found a home to meet our requirements. An old farmhouse needing no decoration at all and situated in a pretty valley in the middle of the green belt.

We moved to Frenchstreet Farm as the first frosts nipped the last rose buds of summer, and we could enjoy fragrant log fires and walks of discovery through the neighbouring woods which glowed in their autumn glory. My father came to join us, deeply wounded by his collapsing marriage, for his wife had run off with Ian Fleming, a character who had been around for some years and who always seemed to me to be very far from the dashing person so often and mistakenly portrayed. Not good-looking or even very attractive, his talk neither witty nor greatly interesting — but then it is never possible to fathom what attracts one person to another.

The ten years between 1948 and 1958 remained uneventful. Events are, however, relative. In the small world of family and farm, of housekeeping and horticulture, small events loomed large. The birth of our beloved younger son completed our family. The tearing-apart of adored young to boarding school; the achievement of a new home-bred cow; the occasional floods which swept through the pigsties; the annual domestic crisis when one foreign domestic couple would replace another. Each time we would hope for an experienced cook, and each time we would discover that the sum of their culinary knowledge was confined to opening a tin, from which ignorant beginning I would impart my own small knowledge of cooking by daily demonstration supported by a few halting words in Italian, French or Spanish. Rowley plodded his daily way to the City. Never failing to turn up, even on Saturdays, nor stopped by winter snows, which regularly threatened to cut us off, and without the use of snowploughs would certainly have succeeded.

By chance our new home marched on one side with that of Sir Winston Churchill, whose new neighbour we then became. At that time Sir Winston owned three farms: Chartwell, French Street and Bardogs. The name Bardogs had caught his fancy. He would say that if he had taken a dukedom, he would have called himself Duke of Bardogs. It had a firm ring to it. His daughter Mary and son-in-law Christopher Soames lived in an attractive house on the Chartwell estate, while Christopher ran the farms with possibly more panache than experience. He also ran a market garden which thrived. The price of lettuce and the qualities of milking cows and Landrace pigs were of absorbing interest in neighbourly conversation.

For ourselves, but with two small fields, a single cow, chickens and a couple of pigs, we made do. This concentration on livestock was the result of a shortage of food. After seven lean years one felt more secure with one's own supply living and breathing about one.

While Rowley addressed himself to the daily grind I dedicated myself to the welfare of our ailing child after dismissing Nannie Brown, who was quite anxious to return to the delights of Hyde Park. With rest, fresh air and good food the little boy made a complete recovery. His convalescence necessitated remaining quietly in the country, allowing no distractions, excitements or strain for a year. During this period we saw more of the Churchills and the Soames's than anyone else. The highlight of our week was the kind and frequent invitations from Lady Churchill to join in watching the Sunday film shows at Chartwell, often followed by an invitation to supper. The films chosen were, invariably, adventure epics, during which Sir Winston would quietly doze. Awaking suddenly with a growl, he would comment loudly on the action, or demand an explanation from his neighbour on what had occurred: a question I always anticipated with apprehension since I invariably sat next to him.

There were frequent dinners with the Soames's in their farmhouse. Once, after a singularly delicious meal, Christopher took Rowley heavily to task for his failure to involve himself in the responsibilities of public life. He became quite heated, to the extent that Rowley felt affronted and almost walked out. Knowing the importance that Christopher placed on good food, it was always a matter of some concern when we entertained him. After accepting abundant hospitality

49

during many weeks of being cookless, we wasted no time in inviting them both to dine the evening following the arrival of a new Italian couple, in whose capacities we entertained high but misplaced hopes. To our increasing mortification the meal commenced with undiluted tinned condensed soup, and continued to a dish of fillets of sole, which were unhappily served in as raw a condition as when they first left the sea. Christopher, who was already showing signs of the gourmet he was to become, took the disastrous meal pretty well. But it took some time before we felt sufficiently confident to invite him to dinner again.

There were many happy interludes between neighbours during these years. The Soames family were increasing fairly rapidly and great interest in them was shown by the inhabitants of Westerham. Mary's reply to our butcher's question as to when baby Jeremy might be due was: 'When the plum is ripe it will drop.' On one occasion dining alone with Mary and her father he asked Mary to sit on his knee after dinner, and then thinking that perhaps I looked rather lonely, asked me to sit on the other one. He had been in a warm and relaxed mood that evening.

In October 1951 a General Election took place and the Conservatives won. Churchill became Prime Minister and Christopher Soames his Parliamentary Private Secretary. Our relations with our illustrious neighbours, however, continued in the same happy way, but with the difference that the conversation became even more interesting to listen to. There were arguments between the Prime Minister, Duncan Sandys, Christopher and Rowley over sterling and what its backing should be. No longer gold. Possibly another commodity. Someone suggested rubber, to Rowley's horror, and he was impudent enough to say that he supposed rubber was being suggested as nothing stretched more readily than elastic. This rather saucy reply cast the PM into a ruminant sulk.

One evening at dinner I was placed between Sir Winston and Robert Menzies, then Prime Minister of Australia. Menzies was engagingly easy to talk to, but when the time came to turn to my other neighbour, only a silence ensued which became increasingly awkward. In desperation I asked the great man if he had done any painting recently. He looked at me with amazement: 'I am the Prime Minister. I have no time to paint.' Our conversation ended there.

Quite often Lady Churchill would hold a children's party at Chartwell for her grandchildren. One Christmas her son Randolph dressed up as Santa Claus. A more benign figure, oozing bonhomie, would have been hard to imagine, as he distributed gifts to the assembled children. But only very recently he had been waging a vitriolic attack on my father, accusing him of publishing pornography in the national press, and dubbing him the 'Pornographer Royal.' He considered there was a slant towards sex in the daily newspapers which he evidently abhorred. One wonders what he might have made of the press today.

During these years I seldom visited London except for some special event. One was a ball held at Buckingham Palace. For such an important occasion I had bought a new dress; not really new, but a model I had found in a sale at a leading couturier which proved to be a little tight. The fashion at that time was pinched-in waists, fortified with plastic rods which held up many layers of voluminous tulle. Therefore the garment was heavy. How much was caused by the dress; how much was caused by the excitement of the event, or the lack of air in a crowded room, or even a combination of all three, but quite suddenly in the Picture Gallery I fainted dead away into the arms of a surprised gentleman behind me. Just before my untimely swoon, which I was relieved to hear later was not altogether ungraceful, I noticed a lady holding a brocade carrier-bag from which poked the face of a pekinese dog. It was Lady Munnings, the wife of the artist. 'The Royal Family quite understand that I am never parted from my little dog,' she disclosed. 'They always allow me to bring her to their parties.' I admired her temerity, and have since never been able to discover how she obtained this special dispensation.

With the sad death of King George VI the new Elizabethan era had begun. Many wondered in which way, under the new reign, the country would distinguish itself in the annals of history. Would we find new horizons, as in the first Elizabeth's time? Could the spirit of adventure once again be felt in the land? We were losing our pre-eminence in world affairs. The Empire was swiftly dissolving. Many comforted themselves with the thought that Britain had always been greatest under a Queen. The Conservative government had won the last election with the slogan 'Set the People Free.' For a while, it seemed, a new spirit was abroad in the land, and with the coming coronation the days of austerity appeared to be over.

As the Coronation Day approached people talked of little else. My father and mother-in-law retrieved their robes from the tailors where they had been carefully preserved in moth-balls, and which only saw the light of day once or twice a century. Then, as if he felt the new reign belonged to the younger generation, my father-in-law quite suddenly died a month before the day. He had been Lord Chamberlain to King George V and through the Abdication to the start of the reign of King George VI. My mother-in-law, in her grief, wanted above all for her son to replace his father in the Abbey. Her wish was granted (places for peers and peeresses were balloted due to shortage of space). So Rowley and I, with mixed feelings of sadness and excitement, took our prescribed places in the Abbey, and watched our young queen perform with immaculate and quiet dignity the ancient ritual of being crowned amid the pomp and glory of the assembled company glittering in their velvets and jewels. And, as if to presage the coming of a brilliant epoch, the news of the conquering of Mount Everest by an englishman capped the expectations of the hour.

The Peers' coronets were as large as soup tureens and firmly fitted the heads of the noble lords with, in some cases, room to spare. But for the Peeresses, heavy little coronets with no apparent means of attachment were expected to be worn. Designed, no doubt, for an earlier age than the flat hair style of the day, the only means of keeping them in place was balance; to keep quite still and depend on gravity.

It was only towards the end of the ceremony that the peers and peeresses, through ancient custom, donned their coronets simultaneously at the hallowed moment of the actual crowning of the monarch. In serried ranks of crimson velvet and miniver sparkling with diamonds, long white gloves gracefully rose together like the necks of a hundred swans. It was, we were told afterwards, a most beautiful and unforgettable sight, but the acute anxiety of keeping our coronets on our heads precluded any appreciation of the scene at the time. With a startling clang one poor lady lost hers, and for the rest of the ceremony we all sat as if cast in wax, firmly concentrating on our headgear which wobbled terrifyingly with every breath.

Later we were invited to stay on a friend's yacht for the Review of the Fleet. This was another extraordinary spectacle. Lines of naval vessels, both ships and submarines, were drawn up in rows as far as the eye could see. At night each ship, with its own supply of fireworks, participated in an orchestrated simultaneous display. Over a great distance, reflections on the water doubled the shafts and sparkle of the fire, making the sight completely unique. The occasion, however, was slightly marred, for I had watched earlier in the day my suitcase slowly disappear into the deep, having been dropped by a seaman from the jetty as we were about to embark. With super-human effort the case was extricated as it gradually sank. Fortunately it was made of rawhide which, being white, showed up. But it was not, of course, watertight. In it was my coronation dress and other expensive articles which the salt water did nothing to improve. We were not able to return home and therefore were burdened with effects not intended for yachts. Rowley was embarrassed to find that while he had only brought grey-flannel trousers everyone else wore white ones.

That year Sir Winston decided to divest himself of some of

his farm lands, and in a letter to his wife Clemmie he wrote, 'French Street Farm has been bought by Cromer for ten thousand. This is a great relief to me. The Nobel literature prize is said to be worth £11,000.' This seemed a strange juxtaposition! The ten thousand pounds were the result of a liquidation of a trust fund belonging to my family, and with it we decided to extend our farming from a single cow to a small herd. It became also a necessary and contrasting interest for Rowley, and eventually myself. The land had not been improved by the generous gift to Churchill from Canada of a tractor more suited to the prairies. With its deep blades it had succeeded in ploughing up not only the soil but the drainage system as well — a drainage system constructed to last by French prisoners of war at the time of Napoleon.

Within my purchase was also the market garden. Walled and with many glasshouses, it had been most successfully run by Christopher who was, by then, much occupied as a very close assistant to his father-in-law. Under our management it sadly became a dismal failure due to cheap foreign produce starting to pour into Britain. The head gardener we took on would proudly tell of the occasion when he encountered Sir Winston and General Montgomery who, after plucking some bunches of grapes, commenced a contest to see who could spit their pips the furthest within the greenhouse. Although it was never known as to who was the victor, in due course a sapling emerged from under a pipe embedded in concrete. Receiving no care or attention, it grew stubbornly to maturity and produced grapes of extraordinary sweetness.

At Chartwell Churchill's partiality for the unusual was to be seen in his flock of black swans and also in his robust herd of belted Galloway cattle. Stumpy and striped, the bulls would delight in leaping some tall gates to court our long-lashed, pretty little heifers, who unfortunately seemed to prefer these outlandish highlanders to their own Jersey mates.

In forming our herd we plunged into buying our original livestock at the Reading sales and, with uncommon luck, bought a young bull from the then Lord Chief Justice's wife, Lady Parker. It proved itself a great sire and was the founder of a most successful herd, albeit a commercial one. Our aim was to build up a herd of cows giving both maximum butter fat and the maximum milk yield, and in this we succeeded. Although farming had flourished in the war, in order to encourage home food production, any losses or improvements could be put against gross personal tax. With sixty head of cattle on only one hundred and twenty acres, we could not hope to cover wages and fodder. Satisfaction came not from profits but from improving the quality of the herd. This happy state lasted until the next Labour government which stopped this advantageous tax situation and, thereby, put an end to our herd. Disappointingly, it was dispersed in 1961.

6

A WEEKEND AT CHEQUERS

In 1953, apart from the excitement of the coronation, we received a telegram from Lady Churchill inviting us to stay at Chequers. My father, who was a friend of Sir Winston's, as his father had been before him, had been asked as well. Since Mary and Christopher would be there too, it would be something of a family party.

We had some difficulty finding our way, as did two of the other guests, Lord and Lady Simonds, the Lord Chancellor and his wife. At the turn of a lane we each stopped to ask the other the way. This encounter cheered us in the knowledge that we were not the only ones. Nevertheless it was with some awe and timidity that we finally arrived at the large Tudor mansion. Our shyness, however, was immediately dispelled by Lady Churchill's warm and friendly greeting which made us feel at ease. Clementine Churchill had a great gift with people old and young. She was charming and kindly, talked animatedly, and showed enthusiastic interest in whatever we might tentatively utter. Many years later Mary remarked that in those letters of condolence that she had received in which was mention of her mother's 'wonderful serenity' she knew at once that their acquaintanceship was slight.

Although Chequers is a large house with many reception rooms, it is not over-endowed with guest bedrooms. As Mary showed Rowley and me to our rooms on the top floor, she told us that mine had once been the prison of Lady Jane Grey, the nine-days queen. It did not prove hard to believe. The first

56

night I lay awake listening to the muffled sighing of the wind and the creaking floorboards, becoming more nervous with every moment. However I was not quite sure that the thought of making conversation to my host for two whole days was not more intimidating than the ghostly room.

At our dinner the evening before we were waited upon by the Women's Auxiliary Air Force. Dressed in uniform, they served us efficiently, but with a distinctive parade-ground manner. The first course was soup, hot and salty — too salty even for manners, and we all gave up any polite pretence. Sir Winston snorted with the first mouthful and called loudly for pencil and paper with which he wrote a very frank note to the cook, while apologising profusely to his guests. It was not until the note had been despatched that Lady Churchill mentioned that the cook had only emerged from retirement, after many years in their service, especially to help out for this particular weekend. Sir Winston was then stricken with remorse for the reprimand he had sent, and remained saddened and silent for the rest of dinner.

It is always difficult for a young woman to know whether to help an aged gentleman to rise or to wait for him to help her. It would seem that the first alternative must be the right one. But I knew that our host belonged to a more chivalrous age, and put great store by gallantry. So when Lady Churchill rose at the end of dinner I took my time while Sir Winston made a great effort to get up as quickly as he could manage to withdraw my chair. For a seeming eternity I wondered if I was doing the right thing and felt that my behaviour was appalling. Here was I, a young and obscure woman, waiting for a venerable, indeed the greatest man of his age, to help her up. My intuition evidently served me well, for he seemed pleased and the rather lengthy process was repeated after each meal. Rowley told me later that after the ladies had retired from the dining room Sir Winston turned to his son-in-law Christopher and said: 'As you are my PPS it is obviously part of your duties to show the gentlemen to the cloakroom.'

After dinner we sat in the long, narrow drawing-room on the first floor, an elegant room full of furniture, but with the impersonal atmosphere of an hotel lounge, the proudest object on display being the death mask of Oliver Cromwell. We were joined later by the gentlemen. The only remnant of conversation that I can recollect was a diatribe from Sir Winston over *The Times*, a newspaper whose policy he clearly disapproved of. I remarked that although it had once been known as The Thunderer, it surely must now be known as The Mumbler. This sally was well received, and the cry went up that I had made a bon mot, a talent much cherished in the Churchill family.

It became clear during the course of the weekend that the reason the Lord Chancellor had been invited down was in order to discuss with the Prime Minister the question of a raise in the salaries of the judges who, it was generally agreed, had fallen out of step with the times and the dignity and integrity of the bench. This subject was discussed freely in the dining-room after the ladies had withdrawn. I understood from Rowley that the PM and the Lord Chancellor wished to give the judges salaries free of tax, as to give them anything meaningful otherwise would have necessitated very large gross increases in their incomes. Rowley had been violently opposed to creating a 'new privileged class,' as he viewed it, and robustly said so, supported by Christopher Soames. He, Rowley, went further, and somewhat intrepidly said that this would be the first step towards the Prime Minister and politicians also becoming a privileged class. Sir Winston was not pleased with this argument, but he must have seen the logic and danger of it, for the proposal in that form was subsequently dropped.

In a small dark room near the front door various lighted tanks of tropical fish were kept. These were shown to us with pride by our host. The more striking had been given names of prominent men and world leaders. I particularly recall a friendly, chunky, black one called Tito. Lady Churchill told us that these fish were the remnants of a much larger collection, of which far the greater part had died on the journey from Chartwell. They had been placed in jam jars filled with warm water, and had inevitably expired from lack of oxygen. Their loss was much mourned by Sir Winston.

We left early on the Monday morning. Sir Winston was not yet up, but on the instructions of Lady Churchill we visited his bedroom in turn to say good-bye. He lay in a four-poster bed smoking one of his large cigars and holding a glass of brandy and water. He looked so pink and white and benevolent. 'What do you want?' he asked, as I nervously entered the room. 'Just to say good-bye and to thank you for a wonderful weekend,' I replied. It was banal, but what else could one say? Remaining silent he just smiled in a beautiful cherubic way.

Shortly after our visit to Chequers the Lord Chancellor, Lord Simonds, a bluff and jovial person, invited us to dine at his official apartment in the House of Lords. Enjoying a magnificent view of the Thames, the residence was approached by way of an ancient lift after traversing a long cement passage with white tiled walls, reminiscent of the London Underground. The apartment was neither ostentatious nor gloomy as one might have expected. We were shown the great seal of England which the Lord Chancellor is charged to look after. It lay in quite a casual way on top of the grand piano. The other guests appeared shortly after ourselves. The introductions were barely audible due to the indelicate noise of plumbing which swiftly brought the dignity of dining with the Lord Chancellor down to a more homely level.

Among the guests were Harold and Lady Dorothy Macmillan. He was at the time Minister of Housing. I found him only marginally easier than Sir Winston to talk to. At dinner I sat opposite Mr Macmillan, who seemed quite unconcerned by the fact that his evening shirt buttons popped undone one after the other at intervals, eventually leaving his chest quite bare. It was, after all, a warm night. This slow revelation, however, was quite mesmerising. I was placed on the left of the Lord Chancellor who had Lady Dorothy on his right. She was wearing a long black evening dress. When I turned to converse with him, to my astonishment I found him calmly wiping his mouth with the hem of Lady Dorothy's dress. His sudden discomfiture on realising what he had mistakenly used as a napkin, and which he hurriedly dropped with an expression of utter horror, made me laugh, but it was not a joke he wished to share, which I thought was a pity. In any case, neither the comedy of the shirt buttons nor the dress used as a napkin had been noticed by Lady Dorothy.

Each year in our local town of Westerham the May Queen was crowned amid general rejoicing and a carnival procession. In spite of his onerous duties, Sir Winston was usually present. He would stand on a platform by the village green to voice his good wishes for the success of the day, while the traffic crawled past, and the passengers on the top deck of the buses would gape like fishes in amazement at the unexpected sight of such a well-known and beloved figure.

It was after one of these annual events, at which I had been given the honour of crowning the Carnival Queen, that Rowley and I received a last-minute invitation to lunch at Chartwell, to lunch alone with the great man and Christopher, as the rest of the family were away. Never again were we to see Sir Winston in such relaxed and splendid form. His mind returned to the days of his youth, prompted by memories of Rowley's Cromer grandfather in Egypt. He enthralled us with descriptions of the Battle of Omdurman, followed by an explanation in forceful detail of the game of polo which, he maintained, taught tactics and strategy, audacity and courage — a sport above all others and of incomparable value to young army officers. Perhaps, indeed, it was the spirit of that game that had won the day at Omdurman.

Towards the end of lunch, becoming more mellow with every moment, Sir Winston urged me, unwillingly, to partake of my first glass of brandy. And Rowley to smoke, equally unwillingly, a large cigar. And as we spluttered and coughed his eyes twinkled merrily in teasing enjoyment. At Sir Winston's eightieth birthday party at number 10 Downing Street a huge cake lit by a bonfire of candles shed a blazing heat. And as Sir Anthony Eden entered the room people respectfully made way to let him pass. It was as if, already, the mantle of power was about to fall upon his shoulders.

In the country, apart from visits to our famous neighbours, life continued in a quiet and ordinary way. Evenings at home were spent watching early black and white television, with a choice of only two channels. I myself seized with relish the opportunity presented by the library of books bequeathed to Rowley to devour the works of Macaulay, Gibbon and many nineteenth century authors.

In 1956 the daily toil of commuting to the City was beginning to take its toll on Rowley. So it was that we decided on purchasing a pied-à-terre in London. Another reason was that Rowley felt that we should entertain business friends, and this was more difficult in the country. This move proved to be a turning point in his career.

The timing of his purchase of a mews house coincided with the Suez misadventure, which followed so swiftly on the heels of the Hungarian uprising. It seemed strange that these events, although quite separate, concerned two countries which in each case had been closely connected with both Rowley's grandfather and mine. Rowley's had virtually governed Egypt for twenty years, while my father had been offered the crown of Hungary. And as my father persuaded his newspapers to support the brave people of Hungary, Rowley donned the uniform of a lieutenant-colonel in the Grenadier Guards to second the motion of the Address of thanks to the Queen's speech in the House of Lords. Asked to do so some time before by Lord Salisbury, Rowley took advantage of the opportunity to support the government on Suez. This venture split every family in the land. More often than not husbands took quite opposite sides to their wives and we were no exception. But, notwithstanding that, it seemed to me that in public, if one's country is involved in hostilities, then whatever the reason, one's duty has to be one of support. It was one of the few active appearances that Rowley made in the Upper House, for he had no wish to enter the political arena, and very much disliked taking part in public debate.

The dining-room of our mews house seated eight people including ourselves, and as soon as the house was ready we started giving small dinners for other young bankers and friends whose husbands mostly worked in the City. It was really high time, for in the country we had neglected this side of business life, which has some value towards a successful career. And in Rowley's case, more than we could possibly have dreamed.

Our younger son started day-school in London where he became friends with another boy called Dwight Makins who came to stay with us in the country. Rowley informed me that he would like to invite his parents, Sir Roger and Lady Makins, to dine. This request I found very disconcerting for I did not know either of them, and Rowley had only a passing acquaintance with him. Besides, Sir Roger was a very distinguished person, being at that time head of the Civil Service and an ex-Ambassador to Washington. 'I cannot think why you should wish to ask them,' I nervously stuttered. 'And anyway, why on earth would such an important and busy man want to be entertained by us?' The invitation was, nevertheless, despatched, and to the surprise of us both, accepted. We were not to know that at that moment Sir Roger was on the lookout for a young banker to fill an official position.

The dinner went off quite well. Both seemed amused at the tiny scale of our entertaining, and when Sir Roger asked, in his bluff way at dinner, if anyone could tell him the name of the Prime Minister of Ceylon (which, for some obscure reason, I knew) an uncanny feeling came over me that, somehow, I had successfully passed some kind of test.

A WEEKEND AT CHEQUERS

It was not long after that evidently fateful dinner that Rowley was asked to go to Washington as Economic Minister.

ECONOMIC MINISTER'S WIFE

A USEFUL CASE OF PNEUMONIA

Returning home to our London mews house from a round of household shopping I found Rowley at once pleased and anxious. I could see that he was also impatient and wished to impart some pressing news. As he had only just returned from a business trip to Liverpool, it seemed surprising. But, unknown to me, he had been summoned the day before by the Chancellor of the Exchequer, Derick Heathcoat-Amory, who asked him if he would undertake a job for HM's Government to be head of the British Treasury Delegation to the USA, British Director of the International Monetary Fund and World Bank, and also Economic Minister in Washington.

The news stunned, and yet, ever since our marriage, I had known instinctively that one day Rowley would be called to do some service for his country above that of simple soldier. I replied: 'So it has come at last, as I always knew it would.'

The assignment was to be for two years and Rowley was given one week to reply. The decision was agonizing. One of our sons was about to take his Common Entrance examinations to Eton; the younger to start at Prep School. The farm to be run, dogs to be looked after. To drop everything, in effect, and to start afresh in a different land. To find new domestic staff, a difficult quest at best. To cater for and to entertain, as yet, unknown people. The prospect soon took on the shape of a nightmare.

We spent the weekend on the Beaulieu River, and on one tranquil, beautiful evening Rowley said: 'The decision must now be made and it will be entirely yours. If you do not want to go, then we shall not, and never afterwards shall I reproach you for it.'

The thought of leaving home and children was distressing, and yet I knew that this assignment would be an important step in Rowley's career and it was not for me to stand in his way. Nevertheless, to be shaken from one's pleasant humdrum existence and into the unknown was traumatic.

Rowley began work at the Treasury in London and, from the start, enjoyed the labour and working with his new colleagues in the Civil Service. For me, preparation for this new life seemed enormous, and I was told that I needed ball dresses, cocktail dresses, and luncheon outfits by the dozen for winter and for summer. Those were the days of hats and gloves, and it seemed I did not possess nearly enough hats. People were full of advice, most of it contradictory. Some told me to put myself in the hands of a well-known couturier who would know exactly what would be required. Others said that going to so many parties made one heartily sick of one's clothes and, therefore, it would be best to buy in great quantity inexpensively. In the end a compromise appeared to be most sensible. In reality, no english materials were at all suitable for the American climate and way of living. They needed to be lighter for both very hot summers and the equally hot central heating in the winter.

The day eventually arrived for the removal of our furniture and effects. Going in advance, they were to be shipped in a freighter called *The American Flier*. They took two months to reach their final destination. The frenzy of packing and sorting out furniture, pictures, ornaments and our entire collection of silver for despatch was a tiring business and they were all to be ready the week before Christmas.

The custom in the Diplomatic Service is never to overlap: a rule likely to have been formed from many years of experience. We, however, were novices and ignorant as well. Rowley's predecessor, Guy Thorold, invited Rowley to come over before his own departure in order to learn the ways of the new job; and Rowley, from inexperience, agreed. No doubt the invitation was kindly meant. Mr and Mrs Thorold, who were quite unknown to us, asked us to stay with them in their house which was to become our home. But I hesitated at the proposal. It did not feel right; and it seemed best for Rowley to go on ahead. It was a decision that we never came to regret, although our plans did not work out quite as expected.

Rowley left for Washington on January 24th 1959 and was duly instructed in his new job which, as he later said, was of no great help since no two people have quite the same approach to their work. At the same time he became involved in the Thorolds' farewell gatherings. They held two huge cocktail parties for their friends and acquaintances which proved an ordeal, as waves of new faces flooded into the house none of whom he knew, and all saying how sorry they were to see the Thorolds go. Rowley was pointed out as the replacement and became an object of curiosity. He felt as if he were somewhere between a bailiff repossessing a house and a trespasser caught gathering someone else's produce. It was an invidious position with an undesirable result. All those strange faces remembered his but he, in turn, could not recall any of theirs. Besides, some were of a persistent disposition and clearly expected to continue the same social intercourse as they had enjoyed before. It became crystal clear as to why the Diplomatic rule of keeping new arrivals apart from those they were to replace abroad was necessary.

In the meantime, back home on the farm, I had developed a cough which very soon turned into double pneumonia.

A call was put through to Washington. At that time the degree of efficiency and perseverance of the telephone operators in America was quite remarkable. Rowley was eventually run to ground in the ante-room of the Chairman of the Federal Reserve Board on whom Rowley was, for the first time, about to call. It could not have been a more ill-chosen moment. The Chairman of 'The Fed' is the nearest equivalent to the Governor of the Bank of England, and to a new Economic Minister an awe-inspiring figure. To be told of an unexpected and serious illness striking down one's wife must have been a shock, and done nothing to help one's equilibrium towards making a good impression. The Americans are, as everyone knows, a most warm-hearted and kindly people, and the Chairman of 'The Fed' was no exception.

While I languished with pneumonia there was no question of a compassionate visit; for no sooner had Rowley taken over the reins of his new job than trouble blew up in world affairs and the problem dropped in his lap.

The job, or more correctly jobs, which Rowley had undertaken, although arduous, had for a long time been steady and quiet with no out-of-the-ordinary difficulties to battle with. Now, almost before he could find his way around his two offices, he suddenly became an essential component in a matter of high policy concerning Egypt, of all places. (This was ironic as it was Rowley's grandfather, the first earl, who had virtually governed Egypt for some twenty-five years. As Sir Evelyn Baring, he had been sent to Egypt as British Comptroller-General of the Egyptian debt. In order for the country to become solvent he reformed the administrative system and, in effect, became ruler under the title of Agent-General).

Since the Suez debacle of 1956 a virtual impasse had been reached between Egypt and HMG in arriving at an agreement to clear up outstanding differences in financial matters which had arisen as a direct result of our invasion of Egypt. The President of the World Bank, Eugene Black, placed great importance on a return to a more normal relationship. He personally thought that John Foster Dulles had been largely responsible for the situation which led to our intervention in Suez, and therefore felt that he should do his best as an American to right the unhappy aftermath. Rowley, as UK Director of the World Bank, then became an essential link in the negotiations since, at that time, there were no diplomatic relations between England and Egypt. Subsequently we heard that there was some amusement and consternation in Egypt when the name of Cromer once again appeared in official documents and telegrams.

It became apparent to Rowley that the differences of approach between London and Cairo were such that telegrams no longer could serve to disentangle the confusion, as both sides were using the same words to mean entirely different things. He therefore decided to fly back to London in an attempt to clarify the issues.

Towards the end of February Rowley telephoned me with the rather surprising news that he would, at last, be returning to England for a few days, but that he would not be able to come down to the country for a day or two as he would be attending consultations in London. At the same time he cautioned me that if any member of the media should chance to telephone, I was to say that he had flown over purely to see me on account of my illness. Governments expect a great deal of their servants and so, I learned, are not above making use of any personal predicament that might be useful to them. So it was that my illness provided a perfect alibi.

The doctors had advised two months rest, but their advice was obviously not to be taken, and I decided to leave with Rowley when he was due to return to the USA the following week after bringing the Egyptian negotiations towards a successful solution. Also there was to be a respite. Rowley was given ten days holiday during which he arranged to take me to stay with a business friend of his at Hobe Sound in Florida.

In those days there were no direct flights from London to Washington. One had to go via New York. Changes in transportation seem to mark the passing years more sharply than other milestones. Destined to cross the Atlantic many times during my life, beginning with a slow steamer, progressing to the great liners, followed by propeller aircraft, then turbo-jet, the Comet, and lastly Concorde, my crossing times came down from three weeks to three-and-a-half hours in forty years.

In 1959 we flew by Comet, and with only a short wait in New York, it was thought to be a rather untiring flight of some eight or nine hours. However, ill luck still dogged my footsteps. The Comet had been plying to and fro without any delay for some weeks past, but on our flight a fault developed about half way across, with the result that we had to land in Newfoundland in sub-arctic weather and in a blizzard. I had been given oxygen on the way over and now, swathed in blankets, was turned off the aeroplane to wait. To our exasperation we missed our connection in New York and had to wait again. In all, our journey had lasted twenty-four hours.

We had arranged to stay one night in Washington at our new home, 2339 S Street, situated in a select area known as the Kaloramas, before taking the night train to Florida. It was not the happiest of arrivals. Weary and depressed, the house itself, although fairly handsome from the outside, was another world once the threshold had been crossed. A gloom descended like an impenetrable cloak in the dark and shadowy hall whence a steep high staircase ascended to the floor above. A landing divided a substantial dining-room from a large drawing-room which, in turn, gave on to a garden. The house was on two levels. The drawing-room contained the heaviest and ugliest furniture imaginable. It was furnished in the manner of an hotel lobby with no focal, point, tables and chairs just scattered here and there. The walls were high and bare, but most curious of all was the colour scheme, or lack of it, for the walls, covers, curtains and carpets all over the house were beige. There was no relief of any kind. Upstairs the bedrooms were no improvement: dark and sombre. The bathrooms old-fashioned, the plumbing positively antique.

The owners of this dismal house were Ambassador and Mrs Cabot from Boston, who let it to the British government while away en poste. It was a great pity that our government spent so much on rented housing, when had they bought it just after the war they would have made a solid gold investment, as the

Chinese did under Chiang Kai-Chek.

Once I was told by an interior decorator that, from experience, quiet, sensitive, rather easily-depressed people went in for light and cheerful colours, whereas lively, buoyant persons were inclined to go for dark and neutral shades. I wondered about Mrs Cabot. Months later she called to ask if I would allow a builder to take a sample of the beige tint for her Boston house as she wished to continue the colour she evidently liked so much. I found her to be an ebullient lady with enormous energy and drive.

Hobe Sound in Florida was a favourite resort for many wealthy and influential members of the Republican administration, and particularly the banking fraternity. But my rest-cure was hardly a rest and we found it impossible not to become involved in the social life of this resort. Maybe it was a happy coincidence to be broken in at the seaside and informally; it certainly provided a link with the many people from Washington who habitually spent their winters there. It was often said that more business was done and big deals and contacts made in the warm sun of Hobe Sound than in many big cities.

Washington, that garden city of attractive homes and wide boulevards, fashioned on the plans of a French architect, was still brown with leafless winter when we returned to S Street. Once we had banished the worst pieces of furniture to the attics and rearranged the rest my spirits began to lighten. We took on a Jamaican couple, Mr and Mrs Henry, who had worked for the Thorolds and also for their predecessors, Lord and Lady Harcourt. We were extremely lucky for they knew what was expected from their job. Mr Henry was known as Henry and his wife as Iris. They understood that certain official guests would fly in at strange hours and require meals. They knew and expected us to entertain frequently and, above all, they were the doyens of the Jamaican domestic labour force in Washington.

The most respected position appeared to mean that Henry

could call on any of his numerous friends to help him and Iris at our parties at any time and with very little notice. It was possibly a little hard on their employers who were usually more junior members of the embassy, but Henry helped them too on his time off. The Henrys were a great blessing, even if at first Iris's cooking was not good. She was wont to cover every dish with a coating of some strong herb chopped finely and looking like newly-mown hay. 'Lady Harcourt liked it done this way,' she would say. I banished all herbs from the kitchen, explaining that we were allergic to them. It seemed better to have none than too much, and I could see that there would be no moderation. The result was a happy one and Iris then proved to be an excellent cook. Her speciality was fried, tinned oysters, and never since have I tasted anything as good. Sole, with roast almonds and lobster tails with rice, was most in demand.

We were especially lucky to have the Henrys, not least because at that time the only good caterers employed whites only, and they were not allowed by their union rules to mix with black waiters or helpers at parties.

It must have been quite bewildering for the Henrys to serve different employers every two years, each with differing views on housekeeping. Mrs Thorold had put great accent on economy which had somehow touched an answering chord in Iris's heart. It took me some time to convince her that where food was concerned economy came second to excellence, but once she understood, she really strove to do her best, although I do not think she ever really quite approved of our extravagant ways. The Treasury gave Rowley a very adequate expense allowance so there was no real need to heavily economise.

Henry himself was a small, slight man with a round friendly face and greying hair. He could look most solemn when on his dignity at parties, or, at least until someone spoke to him, when a delightful giggle would break forth. He could look more disapproving than a Quaker elder at times, with his lips pursed and eyes downcast. That was usually when someone or something offended his idea of order, or when he himself forgot something. If ever an object was dropped or accidentally broken by Henry, the event was swiftly followed by a loud exclamation of 'Ouch!' — the only epithet Henry allowed himself, or thought fit to utter. Both Henrys heartily disapproved of American negroes. In their view they were brash, uncouth and loud-mouthed, and at no time would they permit any social or business intercourse with them if they could help it. 'Trash,' Iris would mutter. She never left the house without wearing a hat, and when we eventually departed I gave her six of my hats which she was absolutely delighted with, and which I knew I would have little use for in England.

The household shopping, I discovered, was never done by telephone. Twice a week Kostos, the uniformed Greek chauffeur, would drive Iris and me to the supermarket. This method of shopping was a complete novelty to foreigners, for supermarkets had not yet invaded Britain. There we would form a small procession. Iris would walk in front, wearing her best hat, and select items from the shelves as she went. These she would place in a double-decker trolley pushed by Kostos, wearing his cap emblazoned with a crown. I would bring up the rear, occasionally guiding Iris in her choice of foodstuffs, and always paying the bill as we left. This pantomime always caused great amusement among my American friends who could scarcely believe their eyes, and considered the sight wholly hilarious.

On the same evening that we returned from Florida, it was arranged for twenty-two British newspapermen to visit us for a drink, our first gathering. They were all Washington correspondents of British national newspapers. Henry Brandon of the *Sunday Times* impressed us most. The correspondent of *The Times* had little to say, was very polite and drove an ancient Rolls-Royce. One came to realise how much our journalists must envy their American counterparts, who became moulders of opinion by way of syndicated columns, sometimes printed in over five-hundred newspapers throughout the land.

They also hold a celebrated position, and the successful columnist is considered to add lustre to any dinner party, however grand.

Rowley was of, but not in, the diplomatic service in the sense that he was not a professional diplomat and, therefore, not a member of that international circuit which is almost a club, whose members more often keep to themselves rather than the people they are accredited to. As outsiders we could not benefit from old friendships and ties with other diplomats, but this lack gave us instead a measure of freedom, and time to choose friends from other spheres. Moreover, Rowley's directorships of the International Monetary Fund and World Bank brought other directors from many countries into our orbit.

The International Monetary Fund was led by a 'Big Swede,' Per Jacobson, who headed an organisation which lent large sums of money to bale out those countries in need of huge loans to ward off bankruptcy. The World Bank lent substantial sums to third world countries for development and help with their infrastructure which, at that time, was a fashionable cause, and gave the World Bank a lustre and renown that the IMF did not possess. This was possibly partly due to the charismatic charm of its President, Eugene Black, who, fortunately for successive British Economic Ministers, lived right next door in S Street. Gene Black enjoyed a good sense of humour. On one occasion he watched a guest of ours dress for dinner. She had forgotten to draw the curtains, being in rather a hurry. Gene was to be our guest that same evening and, on arrival, he told her that he already knew her rather well, which surprised but did not dismay, due to his enormous charm. The fact that she was an english duchess seemed to add piquancy to the situation.

Our first guest was Sir Denis Rickett, a rather austere Treasury mandarin who enjoyed serious music and demanded little in the way of hospitality. Our second was Anthony Barber who was making his first visit to Washington as Financial Secretary to the Treasury. His enthusiasm for all he saw and did was engaging as we took him on various sight-seeing tours. Between our return from Florida and my planned return to England were three weeks, during which I plunged into the social life of Washington as best I could to make up for time lost. It proved concentrated and hectic, and unfortunately the holidays in England were no better and could not have been described as restful.

8

DIPLOMATIC BAPTISM

Social life in the United States probably plays a more important part in oiling the wheels of business and official affairs than in any other country in the world. It was therefore of prime importance to entertain extensively, especially by means of dinner parties, which give more time for relaxed discussion than most other forms of hospitality. We thus set ourselves a course of at least one large dinner party a week and rather smaller luncheons.

But before inviting anyone we had first to compose a list of guests, and since I knew nobody, and Rowley was too occupied to acquaint himself with other than his colleagues in the IMF and World Bank, we had to start from scratch. Already, on my arrival, our sitting-room mantelpiece was laden with invitations from complete strangers, and with their help we would sally forth night after night on what became in the nature of a fishing expedition. We each hoped to return with a new name, perhaps two, of some congenial persons to whom we had been introduced. A reference book was kept and each name entered and accompanied by a description of any useful fact. It was a means of keeping note in order to prevent, if possible, a personality clash or other reasons for incompatibility at our dinners. This practice became my daily evening homework, and without it I do not think that we would have succeeded in our entertaining.

In a surprisingly short time we had collected sufficient names to more than make up our first dinner party. At first it was often the case that the only strangers at our own dinner parties were ourselves, for everyone else appeared to know each other quite well. It gave one a curious feeling of unreality, even embarrassment, to be the odd ones out.

My duties as a hostess were made a great deal easier by the then custom in Washington of guests making their own forays in search of companions after dinner. As soon as the gentlemen had left the dining-room to join the ladies, each would rush to grab the attention of some agreeable female, as often as not leaving Rowley and me standing with no-one to talk to but ourselves; but at least I was saved from many a possibly awkward encounter. This helpful custom tended to lapse over the years and when I returned, as Ambassadress, it was no longer practised, and it was up to the hostess to do the work.

The guest list for our second dinner party astonishes me now as much as it must have surprised our guests at the time. Whether by chance, luck or prescience, or a compound of all three, we managed to gather an almost perfect mixture. Mrs Robert Bliss, one of the great Washington hostesses, who reigned over the social scene with dignity and grace, a staunch Republican and a revered figure. Senator John Sherman Cooper and his elegant and exotic wife Lorraine. The French Ambassador, Hervé Alphand and his beautiful spouse. The Director of the National Gallery, John Walker, a man of enormous charm. The wife of the Secretary of the Treasury, and, among others, an unknown senator whose very name sparked interest on the table plan placed by the front door. Senator McCarthy, not the famous or, more accurately, infamous one, but a new good-looking young senator. A left-leaning Democrat called Eugene (who later ran for President) who, on this occasion, captivated everyone with his natural charm and who, for his part, was equally enchanted with the famed Mrs Bliss whom, he told me, he had much hoped one day to meet and never thought he would get the chance. Eugene, and his wife Abigail, were the leavening, the cement which bound this dinner party together and made it so successful, if not altogether perfect. It was during dinner that Rowley noticed that the Secretary's wife was clearly not herself, and by the time that the ladies had regained the drawing-room she was in a state of collapse. Not recognising the malady I wondered what to do: ring for a doctor? Smelling salts? Burnt feathers? It was a fraught moment. The situation was saved by the wife of an Assistant Secretary of the Treasury who was among our guests and who firmly told me to get her upstairs and order black coffee, which with her help I managed to do. Lying on my bed quite *hors de combat* and plied with black coffee by an understanding Henry she eventually recovered. It transpired that the poor lady had dutifully attended three cocktail parties before sampling our wines, and it had all proved to be too much. One did wonder if alcoholism was a customary hazard at Washington dinners, but it was, in fact, the first and last case that I was, fortunately, ever confronted with.

The Washington Hostesses were an institution and served a useful purpose. They were formed from exceedingly rich ladies who were respected both for their wealth and for their energetic and prodigious hospitality. Some were Republicans, others Democrats and each would entertain members, but not exclusively, of their chosen party as well as the Diplomatic Corps. Their usefulness lay in the opportunity offered for young members of Congress, Diplomats and other newcomers to meet. There was also a recognised but unwritten pecking order, as well as a difference in tempo between them.

In 1959 Mrs Robert Bliss reigned supreme in the Republican camp. She was the *Grande Dame* personified, small and delicate as porcelain, gracious and ladylike, her manners exquisite and her furniture fine French eighteenth century. Her Georgetown house was immaculate, and it seemed to me impossible for any but the most well-mannered to be invited twice. Earlier she had presided over Dumbarton Oaks, her huge private Washington home long since given to the nation.

Mrs Bliss was kindly towards the young. Lunching with her and her husband alone on the day that Jack Kennedy won the election, she made no disguise of her disapproval of the 'rough' Kennedys. 'Do you think he could possibly win?' she asked me with obvious disbelief. 'Do not underestimate the luck of the Irish,' I replied. This delicate-looking lady and her elderly husband, both over eighty, achieved their wish of visiting the monastery atop Mount Sinai two years later.

Second in precedence was Mrs Robert Low Bacon. Equally loved and respected, she was made of rougher material: louder in voice and heavier in manner. The less couth felt more at ease. She lived in an old house in downtown Washington long since abandoned by the residents. Her rooms remained the same until the day she died. It was she who presented us with our ambassadorial leaving present as no doubt Mrs Bliss had performed this ritual for others before us. The Hostesses' positions unquestioned and problems over their succession never arose.

Mrs Perle Mesta led the Democrats as hostess. Her parties tended to be larger and less selective. There were many others in the wings ready to step into her shoes. But, as the years passed, no-one seemed to be an obvious candidate for the Crown and today I doubt whether any single hostess could be so acclaimed, as in those days.

On my arrival in Washington I found an invitation to join International Group Two in place of Mrs Thorold. The Group was composed of twenty women — ten from Congress (five from each House) and ten from the Diplomatic Corps. The Group was very useful to a newcomer in giving her an opportunity to meet some Congressional wives which, with hindsight, had been chosen with extraordinary perspicacity. At our first meeting Lady Bird Johnson put herself out to be friendly to a newcomer and quickly dispelled any feeling of shyness, as did Abigail McCarthy. Later, when it came to the turn of Betty Ford to entertain us in her home, she charmed us all with her fresh enthusiasm as a new Congressman's wife, and with her vivacity and good looks.

The Group met once a month in each others' houses where we would be treated to lunch and served the national or regional dish from whichever place our hostess came. In the afternoon a talk would be given on the beauties and attractions of the Homeland. I felt closer to the American Congress wives that to those of the Diplomats, partly, I think, because they were more natural, friendly and relaxed. The Diplomatic wives seemed never able to forget that they were the representatives of their countries at these meetings and were always rather stiff and over-polite. As was required we all wore hats. The conversation never varied from food, children, education or clothes. It was safe talk if not very stimulating. Many compliments were given and received and never a note of criticism. The Diplomatic wives were well versed and knew well how to handle such gatherings, for never a discordant note nor argument was allowed to enliven the proceedings.

When it came to the turn of Lady Bird to entertain us we were taken round the Capitol and shown rooms not open to the casual visitor. Senator Lyndon Johnson was, at that time, Majority Leader in the Senate, a very powerful position and one in which he was most adept. As a special concession we were taken to his private office where on the wall opposite his desk hung a life-size coloured photograph of himself. On another wall a statement of a personal creed which started 'First I am a Texan' or it may have been '... an American' but went on line after line ending '... a husband,' '... a father.' I wondered about this man. Was he a supreme egoist, or just a simple rustic, or both? We were allowed on to the floor of the Senate Chamber where we peeped into the Senators' desks. Arranged in a semi-circle, they looked exactly like old-fashioned school desks with hinged tops. Names and doodles had been carved on the inside of the lids, just like at school, the difference being that some of those names belonged to famous figures in American history; a strange discovery that somehow seemed to present the past and present youth and boyishness of this great nation.

As a hostess there were many social pitfalls to be avoided. *Place à table* was very strict. Although America is a republic and always lauding democracy and even equality, official status is very strictly adhered to. Fortunately it was not difficult to discover who took precedence over whom for the Washington Social Register edited by Carolyn Hagner Shaw advised one on all the finer points of protocol and etiquette. If that failed, then there was always the Chief of Protocol's office, although I never had recourse to that Department, for Miss Hagner's book was comprehensive and detailed. Her first admonishment, a little alarming: 'The necessity of following protocol in the Nation's Capital is of momentous importance. Do not belittle it.' One was carefully informed 'never to forget that the wife of an official always assumes the rank held by her husband whether he be present or not' and also that 'the husband of a woman official assumes the rank of his wife.'

I liked the reminder that 'when in doubt as to which two people bear the higher rank, it is the best part of wisdom never to invite them to a seated dinner at the same time.' Also that 'personal friendships do not count in official Washington as the ranks of one's guests must be the deciding factor at all times.' From these official strictures followed the fact that it was not just the chief guests that needed special seating but almost the entire table, the lowliest position being mid-centre on the left-hand side of the hostess. In the table of precedence it seemed slightly strange that the Speaker of the House of Representatives should rank higher that an Ambassador of a foreign country, and that the widows of former Presidents were senior to the current Secretary of State.

Most people in Washington were not surprised to receive an invitation to dinner on the basis of having met once, however fleetingly, and as often as not accepted. This may have been partly due to the fact that the population of Washington was mainly a shifting one, with government officials and diplomats continually taking up and leaving their posts, as well as Congressmen losing or keeping their seats bi-annually, as might one-third of the Senate.

To me it was intimidating to ask a number of total strangers to dine but it had to be done. There was, inevitably, one occasion not long after we arrived when all our guests, having met us but once, turned out to know each other extremely well. We joined in the general laughter when someone said that the only strangers at the dinner party were the host and hostess! Fortunately there can be no other country where the people are so warm and friendly to strangers, are eager to meet people and often rush to introduce themselves. This makes the lot of the hostess very much easier.

9

DUTY FITLY DONE

Our two years of duty coincided with the last two years of the fading power of the Republican administration of President Eisenhower. At the time of our arrival John Foster Dulles was Secretary of State. He was in bad health and was shortly to die. There seemed a general lack of purpose in the country. President Eisenhower, although loved by the people, was not quite fulfilling the role of world leader to the degree expected. Many Democrats and some Republicans sharply criticised his methods in our company. It was never wise to agree and equally difficult not to.

At that time in Washington, almost every day, and certainly once a week, a Head of State or Prime Minister was wont to visit the capital in order to call upon the President and, in almost every case, to ask for financial aid in some form or another. The visits of the Heads of State (always accorded their due pomp and ceremony) roused no interest in the minds of the public. Often on my shopping forays downtown the passers-by would be halted from crossing the street by police in order to make way for a military parade escorting a king or president to the White House. It was only if the important visitors were of unusual interest, such as Castro of Cuba, or wives celebrated for their beauty, as in the case of Thailand or Queen Soraya of Iran, that the people showed any interest further than cheerful tolerance at being held up for a few minutes before continuing on their way. This gave food for thought as to what place our great little country filled in the minds of the present-day Americans. Were we just another debtor-nation asking for aid, or were we considered different from the others? The mention of the British Commonwealth always seemed to produce a politely amused reaction. Canada, Australia, India and many others had their own embassies, and received the same formal respect as ours.

Socially, of course, we retained, with France, pre-eminence. The British and French ambassadors' presence at a dinner always gave a certain cachet to the evening — as in London, where the French and American ambassadors hold the same position. In Washington at that time the Russian and satellite ambassadors were barely seen at all.

In our embassy, Rowley's position was a peculiar one. He ranked third after the Ambassador (Sir Harold Caccia) and the Minister (Lord Hood). But unlike the Minister, Rowley was regarded by the-then Ministry of Works as ranking as an ambassador. This meant that we were entitled to use the same white china adorned by the crown as the ambassador, as well as the same white place-cards emblazoned with the Royal Arms in gold. In certain circumstances Rowley was accorded ambassadorial treatment. Rowley had two offices, one in the embassy, which was rather bare and old-fashioned, and another much larger and more modern in the building that housed the IMF and World Bank. Rowley would spend the early part of the morning in the embassy and then, accompanied by his secretary, drive to his other office, which he greatly preferred. He would return again to the embassy in the evening to discuss with the ambassador any telegrams he wished to send. Although Rowley occupied two offices, it took a long time before he was allowed more than one typewriter. The job was arduous, being three in one — possibly the hardest he was ever to have; followed, inevitably, at the end of the day by the everlasting parties which could not be avoided, and which were important to the job.

In the embassy Chancery there existed a curious tradition of demarkation. According to rank the offices were furnished differently. At junior levels only a desk and chair were permitted, which grew according to seniority, when a carpet and tall hat-stand would be included. A Minister's office, however, was not provided with a hat-stand, on the assumption that they had always, in the past, merited some flunkey to divest them of these articles. Rowley, therefore, could never find anywhere to put his headgear, which always amused him. Ten years on, men's hats were no longer worn.

Once every two months I was expected to hold a coffee morning for the British Embassy wives. Lady Caccia was too busy to hold them with any frequency. Lord Hood was unmarried, so the Commercial Minister's wife and I took this chore in turns. One feature of the Diplomatic Corps is intermarriage, which is hardly surprising when one considers that diplomats spend much of their lives away from their own shores. I had expected to find rather dashing, chic and elegant ladies descending on my drawing-room and was astonished to find that most of them spoke with strong foreign accents and were very far from being well-dressed. I could never get quite used to the fact that so many were foreign-born when, after all, they were representing the United Kingdom. Very few seemed to possess the savoir-faire that one might have expected, and the conversation revolved round the usual subjects of children, domestics and food.

On one of these coffee morning occasions a cousin of Rowley's, Fiona Myddelton and a friend of hers, Kate Worsley, who later became the Duchess of Kent, were staying with us after an exhausting bus ride all round the United States, down the west coast as far as Mexico City, and up through Texas to Washington. They were travel-stained and weary when they arrived, their shoes in need of instant attention from the cobbler and their clothes from our washing lady. When they heard that I was to hold a coffee morning two days later for the Diplomatic wives they both sweetly said that they would like to attend, possibly also out of curiosity. Like me, they had expected to find dashing Foreign Office wives and were sadly disappointed. Still, they made a noble effort for half an hour before retiring to the seclusion of their bedrooms.

In May of our first year the McCarthys invited us back to dinner which they held in an hotel. Eugene was the junior Senator from Minnesota and he was keen that we should meet the senior Senator, Hubert Humphrey, of whom he and his wife thought very highly at that time; perhaps one could say he was a hero. Humphrey was certainly very self-important. After dinner he strutted up and down in a very self-sufficient manner, talking loudly but saying little. Why the McCarthys looked up to him so highly made us wonder. Later they became political competitors and no longer friends, for Hubert Humphrey won the Vice-Presidential ticket to Lyndon Johnson's presidency, defeating Gene McCarthy.

Another Washington friend and a great character was Joe Alsop, the columnist. The first time we met was at a small luncheon. He asked me in a loud voice which I considered the most important, 'money or sex?' The question, I felt, was mainly asked in order to disconcert. Giving it some serious thought, I replied that surely it depended on what one already had, for whatever one had, one was bound to want the other. He liked this reply and a friendship began. I remembered that about this time someone asked Joe what he thought of Jack Kennedy. His reply was immediate. 'Squalid,' he simply said, which certainly surprised us, particularly as Jack Kennedy was thought to be quite a friend of Joe's and, in fact, remained so when he became President.

One couple we entertained to dinner fairly frequently was Prescott and Dorothy Bush: he, a most respected Senator, tall and aristocratic, with a gentle charm, and his wife Dottie, who was a small lady of boundless vitality whose eyes sparkled and yet were shrewd. They often spoke of their son, George, but we were not to meet him for some years to come.

Before the war, when air-conditioning was in its infancy, the British Embassy would close during the summer months and move to cooler climes up north. But by 1959 all the embassies remained in Washington. Earlier, Congress sat for only the first part of the year and, indeed even in 1959, recessed for the summer and did not meet until the new year. This would give a dampener to the autumn dinners, for without any politicians they were less lively, and there was less to discuss.

The horror of a Washington summer has to be experienced to be believed. Even to our Jamaican staff it was a trial, for they would say that at least in Jamaica a breeze would bring a modicum of comfort, whereas in Washington the heat would increase during the afternoon and even into the evening. Humid, the air would be like thick, hot soup. Our official car, a rather stately Humber, boasted one small fan in a corner which, however hard it tried, never succeeded in making an impression on the turgid air. One sat in the back dressed in a hat, and trying as best one could to keep one's powder dry, for those were the days when ladies were appalled at the thought of being seen with a shiny nose, let alone a face dripping with perspiration.

At the end of September when the temperature was still high, bankers and finance ministers from all over the world would congregate for the World Bank meeting. Every third year it would take place in some other country, but during our time it was held in Washington. It would be a very busy time for us and our staff. Apart from having house guests, there was a full programme for the wives while their husbands were attending meetings, and each evening countless cocktail parties and receptions were given. The highlight for the ladies that first year was a tea party at the White House held by Mamie Eisenhower. This was my first visit and I was amused to discover that the ordinary guest entered through a side door, while those with the Entrée came through the main entrance, which is quite the reverse to Buckingham Palace. After passing through some stately rooms, we encountered our hostess who was lit by a cunningly placed spotlight, which caused her to glow with a golden radiance. She even looked almost beautiful when in reality she was far from that. Graciously, she lightly shook my hand and smiled. I was not at all certain that she could see beyond the spotlight to whose hand she was shaking as her expression was rather blank. Nevertheless, most people were satisfied at meeting Mrs Eisenhower and very pleased to be in the White House.

Each year it was beholden to the Economic Minister to give a buffet dinner for the British delegation and other officials. We tried hard to make it as enjoyable an evening as possible. A transparent plastic tent would be hired to cover the garden, and with lights placed in the flower beds the effect was attractive. Candles on small round tables gave an air of romance to an otherwise staid party. A man would play a concertina and by and large the evening would be considered a success, or, at least, the first one was. The second, unhappily, coincided with the first ever television debate between the two Presidential candidates in the election, Vice-President Nixon and Jack Kennedy. No American of any consequence wished to miss it, nor, for that matter, did we.

Walter Lippmann and Phil Geyelin had accepted and now felt that they should refuse on account of being journalists, and many others felt the same. We solved the problem by hiring four television sets, each placed in a corner of the tent, with the result that the big debate became the entertainment for the evening. Neither candidate came over well. Nixon had an unshaven look, and Kennedy looked rather callow, which prompted a loud remark from one American lady who said: 'Oh God! Do we really have to get one of them!' The debate was not the only obstacle to the evening. September heralds the start of the hurricane season, and that afternoon a warning that Hurricane Dora was advancing in full force on Washington had come to the notice of the caterers, who immediately wished to dismantle the tent they had only erected that morning. Had they done so the party would have had to have been cancelled; so bringing all the persuasion I could upon them, and with various dire warnings they agreed to let it stand. As the afternoon wore on, the temperature started to soar, and with it the humidity. There was also an uncanny stillness. Dora, fortunately, decided to change course shortly before reaching the capital, and tore off at an angle, just missing us. There was great relief all round and we were glad to have ignored the warnings and gone ahead with the party. The Chancellor of the Exchequer, Selwyn Lloyd, was our guest of honour, and in the end the party was declared a success, even if we had not captured the lively and relaxed atmosphere of the previous one.

Opposite our S Street house lived the widow of President Woodrow Wilson, an old lady who seldom sallied forth from her house. She would watch from a window the comings and goings across the street and one would feel her eye upon whomsoever ventured in or out of our house. One neighbour on the other side from the President of the World Bank was the Ambassador of Pakistan and his family, with whom we did not have the same close relationship. It was not in any way hostile, but now and again they cooked something that definitely was. Some indefinable substance which gave off an aroma that simply compelled us to leave the house. Fortunately it was never cooked in the evening. Therefore our dinners were safe. Also the problem did not occur very often, but was a hospitality hazard just the same.

In those days there existed a Debutante season in Washington, as indeed there was in London, but both were very different. Our daughter had reached the age of seventeen, and much wished to experience a 'Coming Out' in Washington, so plans had to be made. These were easy, if expensive, for a rather commanding lady ran the whole affair. For a fee which was not small, she would give a date on which a party could be held. She would also decree whether it could be a ball, a tea-dance, dinner party or simply a lunch. She would produce a list of the guests to be invited and would do the seating plans as well. It was a system that took a great load off the parents, and was also considered a benefit by the young. It was the organiser's responsibility to know which couples had paired off and who was courting whom. She possessed a valuable list of young men, a number, possibly, strangers, and made sure they went to the parties she had arranged. The young men, carefully chosen as suitable, sometimes bore names that made us chuckle. The season was extremely short and also divided: one part took place during the Christmas two-week holiday, and the other during the Easter vacation, whereas in London the season for debutantes would drag on for three months or more. Short as it was in Washington, one or two young people would become engaged and shortly afterwards even marry.

In November 1960 a farewell luncheon for Mamie Eisenhower and Patricia Nixon was given by the wife of the US Atomic Energy Commission, Mrs John McCone to which I was bidden. Thirty women sat around a horseshoe table. Being very junior in rank I was put at the end, next to Elizabeth Arden. My neighbour was a great friend of Mrs Eisenhower which probably accounted for the perfection of her make-up. Miss Arden's chief topic of conversation was racehorses and I could not wean her on to the subject of cosmetics however much I tried.

Hildegarde, a singer, whose act was to sing popular songs while playing the piano wearing gloves was also famous for her temperament. She arrived late because her aeroplane had been delayed, and this had not put her in a good humour. Conceivably also she was not being paid a fee, or if she was, possibly not enough. At any rate, after playing a short repertoire she stopped and asked Mrs Eisenhower to choose the next song. Mrs Eisenhower asked for 'God Bless this House,' homespun and certainly well-known, but not, as it turned out, to Hildegarde. A silence followed which became awkward, and then Hildegarde confessed with a bad grace that she did not know how to play it. Mrs Eisenhower looked annoyed and the situation was saved by the intervention of Pat Nixon who, fortunately, was able to ask for a known Hildegarde song. It looked very much at one moment as if Hildegarde was quite ready to flounce out. This she was quite capable of doing. Once in London at a party for the presentation of film awards she had refused to sing at the last moment. That situation was saved by Bing Crosby who, by chance, was staying in the same hotel where the film award party was taking place and who, equally by chance, came to hear of her behaviour. Our luncheon ended on a happier note with all the ladies joining in a general sing-song of somewhat corny tunes reminiscent of the end of a school term.

In December of 1960 we were told to move out of our official house in S Street for renovations and, instead, a suite of rooms were taken in the Shoreham Hotel. We bid a sad farewell to the Henrys, packed up the furniture, pictures and trunks and, without much regret, spent our last month in the hotel where we celebrated Christmas with our family of three.

On our arrival at our spacious suite at the Shoreham we discovered the plumbing has seized up due to ancient pipes. This entailed the removal of the bathroom units which remained in the passage of our suite for a month. We were given an extra bedroom entirely for the use of its adjoining bathroom which was still in working order, and thus we continued to reside in the nation's capital. We had a kitchen and cooked a happy Christmas lunch for our little family. The boys spent much of their time tobogganing on the slopes beneath the hotel. The elder of the two attended dancing classes at Arthur Murray; modern pop, do-as-you-will gyrations, had not yet burst upon the world.

That autumn there had been talk that Kim Cobbold would be resigning from the Bank of England, and this gave rise to much speculation as to who would succeed him. In a moment of precognition I told Rowley that I was quite certain that he would be the choice. 'But that is quite preposterous,' he replied with open disbelief. Various candidates were discussed, particularly by Per Jacobson of the IMF, to whom the subject was of burning interest. He would call Rowley into his office in order to speculate on whom would be chosen for this responsible position and the pros and cons of likely candidates would be examined. Two names came up through the grapevine, and Per dismissed these characters with some asperity: 'One is a windbag and the other a lightweight.'

One morning Rowley knocked on his door. He had come, he said, to tell Per that the appointment of the new Governor had been announced. 'Who is it?' Per asked with eagerness. 'It is me,' Rowley humbly replied. The heavens did not collapse, and Per, after some moments, asked him if he knew any of the world's central bankers. Rowley had to admit that he knew very few. 'I will help you,' Per told him. He knew them all and was as good as his word, and, moreover, proved a good friend and ally.

To me Rowley had been diffident over accepting this onerous position. 'I am too young and inexperienced,' he said, but I encouraged him to take it.

During Rowley's two years in Washington he discovered that he got on very well with the Treasury officials. His understanding of Americans had always been mutual and happy. He discovered in himself an outstanding ability for negotiation, and a gift for being an excellent chairman; which he had not before been in a position to realize.

Before we finally left Washington many farewell parties were given, culminating in two large receptions given by ourselves in the Chancery. Arthur Krock, the well-known journalist was inspired to write a panegyrical poem which at one party he stood and recited. The gist of it was as follows:

If Her Majesty's acknowledgement of duty fitly done
Traditionally were writ on a diplomer,
Of all who've served her in those realms where once ne'er
set the sun,
None would the more deserve it than Lord Cromer.
From Francis, who the House of Baring founded,
Through a long line of Viceroys, pro-consuls — a priori,
The Barings have earned Britain's praise unbounded.

High on their 'scutcheon are the bays Maurice, the poet,
  wore.
Evelyn o'erthrew Ismail, the false Khedive.
With such ancestors, such a wife, the question is, what more
Rewards remain for Rowland to receive?
But one there is, undreamed of by his celebrated folk,
The while they scaled the peerage rank on rank,
For not to Northbrook never, nor yet to Revelstoke,
Did the PM give the key to England's Bank.
Imagination they possessed, but never enough daring,
As to've foreseen all Rothschild gold turned over to a
  Baring!

The job of Economic Minister in Washington customarily carried with it on its completion recognition of a KCMG (which had been awarded to Rowley's predecessors). On this occasion it was not offered, and when Rowley made an enquiry, the reply came back that since he was an earl which, politically, was quite bad enough, nothing therefore would be forthcoming.

To one who, through no fault or merit of his own, had an earldom thrust on him through birth, Rowley felt a certain lack of fairness in this decision. Many years later, when offered the Washington embassy he told the Prime Minister, once he had decided to accept it, that he would not dream of going until this past oversight had been remedied, which was immediately done.

GOVERNOR'S WIFE

10

YOUNG BOSS FOR THE OLD LADY

We returned from Washington in January 1961 with our two young sons, having set sail from New York in the *SS United States*. We were not to know that this would be the last time that we would cross the Atlantic Ocean by ship, having done so many times in the past as a matter of course.

On arrival at Southampton the boys and I watched the great ship dock as we stood by the rails on the main deck. Suddenly we noticed a crowd of men hurrying on to the pier with notebooks flapping and others with cameras. As the gangplank was lowered they proceeded to clamber on to the ship. We wondered aloud as to whom they could possibly want to interview. Which mysterious celebrity had lain unseen and unheard during the voyage? It must be a famous film star, we supposed. Later we descended to our cabins only to find that this bevy of newshounds had found their quarry in Rowley. A queue had formed outside our staterooms with the intention of interviewing and photographing the Governor Elect of the Bank of England.

For me a new voyage had begun — one that was to last five years. And those five years were to be among the happiest and most interesting of my life. To Rowley they would certainly be interesting but the burden of responsibility he was to shoulder precluded contentment.

The news of Rowley's appointment was generally well received by the press. With John F Kennedy as the new young President of the United States, it was widely considered appropriate and imaginative for the Old Lady of Thread-needle Street to be given a young boss (the youngest for two-hundred years) and the Prime Minister was congratulated on his choice. Answering criticism in the House from a member of the Opposition, Mr Macmillan replied: 'Although he is a young man, which is said not to be a bad thing now-a-days, he has a long connection with banking matters and he has been one of the most successful Economic Ministers at HM's Embassy.'

Nevertheless Rowley's appointment was, in fact, a compromise. The Bank, the Treasury and the Government each favoured a separate candidate. None met the whole-hearted approval of all three. Rowley was not anyone's first choice or, possibly, second, but he was the only one that was acceptable to all.

Rowley's term of office was to be for five years and to commence in June 1961. Once appointed by the Sovereign, no change can be made by any succeeding Prime Minister until the Bank Governor's full term is completed.

Friends and business acquaintances hastened to tell us how lucky Rowley was. 'My dear fellow, it is the best job going; prestigious and grand and does not involve much work; a sinecure, in fact.' Those were the general sentiments. How wrong they were proved to be.

In Southampton the reporters' questions had seemed extraordinarily trivial. 'In what capacity are you related to Mr Macmillan?' This question seemed to be of paramount interest since one or two of the Prime Minister's relations had recently been given government posts. 'Not in any way whatever,' Rowley replied. 'Sir Winston Churchill is a neighbour of ours, but I do not know what you can make of that.' It was the first of many press interviews, and we began to discover the doubtful benefits of publicity.

Once again it was thought beneficial for Rowley to learn the ropes before the departure of his predecessor, Lord Cobbold, and once again it did not prove useful. There is little value in learning how to act while waiting in the wings. Besides, Rowley needed a well-earned rest of some length between jobs and this was denied him.

Some of the photographs of Rowley did him justice, but one really dreadful picture printed alongside Kim Cobbold prompted the latter to send Rowley a copy accompanied by the following comment:

'A very shady-looking pair to have running a bank, but on this occasion, unlike most others, I think the new one looks worse than the old'!

Before Rowley had taken up his post in Washington he was given leave of absence from Barings bank. Therefore, before accepting the position of Governor, it was necessary to again seek Barings' approval.

The Prime Minister, with this in mind, asked the senior partner, Evelyn B Baring, to call upon him. Thinking that any City bank would be proud and pleased to have one of their members so honoured, Macmillan was astonished to discover that Evelyn Baring was not. The Prime Minister was, in fact, somewhat disconcerted by his reaction. On receiving the news Evelyn Baring rather churlishly replied: 'All right, we will let Lord Cromer go, but after you have finished with him we can give no assurance that we will take him back.' Since at the time Barings bank was still enjoying a reputation based mainly on past glories, and no longer possessed any partners of great distinction, Evelyn Baring's reply appeared to be at the very least eccentric.

Before Rowley took up his new job, his tutor at Cambridge, Mr Gow, invited him to dine in his new rooms at Trinity College, Cambridge. He also invited a number of leading Cambridge economists. As Mr Gow had refused to allow Rowley to switch from Roman Law to Economics when Rowley wished to do so as an undergraduate, and had therefore left the University earlier than intended because he found the subject of Ancient Law excessively boring, Rowley told Mr Gow that if the Bank of England had a remarkable ignorance of Economics under his governorship it would be entirely due to Mr Gow. To which Mr Gow replied in a voice loud enough to be heard by all present, that this was Rowley's saving grace because had he studied under any of these professors, Gow himself would have been scared out of his wits.

The Governor's official abode was small and poky. The original idea was to provide a spacious penthouse flat on the top floor of a section of a large modern building which housed the Government Bond offices. However the Inland Revenue had decreed, in its mysterious and parsimonious way, that the tax that would be levied on the Governor's income for his occupation would be more than his net salary as Governor. Faced with this financial impossibility, the top floor was, instead, divided into inner and outer apartments. The inner, at the end of a very long corridor, was to be for the Governor. The outer, divided into three units, was for the Governor's official entertaining, and consisted of a drawing-room, dining-room, and a large kitchen used only by caterers, bedrooms and bathrooms for official guests and a small flat for a housekeeper to look after them. For ourselves there was an unfurnished living-room which had to also serve as a dining-room; small kitchen and two bedrooms. For this the Income Tax authorities also saw fit to tax the Governor.

With hindsight, we may well have made a mistake to have moved from our comfortable mews house but, at first, we were excited by the novelty of living in the City, and it took time to realise the demarkation between private and official living. There were, however, many small benefits we came to appreciate. The Bank provided its own maintenance men. Any electrical faults, plumbing failures or minor decoration were immediately attended to with the minimum of fuss. But, above all, during the many monetary crises to come, it proved invaluable for Rowley to be living over the shop.

Living in the City was altogether different from living in the West End. The atmosphere was strange and did not feel like London at all. Even the air seemed different. Maybe this was because we were nearer the Thames estuary. Being full of scurrying people during a weekday, at night and during the weekends it was deserted. The nights, however, were far from tranquil. Trucks rumbled down Cheapside on their way to and from the docks. The noise, magnified by the funnel of modern facades, condemning us to the use of ear-plugs.

Most of the city buildings were new due to wartime destruction, but the high-rise had barely begun. Wild flowers still flourished on old bombed sites and between modern offices one came, unexpectedly, on the ruins of old City churches. The old City churches had once been a glory before so many were damaged, but bells still rang and steeples still peeped above the roofs.

From our flat on the sixth floor we enjoyed unparalleled views. To the south were the hills of Sydenham and Beckenham, and from one window the dome of St Paul's was impressively close. Too distant a view to watch the activity of the streets meant isolation, but there was also a comfortable feeling of safety. Curiously, and at surprisingly frequent intervals, warehouses would catch fire, and from our grandstand view Nannie and our younger son would watch the conflagrations being dealt with. The City fires were quite a feature. At one time even the Bank itself caught alight on an upper storey and we rushed out to watch that being extinguished too.

The only entrances to our flat were modest: one insignificant door into Cheapside and another into a large garage. But from the garage an electrically-operated portcullis would proclaim the importance of security in such a building.

Because the lower floors of the building which housed our flat also contained the Government Bond offices, for five years I was able to extract some amusement to questions of our whereabouts by replying that as a matter of fact we lived above the National Debt.

The two official entertaining rooms came under the Head of Establishments and one of the executive directors of the Bank. When Lord Cobbold first invited us to an official dinner he remarked as he opened the door to the drawing-room to every arrival: 'Isn't it absolutely frightful?' accompanied by a booming laugh. He meant the decoration.

It was a room designed by a committee, with the unfortunate result that nothing matched and every item in it bore no relationship to the other. Each member had clearly had his say, and expense had been no object. And because so much money had already been spent, no further expenditure was favoured. One member of the committee had happily thought to give distinction to an otherwise stark, low ceilinged, modern room by purchasing the original wallpaper from the Chinese Room at Panshanger, the home of Lady Desborough (the famous Edwardian hostess). This was a stroke of genius. But, not so happily, shiny satin, smoked glass, crystal drops, tassels and a modern chinese carpet (especially woven) had connived to produce a nightmare. 'A tart's parlour,' remarked quite a few guests.

Something had to be done, but the directors were very reluctant to allow a newcomer such as myself to have a say, although there was general agreement that something was wrong. The majority were completely convinced that it was the wallpaper, when in my opinion it was the only redeeming feature.

It took a little time to persuade those whom it concerned that we really could not entertain amid such dreadful decor for five years and that it would not cost much to make improvements; and finally it was agreed. All that was necessary was to show the magnificent wallpaper to its best advantage, to dispense with the much-patterned carpet and replace it with an ordinary plain one. To be rid of the smoked glass and all the other fancy bits. To take tints from the paper and use them for perfectly plain curtains and coverings. The old curtains were of a fussy pattern and of an indescribable hue.

After a period of grave suspicion the directors professed to be pleased with the results and certainly relieved that the cost was relatively slight.

The dining room was modern, and although inspiring no favourable comment, did not, by virtue of being modern, need any alteration. The fact that few people and no women could leave the dining table unaided was of minor concern, for the modern chairs were weighty.

When Rowley took over the reins as Governor on July 1st 1961 he told me on that first day that he had never felt so lonely in all his life. The grandeur of the Bank, with its huge rooms and marble halls. The pink-liveried messengers standing respectfully silent about the passages. The faces of past and eminent Governors looking sternly down from the walls — all contributed to an overwhelming feeling of inadequacy. This ancient and massive institution, entirely under the charge of one person, himself. It was intimidating.

The suite of rooms used by the Governor and Executive Directors were known as the Parlours. And the largest and grandest of them is occupied by the Governor. His room, dominated by a large table which had been used as a desk for centuries by past Governors, evoked the awesome thought of how much of Britain and her Empire's financial business had been conducted over its green baize top. The thought did nothing to encourage, nor did the fact that on that first morning, not a single piece of paper lay upon its surface, nor was there any mail. In fact, the only reading matter consisted of *The Times* and the *Financial Times* which Rowley had already studied at breakfast.

From nine-thirty to eleven o'clock Rowley sat and studied the walls, re-read the newspapers and felt increasingly and depressingly alone. He never forgot that morning, and when, many years later, Gordon Richardson took over the Bank, Rowley wrote him a note, to which Gordon replied appreciatively that it had been most comforting, for the only piece of paper on the table on his first morning had been Rowley's welcome letter.

After those first interminable two hours of that alarming first day, the tempo radically changed. People began to call, and from then on the pressure of work became more and more demanding.

When my father called my brother into his office in Associated Newspapers to tell him that the wire services had just come through with the news that Rowley was to become the new Governor of the Bank of England, Vere replied with a chuckle, 'What does that make Esme, a Governess?'

The wife of the Bank Governor has no duties, unless it is to provide as serene a private life as she can for her husband with his heavy responsibilities. To learn to wear a smiling face in public in case a gloomy one might be misinterpreted as reflecting anxieties over the pound sterling. To refrain from relaxed gossip in case a stray word be taken as a sign of impending trouble, and even to withdraw from social life during monetary crises. On the other hand, being the wife of the Governor meant sharing much that was pleasant and interesting. Meeting interesting and important people of many nationalities, and perhaps above all, travelling abroad in a manner not remotely possible for an ordinary person.

On July 17th, soon after Rowley took over, we were invited to dine with the Prime Minister. The dinner was in honour of the Governor General of Nigeria, and decorations were requested to be worn, which for ladies at that time meant tiaras if they could possibly find one.

At dinner I was placed next to James Callaghan, whose good-looking face I had only previously seen on the television screen. Turning in my direction, and with a meaningful glance at my jewellery, he opened the conversation by telling me how very hard it had been for his mother to bring him up on less than three pounds a week. Looking him full in the eye I told him that my great-grandmother had struggled to rear a family of eight sons and three daughters on possibly less. But, in spite of that, six of the eight sons had gone on to become millionaires, had provided new jobs for countless people and endowed many charities. Therefore I believed in freedom of opportunity and private enterprise. 'I cannot think what family you can be thinking of, unless it is the Harmsworths,' he commented after a pause. From then on, although we differed in our views, by his firmness and plain speaking he gained my respect and even admiration.

Since the war the general political thought in Britain had been towards security. Security of jobs, health and welfare, very high taxation and, above all a feeling that any form of wealth was something to be almost ashamed of. All political parties seemed to share this view, which had an unfortunate and stifling effect on all forms of enterprise at a time when the country needed to encourage its natural genius for invention and venture, for the nation's coffers were very far from full.

Already, before Rowley had been more than a few days in the Governor's chair, the gathering clouds of a possible monetary crisis could be discerned, and Bank Rate was raised. Per Jacobson, the wise head of the International Monetary Fund, was strongly advising that Britain should reduce her spending, and such counsel was never welcome at Westminster. As we were leaving the Prime Minister's dinner, Harold Macmillan called after Rowley: 'Do we really have to take notice of that tiresome Swede?' At that time we were borrowing from the fund and perforce had little choice but try to do what the Fund suggested. The politicians understandably disliked any belt-tightening. They had for years been cheerfully spending what was left of the wealth of Britain, and some were just beginning to learn that printing more paper money was no answer in the long run. If the Conservative politicians needed some lessons that Mr Micawber knew only too well and if, as it appeared, they did not want to listen, what extra nightmares lay ahead when the Labour Party's turn to take over came? For one's peace of mind it was best to stick to the present and give no thought to the morrow.

Every autumn the Lord Mayor of London holds a banquet

at the Mansion House, known as the Bankers and Merchants Dinner. It is a large and formal affair, the main speakers always being the Chancellor of the Exchequer, the Governor of the Bank of England, and the Chairman of the Stock Exchange. For the Governor, it is his most important oration of the year. In that autumn of 1961 it was also the very first time that I had ever attended a formal City banquet.

The Chancellor was Selwyn Lloyd, a bachelor. I therefore found to my increasing dismay that I would be the ranking lady after the Lady Mayoress, and I had no idea what to expect. The most important of the guests assembled in an ante-room. Then, to a flourish of trumpets delivered by splendidly attired members of The Honourable Artillery Company which heralded our entrance into the banqueting hall, we processed towards the head table watched by hundreds of gentlemen and their tiara-clad wives.

Seated on the left of the Lord Mayor I realised that most eyes were upon us, but relaxed in the thought that as long as I did not actually drop my knife and fork all would be well. Besides, the Lord Mayor was civil and seemed kind. But when, at the end of the dinner, a huge gilt cup was placed in front of the Lord Mayor, who then asked me if I was ready to take part in the Loving Cup ceremony, I replied with dismay that I had absolutely no notion whatsoever of what he might be talking about. He was somewhat taken aback, because at all the City functions this had been an age-old custom — at all the Livery Companies as well, but Rowley had never belonged to any, or wished to. The Lord Mayor hastened to explain; and it seemed really quite complicated. First, the Lord Mayor would turn and bow to me while I curtsied in return; then he would drink from the huge cup and then we would bow and curtsy again, after which it was my turn to drink from the cup and then turn and start the ritual again with my other neighbour. But, most important, after my neighbour repeated the performance on his other side I was not to sit down, but to remain standing and turn my back towards him. This latter posture is apparently an ancient custom originating from the necessity to guard those pledging their friendship from a stab in the back. 'Symbolic of the competitive society,' one Labour Minister quipped at a later date. With shaking knees I managed my part and watched anxiously as Rowley undertook his.

The speeches were, by custom, serious, often technical and certainly lengthy. By the time that Rowley was half way through his speech, the disconcerting sight of quite a few women being aided from the room through lack of air or general boredom was certainly discouraging. Therefore, a year or two later, he requested that women should be excluded from the scene. This came as a disappointment to me for no longer could I share in the only ceremonial event of the year in which the Governor played a leading role.

Rowley spoke out in his speech and gave his honest views, criticising the government, the unions and management. The government for not having a consistent policy, and the others for their outdated customs and practices. This was the first of many speeches that Rowley gave in which he tried to draw the attention of both the government and the governed to our financial plight. It was a brave thing to do, for really no-one likes the unpalatable truth, and certainly not the British when they are in one of their ostrich moods. Sometimes, during the following years, he would ask me if I thought he was right. My answer was always the same. If you know something is wrong and you can put it right then you must speak up. The people have a right to know. This, I am afraid, was never popular with the politicians of the time.

Possibly the chief responsibility of the nation's banker is to watch over his country's reserves; to advise and warn the government of the need to take measures to protect the currency. Rowley felt deeply about this. 'Our money should be honest. Those who save should have no fear of being cheated when they come to realise their savings.' These and other sentiments in the same general vein were given in his speeches from various forums within the British Isles. The following June he said: 'Financing government spending might cause inflation. There could be a manufacture of money quite unrelated to real resources followed by a further decline in the purchasing power of money. These were all severe warnings of the evils of inflation which, in fact, were to come in very much greater severity some years later.

Many thought that Rowley was right to speak out, but the Conservative Government, no doubt, had moments of regret at having appointed him in the first place.

Outside London Rowley's first speech was in Coventry at a dinner given by the Chamber of Commerce. This was the first time we encountered the provinces' habit of retiring from the banqueting hall as soon as the meal was finished and before the speeches started, later to reassemble at their tables, by which time the atmosphere was dead and Rowley would have the unenviable task of bringing it to life again.

Rowley's speeches were given quite wide coverage in the newspapers and this, we discovered, brought some unwished-for attention. For almost directly afterwards our house would sustain an attempted robbery.

Every month the world's leading central bankers gathered in Switzerland for the board meetings of the Bank of International Settlements in the quiet provincial town of Basle. That there was a curiously fraternal bond between the governors of the various nations' central banks was clearly discernable. Each was the guardian of his nation's financial wellbeing and each was aware of the profligate tendencies of governments, whatever their political hue. The meetings were a source of strength to each one of them, and all were aware of the fragility of the world's monetary system. Their confidence in each other was personal and based on the prestige of each nation's bank and not on that of their governments.

Accompanying Rowley occasionally to Basle, I came to know and admire most of his international colleagues. All were men of wisdom and integrity who had risen to the top

110

through sheer brilliance and hard work. If they had, at first, entertained doubts over Rowley's appointment, mistakenly perhaps thinking him just a privileged scion of the British aristocracy, it did not take long before they realised their error and found him a worthy colleague.

The Annual General Meeting in June usually coincided with the publication of the Queen's birthday honours list. It was a great surprise, and even more so since most of the central bankers came from republics, to discover that the list was carefully scrutinised and freely commented on during the large annual lunch party. It came as a shock to them when Harold Wilson recommended to the Queen to honour the Beatles with the MBE. And we both had a hard time excusing what in their eyes appeared to be no less than a facetious exercise in frivolity. This, in turn, made it even harder for Rowley to convince them of Harold Wilson's serious and responsible intentions.

There were some short visits to Europe apart from Basle during our first year, one particularly memorable being the World Bank meeting in Vienna. We were all greatly spoiled by the Austrians who were keen to give us the best time possible. The palace of Schönnbrun was opened up for an evening party. Candlelit and with appropriate music we all dined in evening clothes in great splendour. Every day, after the meetings, receptions, dinners, concerts, opera and the Lipizzaner horses were all for our pleasure.

Some time the following month I lunched with Sissy Ormsby-Gore. Her husband had been appointed our ambassador in Washington and she wanted me to tell her all I could. She was both nervous and scared at the prospect, but a more charming, sweet, intelligent and gentle person would be hard to find. 'What can I do to make them like me?' she asked. 'Just be there,' I replied. She was a very devout Catholic and I think her faith helped sustain her and others through the traumas she was to experience in Washington.

About this time we asked the Governor of the Bank of

111

Australia and his wife to lunch in the country as they were on a visit to England. It was the first time I had met them. Our cook had come out of retirement to help me. She had worked for my father for years, and was of the old school. We also arranged to interview a prospective gardener and his wife. Most unfortunately, poor Mrs Williams confused the two and showed the Governor and his wife into the staff sitting-room before telling me that a Mr and Mrs Coombs were waiting for me to interview them. Horrified, I rushed along and with profuse apologies escorted the Coombs to the front of the house. There was really nothing I could say but the truth, and they both took it very well. Nugget Coombs even said that his father had been a jobbing gardener before emigrating to Australia, which somehow made one feel even more embarrassed. Nugget was a very distinguished Australian and greatly revered. He was also a modest man of simple tastes. He remarked to me that he hoped that we were going to serve cabbage for lunch as it was his favourite. Fortunately we did, although Rowley has always said that it was not a vegetable that was at all suitable for guests.

The autumn of 1961 saw the death of Ruby, Rowley's mother. A daughter of a Viceroy of India, she had just lived long enough to see her son become, if not a Viceroy as she had ardently hoped, at least a kind of Governor. Rejoicing in that distinction she died content.

About the same time as that sad event I regretfully sold my dairy herd for, unfortunately, their upkeep was becoming increasingly costly.

11

CALLING ON PRESIDENT DE VALERA

There were many pleasures reserved for the Bank's Governor and his wife, not least an annual invitation to sit in the Royal Box at Wimbledon, to witness the semi-finals and enjoy the delicious tea provided; to launch a huge oil tanker for British Petroleum; invitations to the State Banquets given by the Sovereign for visiting Heads of State at Buckingham Palace. These latter invitations were a special treat. The first one that I attended still shines out above the others as the imprint of first experiences usually do.

The Head of State was the President of the Republic of Liberia and his wife, Mrs Tubman. This was the country to which the slaves from the southern States of the USA had returned to govern their own land. Knowing none other, they adopted the same way of life they had experienced in America, with the difference that they then owned their own slaves brought into captivity from other parts of Africa. Slavery ceased, but those in authority who could afford it, still quaintly clung to the formal attire of shiny top hats and tail coats worn by the plantation owners of the past.

The gold plate, exquisite porcelain, profusion of flowers and the general splendour of the Palace scene, enhanced by the graciousness of the Royal Family, bestowed upon the representatives of this tiny country a touching contrast. The Honourable E Reginald Townsend, who liked to be addressed by his full name and title, proved to be a short very-black person of great dignity. The title Honourable being a title of

113

distinction in the United States, it was retained in Liberia.

That month Selwyn Lloyd was suddenly dismissed from the Exchequer, among other extensive government changes made by Harold Macmillan during what became known as 'the night of the long knives.' Rowley was sorry to see him go for he had acted responsibly as Chancellor and had done what had been necessary in the face of unpopularity, which may or may not have been the reason for his dismissal. To curb the over-ambitious claims of the Trades Unions Selwyn had introduced his electorally unpopular and uninspiring 'Pay Pause.'

Harold Macmillan, with the ghosts of 1926, the slump and the dole queues haunting his judgement and, being above all a consummate politician, was looking ahead to the next election and how to win it, even if that meant papering over the cracks of financial decay.

Reginald Maudling was given the Exchequer. He was an unknown quantity to us. He seemed able and businesslike in his other official positions, and he was undoubtedly amiable, and evidently popular with the public. Doubtless he would be a good Chancellor; at any rate we hoped so. In order to get to know him better we invited him and his wife Beryl to stay with us in Kent. We spent a pleasant day walking and talking and trying to discover what sort of person he was. Delighted to have been appointed Chancellor, he appeared full of confidence and bonhomie. Did he realise the seriousness of our financial situation? Did he have his own thoughts towards the solution of our monetary difficulties? If he had, he showed no signs.

I remember remarking that governments could not act the role of Father Christmas for ever, especially without a sackful of toys, and noticed the set of a very firm chin. After they left Rowley wanted to know what I thought of him, and I replied that I did not know and that he seemed rather an enigma. Rowley agreed, and neither of us felt happy.

After the redecoration of the official entertaining rooms we started to hold dinner parties. We gave about three a month on average. If we had a policy, it was to bring together leading personalities in many fields. Some, not seeming compatible on paper did, on meeting, get along very well, and certainly enlivened the parties. Barbara Castle with the President of the World Bank; Ted Heath with Alastair Burnet; Henry Moore with Cecil King; Sir Frederick Ashton with Rab Butler; Enoch Powell with Humphrey Trevelyan, and many other permutations. It was fun composing the lists and interesting to see how they worked out.

The directors showed their confidence in my choice of decoration to the extent of allowing me free rein in buying some ultra-modern pictures to hang in the dining-room. Happily, I made haste and repaired to a well-known avant-garde gallery and chose a Paul Nash and two Alan Reynolds, while enormously appreciating this opportunity to make such an enviable selection. It was curious, and yet not extraordinary, to discover that where members of the Conservative government admired the traditional drawing-room, it was the modern dining-room, with its abstract pictures, which appealed to the Labour members. Either way, the abstract pictures always produced comment, particularly the Reynolds, for a suspicion always arose that they might have been hung upside down. Subsequent Governors relegated them to the store-rooms and preferred something more classical. But the Bank had, unwittingly, made a good investment.

Our guests were always directed to arrive at the Watling Street entrance of the Bank. The start of Roman Watling Street is an obscure and narrow lane, from which a ramp descends into the subterranean garage of New Change, a workmanlike garage containing our modest front door. Watching for the kind of entrance thought appropriate to the dignity of Governor, most guests would pass it completely by, only to be frantically pursued down empty streets by top-hatted and pink-liveried messengers who would breathlessly succeed in turning them back. The contrast between the grandly clothed and respectful messengers with our humble entrance, provoked sufficient amusement to give a good start to the evening.

In October of 1962 we made the first of our overseas official visits from Governor to Governor. We chose Ireland, to which neither of us had ever been, and which no Governor of the Bank of England had ever before visited in an official capacity.

The warmth of our reception in Dublin and the sheer vitality and gaiety of the Irish quite took our breath away. Their beautiful city, reminiscent of London thirty years before when horse-drawn carts were still prevalent in the streets, evoked nostalgia. We met many people, but attempting to discover their political differences was difficult. The Fianna Fail and the Fine Gael, apart from sounding alike, appeared at the time to have similar policies. People, they said, voted mainly for historical reasons. The more explanations I received, the more confused I became. But one thing was certain; all were friendly and easily given to laughter.

Fianna Fail was in power at the time of our visit, and the members of it seemed quieter and more subdued; possibly more conscious of their dignity than the Fine Gael shadow ministers, who were decidedly boisterous.

The evening of our arrival the Governor of the Central Bank, Dr Moynihan, gave a reception in our honour in order to meet the leading banking personalities, and even in this proverbial, stuffy section of society, the Irish bankers were easy, relaxed and thoroughly enjoyed the occasion of a party, for it was a very merry one.

The Central Bank of Ireland was then a rather new institution, doing only note issue and a few other central bank functions. Any other activities came under the Bank of England. The Bank of Ireland (not to be confused with the Central Bank of Ireland) Court Room had been the chamber of the Irish House of Lords, and still keeps to this day the mace, which is displayed with some pride to visitors.

After the House of Lords was dissolved early in the nineteenth century, the Irish mace mysteriously disappeared, only to surface again in a 1920s Sotheby's sale catalogue. The Bank of Ireland thought it appropriate to bring it home and bid accordingly but, to their consternation, a competition arose from another keen bidder, resulting in a much more inflated price being paid by the Bank, who were determined to obtain this prize. On returning to Ireland, and much to their amusement, they discovered that the under-bidder had been none other than the Government of the Republic of Ireland. Ever afterwards the Bank would remark to distinguished visitors: 'You see, we had more money than they did.'

The Irish seemed very concerned that we should enjoy and like their country, but when I remarked, jokingly, that maybe Rowley and I might go so far as to live there, for I had liked what I had seen so much, the reaction was suddenly decidedly cool.

A meeting was arranged between the President of the Irish Republic, Eamon de Valera, and my husband, escorted by Dr Moynihan. I also attended, although how I came to be included remained a mystery. We drove through lovely Phoenix Park to Arus Anllachtaran (the presidential palace) which had once been the residence of the Viceroys. It is now called by an impossible gaelic name, which someone attempted to translate, the result being The House of Cream. A rather seedy-looking ADC answered the door and asked us to sign the visitors' book, which was lying on a table in the hall, and beside which hung a striking oil painting 'Men of the IRA.' This gave me a frisson as I thought of all those bomb incidents in London when I had been a schoolgirl. And this was before the much more terrible bombings that were to come.

Rowley warned me on no account to mention prison when talking to President de Valera. I was rather annoyed and I sharply told him that I did not usually start conversations in that way and, in this case, would have more tact. We were ushered through a magnificent Georgian drawing-room and after waiting for some fifteen minutes, an army officer asked

117

us to follow him into the President's study, where we found Mr de Valera sitting behind a large desk. He rose as we approached and proffered his hand which we had been warned to grasp for his eyesight had failed and he was almost totally blind.

We sat on chairs around his desk feeling nervous and wondering what to say. Mr de Valera had just celebrated his eightieth birthday and at first just seemed an ordinary, rather stiff old man; but as he thawed he started to radiate charm until after only a short time we were both rapt — in fact, spellbound, by all he had to say. Almost his first words were about his time in prison (I could not resist making a face at Rowley). With humour, he talked about it with what, incredibly, appeared to be genuine nostalgia. That he raised the subject at all was certainly a surprise and might well have caused embarrassment since it was we British that had put him there, but somehow he made it seem quite the most natural subject to talk about. He told us that when at first he had been imprisoned, and after realising he was not in a position to give any help to his wife and children, he accepted his fate and settled down to make the most of his time there, by taking the opportunity of improving his mind, studying books from the extensive prison library; and the time that was given him to do so would never have been possible at home. For he now had complete freedom from worry and interference. He also acquired a taste for hot gruel which the prisoners were given first thing in the morning, and never in his life had cocoa ever afterwards tasted so good.

De Valera discussed economic affairs lightly and with humour. He seemed particularly anxious to find out the relative status of the Bank of England versus the British Treasury, ambling around the point, until finally asking outright: 'Who has the final word?' My husband artlessly replied, 'The Government.' Mr de Valera told us that one of his sons claimed that economics shaped history, and he had told him that it had not been so at all in Ireland.

At the end of our interview we were asked if we would pose for photographs with the President, which we were happy to do. De Valera spoke, as we were leaving, on the great importance he placed on the gaelic tongue. He wished it to be spoken by all Irish people and had, in fact, made it compulsory in all the schools. However, most Irish people I spoke to declared it to be a complete waste of time. We finally left Mr de Valera's presence feeling buoyant in spirit and appreciative at having had the opportunity of chatting with such an attractive personality, conceivably even a great man, in spite of the many controversial and less-praiseworthy sides to his character and past career.

On our last evening we were entertained by the Minister of Finance, Dr Ryan, at a very imposing mansion that had once been the Dublin house of Lord Iveagh. About forty people sat down at a long table in the dining-room. I had been told by various women on arrival that the party would be dull and formal, and that no-one was expected to enjoy themselves. I sat between the Minister and his shadow in the Fine Gael. The food was excellent. Everyone except Rowley and I had been given an individual menu in gaelic, which only a few were able to read. Ours were in French, and not a few of the guests asked permission to glance at them. The main course in gaelic was SICIN ROSTA ar BHAGUN with a number of accents over the vowels. Probably one could have guessed that one, but MANGLAM BEARDOIGE defeated us completely.

I asked the Minister and his opposite number if they considered themselves Europeans, for at that time Ireland was keen to become a member of the Common Market. They both replied that they did. We agreed that eventually a common language must come into use. I asked them which one. They both firmly replied French.

In the drawing-room after dinner a little old man with a deaf-aid came and perched on the arm of my chair. He was nimble and small and might have been an elderly leprechaun. He was Sean O'Kelly, who had been the second President of

Ireland, which office he had held for fourteen years. A merry, pixie-like person, with charm, he laughed a lot. He told me that during his days as President he had given numerous parties which had never ended before 3.00 am, and that he had always stayed up to enjoy the last gay moment. He proudly wore the emblem of the Chevalier of the Légion d'Honneur, which he laughingly told me had been given to him by the French for the excellence of his table and his knowledge of wine during his presidency.

Rowley and I left what appeared to be a most successful party at about eleven o'clock, as we had to catch an early plane the next day. I mentioned to my host that I hoped our departure would not have the effect of breaking up the party. He replied with a smile that I need not worry for he was certain that the evening had a long way yet to go. The guests did seem to have settled down and clearly had every intention of making a night of it.

The following month we made a trip to visit the Canadian Governor in Ottawa, visiting Montreal before and afterwards for Rowley to see, and both of us to be entertained, by the Montreal bankers. Montreal was still at that time the centre of business in Canada. From there we took the night train to New York for two nights of more bankers' hospitality, before continuing on to Washington where we stayed at the Embassy with the Ormsby-Gores. We did not see very much of our hosts as every meal and cocktail party was taken up seeing old friends. But I saw Sissy enough to realise how close they were to President Kennedy; indeed the embassy seemed to be filled with childish activity and laughter, as the younger generation of Kennedys and the younger Ormsby-Gore children flew down a huge upstairs passage. Sissy did accompany me out to tea with the venerable Mrs Longworth in her time-capsule house, where the silver kettle, nestling on its paraffin flame, blew up, to shower us all with boiling water. Completely unruffled, Mrs Longworth totally ignored this interruption.

CALLING ON PRESIDENT DE VALERA

The chairman of the Federal Reserve, Bill Martin and his wife,
were no strangers to us, which was a help to Rowley.

12

THEY WANTED A NOVELTY

In May 1963 Mr Korovushkin, the President of the Bank of the USSR, the Gosbank, decided to call upon the Bank of England. This was the first visit by a top official of the Gosbank since the Russian Revolution. He brought his wife with him. His daughter and son-in-law were attached to the Soviet Embassy in London. We were expected to entertain them in the country and also in London. News had reached us before his arrival that neither he nor his wife spoke english or any other language, so all communication took place through John Stevens of the Bank, who was fluent in Russian, or Mr Korovushkin's son-in-law.

Rowley and I were slightly apprehensive about this visit since it was to be the first time either of us had met a senior Communist official. The first problem was how to entertain him in London. Advice was given that a musical entertainment would be the most welcome, but not one that would be too high-brow. Therefore 'The Black and White Minstrel Show' was recommended. It did not seem to me to be a very tactful choice, partly because all the performers were white dressed up as black, that it was an American import, and I wondered if Mr Korovushkin would understand. The show was known to be one of the most successful of its kind in London at that time, which may have been why it was chosen. Whether Mr Korovushkin or his wife enjoyed it or not, no indication was given. Our lunch for them in the country proved even more difficult. We had been warned that their table manners might not be quite what we would expect; that peas would most probably be eaten off a knife (not that we would have minded!)

In spite of John Stevens' and the son-in-law's swift ability to translate, conversation proved extremely difficult for Mr Korovushkin was a most unco-operative and taciturn personality. Besides, he lacked both humour and any social grace. Whatever subject we chose to mention always produced the reply that in the Soviet Union everything was better, larger and more efficient. He could find nothing to praise in Britain.

He stayed at the Savoy Hotel in London. Also at Gleneagles in Perthshire, where they did him the honour of running up the Hammer and Sickle on their flag pole, much to the amazement of their American guests. And he was accompanied to Scotland by Jasper Rootham, a genial and urbane official from the Bank who was also an expert on Russia, who felt discouraged and distressed, for he knew many polite and attractive Russians. Poor Jasper became the recipient of both his and his wife's complaints.

To Rowley and me, Mr Korovushkin was the representative of his people, for we knew no others, and he was therefore to us a typical example of the rest of his countrymen. It was with no sense of loss, but with a certain degree of curiosity, that we later heard that Mr Korovushkin had been removed from his position as Chief of the Gosbank and sent to Siberia very shortly after his return from England. We speculated that maybe after all he had become infected with western ideas, which seemed rather unlikely, since he was the most intransigent of men. His disappearance did seem strange, and the only chink of light that shone on this mystery was a rumour of decidedly human proportions: that his wife, his second, also his secretary and a great deal younger than himself, had, on her return to Russia, gained the animosity of wives of more senior officials by her uppishness and condescending manner. So the husband was demoted and sent off to look after a small branch in the East with the purpose of bringing his wife down to size. Whether this was true or not, Mr Korovushkin's visit and subsequent removal coincided with a new direction in Soviet policy: that of allowing their officials to make visits to the West. Possibly it was realised that a representative abroad should be a person capable of making a good impression.

Before Mr Korovushkin departed from England he invited Rowley to visit the Gosbank in Moscow as soon as it might be convenient. After his removal the invitation was instantly renewed by his successor, and quite a considerable amount of pressure was exerted to persuade us to make this return visit in the autumn of 1963, but which we were not able to do until June 1964.

That autumn of 1963 Harold Macmillan relinquished the premiership due to ill-health and was succeeded by Alec Douglas-Home whose appointment, though generally welcome, was greeted by surprise by many, and in particular by Rab Butler, who therefore lost his final chance of becoming Prime Minister. Sitting by his side at a dinner at Lancaster House for the Prime Minister of Luxembourg he remarked, rather quaintly, and with touching despair: 'You see, they really wanted a novelty.'

The next week we were invited to dine by the new Prime Minister at Number Ten in honour of the Prime Minister of Iceland, and there I met Harold Wilson for the first time. I was seated between him and Patrick Gordon-Walker, the then shadow Foreign Secretary. I remember an animated conversation with Mr Gordon-Walker about the Queen's official birthday celebrations in various embassies abroad. 'When I am in office I shall see that they are discontinued,' he said. 'But how shall we reciprocate other countries' National Day Celebrations?' I asked him. 'If they are sensible they will follow suit,' he replied in a very English way, quite forgetting our diminished place in the world. 'In Washington the Queen's Birthday Party is the leading social event of the year, enjoyed by a multitude of American officials,' I pleaded, 'and they will not understand if the party is abolished. They will consider it an ungracious act, to say the least.'

This dialogue caused much amusement to his other neighbour, Lady Caccia, who remembered well my dread of the parties, on account of the long stand in appalling heat. However she joined in support of my argument. Making, nevertheless, no headway whatsoever, I appealed in desperation to Harold Wilson. He listened and replied with care: 'It is quite easy. We shall see that only one of the Queen's birthdays are celebrated,' which neatly ended the argument without a commitment to either side.

Mr Wilson was an easy conversationalist, relaxed and by no means contentious, quite unlike my other neighbour. We discussed simple matters of day to day living. 'I need ten hours sleep at night, but can manage with eight,' he told me. 'But surely, if ever you are Prime Minister, you will be lucky to be left undisturbed for that length of time,' I commented. 'I will insist upon it,' he replied. Noticing my glance at a jug of water close to his plate he revealed that 'they know my habits, for I drink a lot of water and I also eat a lot of salt.' He gave me the feeling that he felt quite confident that before long he would be presiding over the same dinner table instead of Sir Alec. 'When I am Prime Minister I expect you will come to some of my parties,' he kindly told me. But in all of his six years in Downing Street he never included me in a single invitation.

At the end of dinner all the politicians present rushed off to vote in a division, but strangely, although all wore dinner jackets, the Labour members changed theirs before appearing in the House of Commons.

A few days later the golden promise of a youthful leader lay shattered in the assassination of John F Kennedy.

One week later we were in Washington staying with the Ormsby-Gores. I reached the embassy ahead of Rowley after a short visit to Canada, and spent that same evening with Sissie and Arthur Schlesinger alone. They were still shocked and beaten by the blow and trying to comfort each other as best they could. It was very sad to witness their personal grief for they had both been such close friends. Outside President Kennedy's immediate circle parties, surprisingly, continued to take place, and no sign of mourning was evident. It was not that the people grieved less, but that life continued as usual. The shock-waves of Kennedy's death shook the world, and somehow one thought that the most shattered spot would be Washington. But this was not the case at all, except in some quarters.

Dinners were given for us every evening. The Chairman of the Federal Reserve, Senator and Mrs Sherman Cooper, the Doug Dillons and others, kindly gave their usual generous hospitality with luncheons and cocktail parties.

During the summer there occurred happy and tragic family events. First our daughter's marriage; then an appalling accident with a go-cart involving our elder son; followed by the tragic death of my nephew in a car accident, and as a final blow at the year-end, our younger son hurt his leg and remained in plaster for months.

The financial scene had remained fairly steady (although Rowley was becoming less and less enchanted with Chancellor Maudling who did not wish to risk unpopularity by curbing public expenditure despite this fast becoming a real necessity). It was not a year that we were sorry to leave.

13

TREATED IN ROYAL FASHION

Bank of England foreign visits were very special. Special because, as guests of Central Bank Governors, we were warmly welcomed, not only into their respective countries, but into their homes. We were able to see their land, and their way of living in a manner not available to a tourist; to meet and talk to some of the leading personalities in Government and, in a short space of time, appreciate their pleasures and sympathise with their problems, as one might do within a family.

Rowley received an invitation from the Government and State Bank of Pakistan for us both to pay a visit to their country early in 1964. It was to be an official visit, but how official, and in what special way we were to be treated, neither of us had an inkling.

Before leaving England we asked government officials whether we should take some gifts for our, at that time, unknown hosts. Their reply was negative, which was a pity. Many occasions arose when it would have been at least polite to exchange presents instead of only receiving them. (To have declined them would have been considered offensive).

It was our first visit to an eastern country. In a state of total ignorance, and with some trepidation mixed with some excitement, we left a cold and wintry England, thinking that the Indian sub-continent would be warm, if not tropical. We took only light-weight summer clothes.

On arrival in Karachi, after a night flight, we were met by the Governor of the Central Bank, Mr Hasnie, whose first remark was: 'Welcome to our underdeveloped country.' Judging by the fleet of cars, uniformed chauffeurs and personal bodyguards dressed in dark-red and golden turbans, sprouting fans of starched cotton, one could hardly have described our welcome as underdeveloped.

We were to stay with the Governor in his official residence, which was occupied, not only by his wife, but also, as in most Muslim households, by their married sons and daughters-in-law, who remained unobtrusive and rarely spoke.

Our three days in Karachi were full, Rowley meeting businessmen and delivering lectures, while I, given a programme of my own, was taken on tours of welfare and craft centres, hospitals, schools and all kinds of other interesting institutions which alerted me to much that I had not hitherto known. Touchingly, I was treated to a concert given by a blind orchestra, the music weird to my ears and the instruments strange; a maternity hospital, simple and somewhat primitive but likely to have been a great improvement on previous conditions. The mothers, in anticipation of this visit, displayed all their male babies with genitals exposed for my admiring inspection, while those who had, to their clear disappointment, given birth to females, looked ashamed and tried to hide them. At that time the authorities were still trying bravely to cope with the multitude of impoverished and illiterate people who had over-run Karachi since Partition. It was an uphill task, but the enthusiasm and energy of the better-off Muslim ladies was most impressive.

Rowley and I were given a personal bearer called Shafi. He looked grim, fierce and wild, but surprised us by his solicitude for our welfare. Like a nanny, he poured milk into our tea, sugared our cereal and looked after us with gentle care, always ready with a fresh bottle of Evian water should we be thirsty. He did not, however, like cleaning our shoes because they were made of leather, and possibly pig, which animal is considered unclean by both Muslims and Hindus.

The climate in Karachi was cool, only to become colder as

we travelled north. I already realised that my clothes were inadequate. A light summer coat now served also as a dressing gown. My two light wool suits were worn alternately. Most evenings required a long dress, which anyway looked softer and more in keeping with the flowing and colourful saris which were all about me.

A picnic at the Bank beach hut was planned with a camel ride beforehand. The picnic proved to be a carefully organized feast; waited on by five footmen in livery. The hut had been freshly painted for our visit, as had the near sides of the neighbouring ones.

The Central Bank itself boasted a Banking Hall panelled in onyx, a marble of translucent green, quarried in Pakistan. A grand and formal banquet was held there, the ladies and gentlemen keeping firmly apart when not seated at the table. It was not long since the days of purdah, and still in the country districts this custom was strictly observed.

After a dinner party at the Bank House we took our leave, accompanied by the guests who did not wish to miss seeing us off on the Khyber Mail Express.

In Pakistan the railway station is a place of great social activity and everyone turns out to speed the departure of families and friends or to greet new arrivals. We had no previous idea of what to expect, but as our car drew up a mob of people surrounded us, and excitedly popped garlands of flowers over our heads. Music played and an arc lamp lit up the scene for a movie camera to take pictures of the event. A great number of people shook us warmly by the hand. We had never experienced such a send-off nor ever would again.

A special railway carriage had been fumigated and carefully cleaned for our use. Orders were given to repaint the outside, but the over-zealous railway workers saw fit to repaint the inside as well. This caused great concern to the Hasnies, who were accompanying us, for a very strong smell of new paint permeated the carriage which, being air-conditioned, was not easy to dispel. Our accommodation was, however, luxurious, with a drawing-room, two sleeping compartments and a bathroom (even if the latter did not function) to ourselves. There was also a kitchen and staff, besides the faithful Shafi.

The next morning we arrived in Bahawalpur to visit the Nawab of Bahawalpur. On our programme a long list of names had been printed on one page, which we took to be a group of people whose names we should memorise before meeting them. Instead, they proved to belong to one: the Nawab himself.

We were met by a very upstanding gentleman in a fez who was said to be Prime Minister, but who reminded us of the Grand Vizier of childhood stories. He was accompanied by a dashing major with a flashing smile and other junior officers of the Nawab's own special army of seven hundred men. As we drove to the main palace, the Prime Minister told Mr Hasnie that one of the orders held by the Nawab had been omitted from the titles in our programme, which caused poor Mr Hasnie great consternation.

Sadiq Garh Palace is built of white marble and set in a lovely garden. It is known as the crystal and carpet palace because of the audience chamber which is equipped with masses of furniture entirely made of glass, as well as huge chandeliers hanging overhead. Whilst we were changing for dinner, an earthquake tremor (common in those parts) was felt. This caused the chandeliers to swing, and throughout the palace a loud tinkling noise could be heard. The Nawab had specifically asked us to visit him as he had been an ADC to the Prince of Wales on his visit to India in 1921 when my father-in-law had been Chief of Staff.

The private army was commanded by a Brigadier, a military figure with a white beard and wearing a fez. He held himself superbly and was constantly admonishing the major whose shoulders were inclined to sag, and who was given to washing his hands when excited.

We were greeted in the Hall of the Palace by the Nawab himself, a small but dignified figure. The meeting between him and Mr Hasnie was most touching, but I was startled by the sound of a bag of coins falling on the marble floor at the Nawab's feet. This had been thrown by Mr Hasnie before bowing low and kissing the Nawab's coat and salaaming. He was in turn greeted with affectionate condescension. The bag of coins was completely ignored, the significance of which I was never able to discover.

We were shown into a large sitting-room and sat on either side of the Nawab, who ordered coffee and proceeded to talk. Around the room a number of gentlemen wearing the fez sat on chairs. They did not speak, and clearly each had his appointed position, for in some cases they sat back to back, those nearer to His Highness being of higher rank. The palace was as cold as the tomb. An all-pervading icy dampness penetrated one's clothes. The sun was shining brightly, but not a single beam penetrated the dark curtained room.

After about an hour we were shown into the chief suite of state rooms. They were huge, darkly furnished and very chilly. In the cavernous main bedroom a huge Victorian bed stood in the middle of the floor. Each room was lit by one solitary twenty-five watt electric bulb.

At mid-day we joined a cortège of three khaki-painted Ford vans enclosed with strips of sticking plaster over the windows, excepting the windscreen. These served the double purpose of keeping the sun's rays out while obscuring the occupants from being seen. We set off at a spanking rate in the leading car for the Nawab's Red Fort situated about sixty miles away in the great Indian desert, where it had been arranged for us to lunch. We were accompanied by the Prime Minister who sat beside us and never drew breath. We drove along a narrow lane which soon became no more than a dirt track, occasionally divided by steep ditches and gullies which we flew over in the manner of a steeplechase, hanging on like grim death and falling back into our seats as if they were saddles. Behind us an enormous cloud of dust prevented the cars behind from being within a mile of us. We drove in this fashion through the desert until far on the horizon we glimpsed the outline of the fort. Nearer to us appeared one of those desert wonders, a huge mirage, with even a few scrubby trees which grow in those parts reflected in it.

The Red Fort was enormous and had once been the desert city of an ancient ruler. It was surrounded by ruins of what must at one time have been a large town. On one side was the muddy pool of the oasis surrounded by palms, with groups of people washing their clothes and filling goat skins with water; on the other, enormous herds of stationary camels with small camel trains disappearing into the distance.

We lunched in an old pavilion near the water hole, in a room exquisitely decorated with mosaic. Most of the party being Muslim, and observing Ramadan which unfortunately coincided with our visit, either discreetly disappeared or sat with us and watched without consuming or drinking a morsel themselves. From dawn to dusk they could neither eat nor drink, but this did not impair their keen sense of fun, or their efforts to give us as good and lavish a meal as their generous hospitality dictated. No-one saw fit to inform us that our visit would clash with the feast of Ramadan until it was too late to change the plans.

Beside the old fort was a walled garden enclosing the tombs of the Nawab's ancestors. A place of extraordinary tranquillity. The Nawab had been married four times, twice to Muslims and twice to English women. His first English wife, to whom he had been devoted, was buried here in a marble tomb near to his other wives. After she died, we were told, the Nawab remained sitting on her coffin weeping bitterly for forty days, and was inconsolable. He left for England shortly afterwards, as was his custom every summer, returning in the autumn with a new English bride.

It was late in the afternoon by the time we returned to the palace and the sun was setting. It had become exceedingly cold. We retired to our room to change for dinner with our teeth chattering. Our large and imposing bathroom appeared to lend the best means of thawing out although it was icy cold. But the water was not. I ran a bath until it was full of warm water, but to my horror it was only too obvious that, somehow, the hot water pipes had become entangled with the sewage system. All the same , a quick dip was the only answer to the intense cold. Besides, one did not want to come down with flu. Afterwards one was at least warmer, if not cleaner.

Dinner was a very formal affair, the table laid for thirty or more people. They were all (besides ourselves, the Hasnies and the Nawab) members of the Household or Mr Hasnie's entourage. Mrs Hasnie and I were the only women present. Throughout the dinner we were regaled with the strains of an eastern orchestra, playing in an adjoining room, but never actually seen. We were waited upon by a number of splendidly uniformed footmen, who could not disguise their disappointment if we did not help ourselves liberally from every dish. Fortunately the food was good. The Prime Minister kept up a lively conversation throughout the meal. The Nawab was gracious and talked a great deal himself, but everyone else maintained a respectful silence.

Two quite beautiful lengths of material were sent to Mrs Hashnie and me. Mine was made of real gold thread and was quite lovely to behold. Mrs Hasnie's was of white lace which I rather envied, and wished later that I had exchanged. Later on, when I knew Ismat Hasnie better, I discovered that she disliked wearing white because, she said, it made her skin look darker. Evidently she came from South India and was ashamed of the tint. Her husband's skin was much lighter. In the end, on our last night before our departure from Pakistan, I managed to persuade her to wear it and she looked magnificent for she was a very good-looking woman, and also a very nice one.

After this very formal dinner we made our departure. This was the first time I caught a train wearing full evening dress, made even more bizarre by having to pick my way over sleeping bodies and impoverished families cooking their food, all crowded together while two soldiers stood guard outside our carriage. Our carriage had been uncoupled from the Khyber Mail Express and recoupled to another train on a different siding whose destination was to be Rawalpindi.

We arrived to the now-customary greeting of many garlands of marigolds. Dinner parties were given but the climate remained cold. An electric fire was quietly placed by my side wherever I sat, and always without talk or fuss. One's comfort seemed paramount, with the exception of my bed, which was an Indian one: just a slatted frame covered with a hard thin mattress, no doubt like all the others. It was best to say nothing.

Many Pakistanis have an endearing way of getting their expressions just a little bit wrong, which engenders gusts of laughter, and everyone joins in the general amusement. At the end of one anecdote someone declared after a pause, 'Of course, he hadn't anything on,' when he actually meant, 'Of course, he was having me on.' One of Mr Hasnie's party, referring to our joining the train, explained that it was much better to travel 'Upper Class' than 'Lower Class.'

We spent one day in Taxila, Alexander the Great's city whose date was three hundred and twenty-six BC. Even the inkpots, cooking utensils and musical instruments in the museum were in a perfect state of preservation.

At seven o'clock in the evening we were to be entertained by the President (Ayub Khan) at a reception in our honour at the Presidential Residence. About five minutes after our arrival two blushing and demure young ladies appeared in richly-hemmed saris. They were the President's daughter and daughter-in-law. There was an excited murmur of voices at their appearance. This, apparently, was a rare event. In Pakistan it is considered a very great honour if the host's wife is present and even more so if he should also produce his grown-up daughters. Mrs Hasnie was quite overcome with delight. No man in the party dared to venture close or speak one word to either lady. Shortly afterwards the President appeared. He shook Rowley warmly by the hand and said, 'My dear fellow, we met in London.' The beautiful young daughter of the President had recently had her nose pierced and proudly wore a solitaire diamond by the side of one nostril. The junior Cabinet Minister present had a young and beautiful American wife who was attired in Swati clothes. She wore a silver ornament over her forehead which also stretched to the back of her head over a central parting; she sported a long silver necklace over a black tunic and trousers, with a colourful shawl thrown over her shoulders. She looked sensational. But the other ladies, dressed in their classical saris, tried not to look shocked, but signally failed.

After the reception we drove about forty miles through fairly wild country to Wah for dinner and to spend the night with Sardar Barket Khan, a large landowner and a director of the Bank. Barket Khan proved to be a tall fierce man with a large black moustache. His house was very cold. The drawing room was relieved by a huge wood fire burning brightly and would undoubtedly have warmed the room if the windows had not been left open. Dinner was a bit of an ordeal because the main course was fish and, unfortunately, was as raw as when it had left the water. I thought that perhaps it might be a new way of smoking fish, but there was no way of separating the bones from the flesh, however much one tried, and those few morsels I managed to extricate tasted quite nasty. Mr Khan suddenly broke into rapid Urdu, and then asked me if my fish was as uncooked as his. After a time more was produced but, unhappily, with no improvement. It was thought that his cooking fire had gone out and that the simpleton cook thought he might just get away with it. Mr Khan was so willing to please and, in spite of his wild looks, so agreeable, that one felt really sorry over the failure of his dinner.

The next morning we set out on the long drive to the valley of Swat, crossing the Indus river at Attock. Then through a long wide valley which gave occasional glimpses, through a break in the hills, of distant snow-covered mountains. The scene evoked pictures of glittering lances, jingling harnesses and the clop of hooves as units of British cavalry were moved up to the frontier posts during the wars and skirmishes around the turn the century. Our car stopped at a bleak cross-road where a portly figure materialised holding a large bunch of wild narcissi and some papers, among which was a letter from our son Vivian. He presented me with the deliciously-scented flowers whose fragrance perfumed the car the whole way to Swat. This gentleman was, evidently, the local branch manager of the Bank from Mardan who had hurried to catch us up. He then joined our motorcade which by this time had grown to six cars.

At Mardan we stopped to take coffee with a rich merchant and the male members of his family. A table was laid out with a veritable feast which we could hardly refuse. Servants appeared bearing gifts for the Hasnies and ourselves. Two very finely woven Kashmir shawls embroidered with gold thread for Ismat and me. And heavy woollen Pathan overcoats for the men. Both gifts were indeed welcome, especially as we were proceeding not only further north, but reaching higher altitudes as well.

I asked Mr Hasnie, after we left Mardan, if in fact we had eaten lunch. 'No,' he answered. 'We will eat at a road house further on.'

Mr Hasnie never spoke much of what was planned ahead. He was always modest, and only vaguely mentioned, in a very understated way, the many exciting events he had in store for us and which must have caused much careful thought and planning. The result was that each day unfolded in a series of glorious surprises. It was a journey from a story book.

We were joined by a military escort which led us towards a mountain range and up a narrow and twisting road until we came to the top of a pass. This pass is called Malakand and is the regimental headquarters of the Ninth Frontier Force. The headquarters stand in the most superb position commanding a breathtaking view of the lower lands of the North West

Frontier Province. On the other side are tribal lands which led to the then tiny Kingdom of Swat. It was at these headquarters that Sir Winston Churchill was stationed as a young man. The Mess was full of trophies and souvenirs of past campaigns, and in it was served a huge lunch of many courses. The officers watched us as we ate, urging us on to eat more, while they themselves ate nothing because of Ramadan.

The next leg of the journey through tribal lands was on an exceedingly dusty road. Every so many yards or so a soldier lined the route, presumably for our protection, although nothing was said. The President of Pakistan had lent us one of his official cars. It was large and black and driven by a dirty, shifty-eyed man in a grubby uniform. All the way from 'Pindi' he drove us at a very fast pace with total disregard for the numerous carts and animals which we passed on our way. Often we had moments of acute anxiety, but he never slackened speed. As we neared Swat there were traces of snow and patches of ice on the track. Inevitably, on coming round a corner, we saw a horse and cart trotting gaily down the centre of the road. We spun round quite out of control, hitting the cart broadside on, but, fortunately, just missing the horse, which had anyway collapsed from sheer fright at the impact. At once a crowd of excited and angry people gathered. But our driver left the car and shouted even louder. The effect was electric. In moments the cart and horse were pushed aside and we continued on our journey. Rowley and I felt so sorry for the people that owned the cart, not to speak of the horse. After this incident Mr Hasnie ordered another car to go ahead of us. He wished to put our safety ahead of our comfort, and we were obliged to submit to the appalling dust raised by the first car.

At Swat we were to be the guests of His Highness The Wali, who was kindly accommodating us in his hotel. The doors of our rooms opened straight on to an open yard covered in snow. We were given a bedroom, sitting-room and bathroom. The latter contained two outside ill-fitting doors and was arctic. Both rooms had fires, which blazed with sweet-smelling logs. They were the only form of heat. After all, in the old days that was all an English country house provided.

Swat is a small mountain country amid the far western range of the gigantic Himalayas as they start to merge with the Hindu Kush. It contains a long fertile valley of about one hundred miles in length with a population of 600,000 people. It was ruled by one man, The Wali, who had complete power of life and death over his subjects. He was chief administrator and sole arbiter on all questions of law, order and finance, the basis of the economy being timber and emeralds. His justice was his own, guided by Islamic law. He was also a most enlightened ruler. He lived modestly, introduced free medicine, and built hospitals and schools; even a university, and all free. He was proud too that no tax was levied at all.

We expected the Wali to be a fierce-looking, wild man from the mountains with little to say beyond a few gruff words. Instead, he surprised us by being clean-shaven, urbane and sophisticated. He greeted us at the front door in an easy friendly way. Mr Hasnie could not believe it was the Ruler himself and thought it must be one of his retainers.

Mr Hasnie asked the Wali if all his family were in Swat, and then appeared to be very shocked when the Wali replied that he had not the faintest idea, as they all lived in separate houses, and therefore they might well be away. He did admit that he always knew the Crown Prince's whereabouts, for reasons of State. But both Mr Hasnie and Ismat looked horrified as it was obviously not done in properly conducted Muslim families for the members to live apart.

The Wali told me that he disliked intensely passing the sentence of death on his subjects, and only in the case of premeditated murder did he do so, and then only as a strong deterrent, and to appease the members of the unfortunate victim's family. It had not been long since the penalty for theft meant losing a hand or foot. Now, convicted criminals were imprisoned in chains, but in order to make their lot less miserable, it was arranged for music to be played by the prison band while they worked in the quarries.

There was no pomp or ceremony about the Wali. Our dinner was western in style from the soup through to ice cream and then rounded off by a savoury. It was only at the end of dinner that one of the Wali's own court suddenly heeled over and was violently sick, becoming rapidly unconscious and then black in the face. No-one spoke for about a minute, while two attendants rushed to remove him from the room as swiftly as they could. The Wali never mentioned the incident and quietly withdrew to the drawing-room, nor did any of us like to allude to it either. But that did not stop us wondering what on earth had been the cause. Cholera? Poison? It was best to put it out of one's mind.

The next day we left for Peshawar. A military escort again accompanied us as far as Malakand. There a new guide from the State Bank met us, and was placed in our car, where he proved to be a great talker and oozed bonhomie. He was a little trying because his gregariousness took the form of a running commentary on all that we passed. He made endless remarks, such as: 'That is a field over there and here is an avenue,' or: 'that is a house with three windows and a door.' When Rowley, getting exasperated, told him that that much he could see, but what was it? the poor man started blustering and then admitted he did not know. But at the end of thirty-six hours it became plain that he had a genius for organisation and showmanship.

On the way we stopped at a Circuit House which in the old days was kept solely for the use of english judges and officials. It was an eighteenth century colonial house set in a garden. The inside, however, was very dirty and down-at-heel, gloomy and poorly furnished. Snakes in the bathroom and bats in the bedroom. I did not look in some dark corners too carefully for the cobwebs were larger than any I had ever seen. On re-entering the garden we found a white cloth-covered table laden with food, which had appeared miraculously. Bearers were still unpacking a china tea set, and when all was ready we sat down to be waited on in the style of a long-gone english house party, taking tea on the lawn — with the difference that we were in the middle of a vast and empty plain.

Government House in Peshawar was to be opened especially for us. In the days of the British Raj it was the official residence of the Governor of the North West Province, since when it was used only by the Governor of West Pakistan on his occasional visits. Although a splendid house, the rooms seemed dead and empty. They were vast. And from the walls portraits of past Governors looked down. Throughout one felt an atmosphere of sadness, a house with its face turned to the past: an almost tangible longing for past glories, for the pomp and circumstance of the British Raj. The people, too, seemed to possess this feeling and for one long magical day appeared desperately anxious to recapture the formalities and grandeur of the past. Pathan hospitality is famous and these generous and proud people wanted to show us that they knew how to treat honoured guests, and that being British it was to be in the manner of a visiting Viceroy and his Vicereine. It is true that word had reached them that Rowley was the grandson of a Viceroy, Lord Minto, whose rule was distinguished by his insistence on the pacification of the Pathan tribes.

From our rooms our new guide came to escort us to the drawing-room where, to our utter astonishment, was a large collection of objects and ornaments. They were all displayed on a long table. When the Hasnies appeared, the guide, with the help of two bearers, started to distribute this extraordinary assortment of things. First of all Mrs Hasnie and I were placed in two armchairs. Then a shy little woman came forward. She was introduced by the guide, with a sweep of his arms, as his wife. She then presented me with an embroidered stole, two gauze scarves, a pair of embroidered slippers and a gold cap, after which she was abruptly ordered by her husband to return home. The bearers then came forward and laid at my feet a quantity of miscellaneous objects. Most of the presents had evidently been collected by our guide from various local industrialists and businessmen. He assured me that he had refused twice the number of gifts as not being worthy of us. I had a small suspicion that some of these presents had arrived in the hope that an invitation would be issued for the following night's big party. I had heard that there had been quite a jostling for invitations, and no doubt the guide had enjoyed the sorting-out of those to be invited, and the returning of presents of those who would not be.

Among Rowley's presents was a cap made from the coat of an unborn lamb. This was considered very special as the pelt of an animal not yet born was thought to have a fine sheen and be extra-soft.

The next morning we set out for the Khyber Pass. Many tribal chieftains were gathering in force to meet Rowley at Jamrud. They wished to welcome him to their tribal lands. There was also to be a small ceremony. They would offer Rowley a sheep or goat which he was to touch on the head before shaking them all by the hand. They did not speak english and Mr Hasnie was the interpreter. I was told to stay in the background and on no account to come forward, to keep my eyes downcast and to generally behave in the modest manner of a Muslim lady. By this time, in any case, I had become used to following Rowley demurely a few paces behind.

On arrival in Jamrud we were greeted with a smart salute by a company of soldiers. Quite close to them stood a row of the fiercest looking men I had ever seen and armed to the teeth. Each, however, was holding a garland of flowers. At one end of the line stood a goat clothed in gaily-coloured hand-kerchiefs which was duly offered. Rowley then slowly walked down the line of Chiefs shaking them by the hand and, as he did so, they each gently hung their garland of flowers around his neck. About two-thirds of the way down it looked as if Rowley would become totally submerged in blossom. His head was fast disappearing. Fortunately, his secretary, Mr

Rose, realising the embarrassment this would cause, leaped forward just in time before his head became lost to view, and to Rowley's extreme relief. When the last hand had been shaken a bearer came forward with two wicked-looking daggers on a tray. One was presented to Rowley, and the other, to my great surprise, to me. Their blades were as sharp as razors and their ends were honed to a vanishing point. The only flaw in the appearance of this wonderful gathering of wild and warlike men was that quite a few wore horn-rimmed glasses.

Jamrud is the gateway to the Khyber Pass. The Pass itself is colourless and treeless and consists of brown mountains and stark rock. But at each turn of the road a small fort can be seen on every hilltop, and in the valley, fortified villages, all as brown as the earth. Each village is guarded by tribesmen with peepholes, for even now the tribes continually raid each others' camps and continually engage in skirmishes. Time appears to have barely altered the place and history impregnates every hill and rock as if the present and past were merged into one. With no effort of imagination one could picture the scene with as it must have been. The zing of the snipers' bullets ricocheting over the rocks and ravines. The many British regiments winning honours in scores of small battles in their bids to occupy commanding positions on the hilltops.

At the border with Afghanistan, the Afghan guards made an unhappy comparison to the disciplined and smart uniformed Pakistani troops. The Afghans had once been smart too, but under the influence of her powerful neighbour, the USSR, her soldiers were dressed in drab grey and looked as dejected as their clothes. After Rowley had stood on a box to take the salute from the Pakistani Border Company guards we repaired to the terrace of the custom house where, once again, our guide produced, as if by magic, a table groaning with food and refreshments. Not that we were to be denied lunch, for we were served that too at Landikotal, the regimental HQ of the Khyber Rifles, on our way back.

That evening was to be the great party, a sit-down dinner for ninety people with all the most important personalities in the area. On entering the huge drawing-room we found the guests all lined up to be greeted, each in turn, as if we were royalty. The women, all clad in their best saris, looked like a flock of tropical birds, strong colours of every hue and glittering with gold. Some indeed outshone the others for the edges of their saris were of silver tinsel such as that with which we decorate our Christmas trees. These were Attock women who were known to love adornment and as much glitter as possible. There was, however, a certain disapproval in the glances from the other ladies.

At dinner I sat between the Chief of the Pakistan Air Force and a politician whose wife had been offered a candidature for the Assembly in a more developed part of the country where, I was told, she would certainly have been successful.

Her husband persuaded her to refuse the opportunity, for had she been victorious he would have lost his seat because he represented an area where it was unthinkable for women to either be seen or even heard.

After dinner spotlights lit up the lawn outside. An oriental band started to play, which included the extra wail of the bagpipes. And on trooped a body of wild-looking tribesmen carrying naked sabres. They performed a fast and vigorous war-dance with swords flashing and hair tumbling. It was tremendous in its energy, virility and fierceness. They were followed by another tribe, dressed differently, who carried rifles. Their dance was equally energetic and interspersed with loud bangs and wild shrieks. Somebody said that each tribe was keenly competing with the other and hoped this would not lead to bloodshed afterwards.

The next morning we were seen off at the airport by our guide who made a formal speech of farewell on the apron. I heard, after we left, that he had described me as 'a perfectly lovable woman' and that Rowley and I had been referred to as 'The Lordoms' while in Peshawar.

In Lahore we stayed with the Governor of West Pakistan, Nawab Khan of Kalabagh, the head of an ancient feudal family. Our accommodation was immaculate as was everything else at this Government House. Here our faithful bearer, Shafi, took his leave, but he was followed by a smartly uniformed bearer who was strictly supervised by an excellent Goanese butler.

There were dinners and luncheons, and again I was given a separate programme. Visiting more hospitals and craft centres and other places of welfare interest. I was made an honorary member of the Pakistan Girl Guides, while not admitting the fact that I had never even been a Brownie (called Bluebirds, for obvious reasons, in that part of the world). Much work was being done for those children blinded by smallpox (now so happily an eradicated scourge). At the Red Cross Blood Donors Centre I was shown with pride a bottle of blood from a very rare group. The next day the newspapers reported me as saying that 'it was the best equipped clinic that I had ever seen,' as indeed it was, for I had never seen another. At a handicraft shop I made a costly purchase of a Swati cloak and was rewarded by a very friendly hug from a senior woman Cabinet Minister.

Lahore, the old capital of the Punjab, is a beautiful city, and much time was taken in sight-seeing. We dined on our last evening with the Governor, a dignified gentleman with a long black moustache. He was a man of extensive knowledge and sound common sense. He also possessed a quiet dignity and a sense of responsibility born from a long line of rulers.

The next morning we made our final departure. Garlanded, we bade goodbye to the Hasnies and their entourage. I know there were tears in our eyes, and I would like to think in theirs as well. Certainly the local newspapers spoke of an emotional farewell. We certainly owed them, and all we had met, our gratitude for showing us their country in a manner completely bewitching and so extraordinarily grand.

14

WHITE NIGHTS AND GOLDEN DAYS

1964 seemed destined for distant travel. In June we set off once again. Like Pakistan, our visit was in response to an official invitation. The new Governor of the Bank of Russia, Alexei Poskonov, had renewed the invitation given by his predecessor with some insistence. It was, evidently, the first time in history that a Governor of the Bank of England had visited Russia. This alone made it seem worthwhile — to make new ground in a country that few had visited (for there were no tourists from outside the Soviet Union at that time) was irresistible. Admittedly, anticipation was mixed equally with excitement and apprehension. Excitement of the unknown and apprehension of what that might mean. It seemed to surprise our friends that Russia possessed a Central Bank at all, possibly because Communism and Banking were widely thought to be antagonistic to each other.

Our flight by BEA Comet was cloudless. As we moved in from the Baltic the tapestry of the Russian countryside unfolded: vast, dark forests hemmed in by huge brown fields. A sparsely populated land speckled with lakes and, very rarely, a road.

The first setback was on the aeroplane itself. A burly and ferocious-looking official took our passports and visas, and as I passed him in order to disembark his arm shot out to stop me from making any further progress. He pointed to the photograph on my passport and then to the one on my visa. They were different. Each had been taken at different times and this aroused suspicion. Meanwhile, Rowley had preceded me down the steps and was being greeted by a crowd of people. When they finally looked up to find that I was unable to leave the plane, word reached the official, who rather ungraciously let me go.

When I eventually alighted a bunch of flowers was pressed into my hands by a young woman with red hair; then a short, rather nondescript, middle-aged man proffered his hand with an important manner. This was Alexei Poskonov, the President of the Gosbank and Rowley's opposite number. He had about him the air of a great man. He had previously been head of the Treasury, but on his appointment as head of the bank he was given the power of immediate recourse to the Presidium and not by way of the Treasury as had been the custom before. This made his position a more powerful an influential one. A widower, his married daughter undertook the duties of hostess. Known as Miss Poskonov when acting in that role, she became Mrs Kritsky when with her husband.

At the airport it was the young woman with red hair who was Maya Poskonov. The airport at that time was small and modest. We were hustled past a few shoddy buildings to a string of black official-looking cars where Rowley and Mr Poskonov embarked in the first, Maya and I in the second, Jasper Rootham from the Bank of England in the third with officers of the Gosbank, and our luggage in the fourth. We were followed by the British Ambassador and Lady Trevelyan who had also been amongst those to greet us. Fortunately, both Rowley and I were accompanied by an interpreter or conversation would have been impossible. As it was, talk did not come at all easily. It took time to get used to speaking through a third person, but by the end of our visit, chatting in this manner became second nature. In fact, by the time we reached home, we missed the opportunity given to think more carefully of a fitting reply.

It was decided to put us up at the Sovietskaya Hotel in a suite of three rooms: a study with an enormous old-fashioned desk and black leather sofa with two armchairs, all as hard as nails; a sitting-room with a table, straight-back chairs and an upright piano. The effect was one of unrelieved gloom. The bedroom was more ordinary, with twin beds and a wardrobe; the bathroom grandly decrepit.

Unpacking proved difficult as there were no drawers. Two small ones by the bed were full of old paper left behind. There were no waste-paper baskets for the simple reason that paper hardly seemed to exist, and was certainly never thrown away. My soiled Kleenex were never removed by the maid, possibly because she had never seen any before. Tissue paper was an object to marvel at.

These hotel rooms were the best available at the time and fortunately, judging by the expressions on the faces of our hosts, no doubts as to the excellence of our accommodation shadowed their thoughts, although our own faces must have given away something of our dismay at the sight of these hot, dark and musty rooms.

Mr Poskonov had thoughtfully made no arrangements for our first evening, but the British Ambassador did give us a tentative invitation to a quiet dinner at the Embassy and we decided to accept it. We sat peacefully on the spacious Embassy balcony, while curiosity gave way to wonder as we watched the sun setting over the Kremlin. That fortress so feared and of grim repute, but also of great beauty. The rose-pink walls glowed, and many golden domes gleamed in the soft evening light, repeated on the face of the water beneath. We sat enchanted by the scene, for the view from the balcony is arguably the finest in Moscow; looking across the river at the yellow-walled Armoury, the seven churches and the palaces within that formidable citadel. Strange and contradictory, it was a perfect introduction for a newcomer to Russia.

On our way to the embassy we were surprised by the number of people thronging the pavements. The streets were very wide and the traffic sparse. On our return the old lamps, each grandly bearing clusters of four lights from which only one shone, hardly gave much illumination to the darkened streets.

The next morning we breakfasted in our hotel on dry bread, jam and milkless tea. Rowley and I had separate programmes. He to the Gosbank for discussions, while Maya Poskonov and a Mrs Matyenka (who worked in the European sector of the Gosbank and acted as interpreter) came to fetch me.

Our first stop was a kindergarten where children between the ages of three and seven were deposited by their mothers on their way to work. My first surprise was to discover that this convenience was not free. The mothers were expected to pay, perhaps not a great deal, but something towards the provision of a facility of this kind. I was probably shown one of the better examples, but it was certainly one of the best kindergartens I had ever seen. Clean, neat and tidy with plenty of toys, birds, goldfish and even a box of mice. It was indeed very well equipped. The Principal told me that the most important lesson taught was one of behaviour, that the children were strictly educated in tidiness, obedience and to be respectful and thoughtful to one another. It is at this very young age that those virtues are the most easily acquired, I was told. I learned also that the Soviet state educates a child for ten years, the obligatory age is from seven to seventeen, instead of from five to fifteen as it then was in England.

The next stop was a modern hospital. There I was shown around by the Chief Medical Officer and Superintendent, who was a woman. She possessed an air of great authority and a pair of shrewd and intelligent eyes. I was not yet accustomed to speaking through an interpreter. Therefore my conversation was rather forced and spasmodic. However I learned that there were virtually no male doctors in the USSR. It was a career considered suitable mainly for women. Only surgeons were men.

The lady doctor wore a white kerchief about her head and a plain white overall, which I also noticed was worn by all the other members of the staff, be they doctors, nurses or maids. I asked the Superintendent if there was any distinction in uniform between the senior and junior nurses, or indeed the ward maids. She appeared quite mystified by my question until I described our customs in England. She then laughed and said that everyone in the Soviet Union was equal and therefore all hospital uniforms were alike and there was absolutely no distinction between one worker and another. I then asked how she managed to distinguish the senior nurses in an emergency, and she rather bitingly replied that she knew every nurse by name, and therefore it was unnecessary for them to be dressed differently. It was a very large hospital and the staff must have been exceedingly numerous.

The women patients occupied small wards with four beds in each placed head to toe along each wall. There were no bedside tables, earphones or any comforts that I could see. The operating theatre, which had only recently been finished, was already shedding tiles from off the walls. If the medical attention was good, the dreariness and discomfort made me extract a promise from Rowley that if, by some mischance, either of us were taken ill, then the other would see that we were immediately flown back to England.

The next port of call was a new department store. I was told by Mrs Matyenka that I would find many things I would want to buy. This, I felt, was bound to prove embarrassing, which it did. There was nothing one could have purchased unless from dire necessity. All the goods were shoddy, tasteless and strictly utilitarian. I left with my purse unopened, although I would have very much liked to have bought something just to please them. The payment for any purchase was most complicated: the customer would queue at a desk to buy a coupon for the amount priced on the article, and then queue again for the article. All the accounting was done on abacuses; not a cash register to be seen.

The Red Square came next, and then St Basil, with its huge asymmetrical domes, built by Ivan the Terrible who had the

149

architect blinded for his pains as he did not wish this work of art to be repeated. Mrs Matyenka did not agree that the Czar was 'Terrible.' She said that, on the contrary, although a rather severe autocrat, he was one of the best rulers in their history.

By this time it was two o'clock and there had been no mention of lunch. It was then that I discovered that unless a formal meal had been arranged, in which case everyone was punctual to the minute, no-one seemed bothered by the idea of lunch and were quite surprised that anyone should want to eat at a prescribed time.

By the end of this very long morning we had become quite friendly and Maya announced that she thought that I was exactly like a heroine from the last chapter of *The Forsyte Saga*. I was not at all certain which character she meant, but decided that as she had used the word 'heroine' it must be favourable. I asked Mrs Matyenka if fat men were admired by the women of Russia. She replied: 'No, nor tall men either. We like muscular men like athletes and ballet dancers.' Maya and Mrs Matyenka finally left me at my hotel at four o'clock with the instruction that I must be ready to leave the hotel at six for an evening at the Opera.

We were fetched by Ludmilla, who was acting as interpreter between Rowley and Mr Poskonov, in a large black limousine. This rather sinister-looking car had been put at Rowley's disposal and caused some interest wherever he went. Ludmilla was a pretty, dark-haired girl with huge eyes and a full mouth. She would gaze in a sultry fashion between slightly closed lids like a basking cat. As I also received these sexy looks, I decided that she was only trying to copy some film star she had seen, and sure enough, when I knew her better, she confided that her ambition was to be in movies. She had tried unsuccessfully, but her face was not considered to be sufficiently Russian. She was evidently half Polish and half Armenian. Although she had a very good command of english, her great shortcoming was her lack of humour. She was, unhappily, quite unable to translate any jokes or witticisms, and invariably lost the point in a story, which was very unhelpful. Without the twinkling eyes of Alexei Poskonov it might have taken a long time to discover that he possessed an excellent sense of humour.

At the Opera House we were met by an official who escorted us to a grand staircase where we were handed over to another official who, in turn, was replaced by someone more senior who ushered us to the open door of a sitting room, the interior of which brought us sharply to a standstill with a gasp of amazement. The walls of the room and the upholstery were covered with scarlet silk brocade; the furniture and baroque decoration was wrapped in gold leaf. It was as sumptuous as a throne room. In the middle stood Mr Poskonov with other senior Bank officials, all dressed in sober, grey lounge suits. Maya, on the other hand, was resplendent in gold and white brocade with a brooch in her hair. No sooner had we been made welcome that the double doors at the other end of this splendid room were opened and we found ourselves in the centre of a huge box. It was the ex-royal box of the Bolshoi Theatre and Rowley and I sat in the middle of the front row. As the lights were slowly dimmed a strange sensation swept over me. Here in this magnificent auditorium and on this very spot Czars and Czarinas had sat before us. Here in the darkness was the splendour of Imperial Russia. The surroundings were the same, the performance probably identical. The performance shown was of the *Queen of Spades*, and giving even more credence to the idea of by-gone regal ghosts was the imposing entrance on the stage by Catharine the Great, which the audience particularly seemed to appreciate. Between acts we were treated to a repast of caviare, cold ham and ice-cream. The theatre was full and, one understood, great competition was entered for tickets, most of the audience at that time being tourists and party officials from other parts of the Soviet Union.

Jasper Rootham spoke Russian fluently. He was also a good

teacher, besides having an uncanny knack of knowing just the phrases that might come in useful. He coached me by writing down phonetically various sentences each day which I would then memorise. If an awkward moment occurred I could then venture a remark in Russian, which was most popular, and certainly caused amusement.

The following day there was a big lunch at the British Embassy. It was all rather stiff and formal. The Deputy Foreign Minister was a woman. At first sight forbidding and austere, with her shiny face and hair scraped back in a bun, she looked like the woman who cut off their tales with a carving knife in the nursery rhyme. At the end of lunch I spoke to her in Russian using one of the phrases I had learned from Jasper. I told her how glad I was to be in Moscow. The effect was quite astonishing. She melted into happy laughter and her face lit up with kindly animation. The forbidding creature of a moment ago disappeared in a flash. She then spoke a little english, the knowledge of which she had previously kept hidden. In the afternoon we made an extensive tour of the Kremlin with Mr Kudryavtsev who was number three at the Bank. Our tour took hours. There was no special plan and we seemed to go round in circles, but how lucky we were to see the churches and other sights before they became over-whelmed with tourists from the west many years later.

Towards the end of our tour of the Kremlin we were taken through a guarded gate to a building housing the central government offices of the Supreme Soviet. Here we were very privileged, as we were permitted to see Lenin's private flat: not open to the public, and yet kept as a national shrine. All immaculately cared for since his death, down to his pens and pencils. The flat was small and austere; a study from which Lenin governed; a kitchen and three small bedrooms. He lived there with his wife and sister. They had no communal sitting-room and only four chairs and a small table from which to dine, partitioned off from the passage. Lenin was ascetic, unconscious of his surroundings. He did not appreciate either comfort or taste. A woman guide of some ferocity jealously guarded this sacred domain. Absolutely nothing was allowed to be touched. At one moment Ludmilla leaned her arm on the back of a remarkably ugly black-leather chair, and was startled to receive a sharp rebuke from the dragon of a keeper. There were many left-wing books in english, which tongue Lenin could speak as well as a dozen others. And a curious feature of the flat was its rather sterile atmosphere: no remnants of a personality had been left behind with the owner's belongings. His apartment in Leningrad also possessed that same empty feeling.

That evening a dinner in a private room at a Moscow restaurant was held by Mr Poskonov. This was the first occasion that we encountered the Russian custom of drinking toasts. They began almost before we sat down, and preceded by a short speech, they continued throughout the meal. Fortunately for Rowley our host gave him the most valuable advice. He suggested that with every sip of vodka or Russian brandy another should be taken from the bottle of fizzy water which would be near him on the table; this had the effect of neutralising any alcoholic effects. Without this kindly advice it would not have been remotely possible to keep sober, for the amount of liquor consumed was enormous. Rowley, in particular, had to be seen to empty his glass after every toast.

There were eight courses, each accompanied by a different wine. The Russian temperament seems to need a stimulant, for with the encouragement given by alcohol, our friends expanded and became cheerful and talkative. The Finance Minister was present at that dinner, a jolly fat man who was proud of his youthful appearance, which he disclosed was due to a bottle of Georgian wine which he consumed daily, and which was known as the 'wine of life.' Mr Poskonov himself was almost sixty and kept himself in trim by roller-skating in the summer and skiing by moonlight in the winter. He confirmed that in parts of Georgia some people lived to a hundred and sixty, due to daily doses of the 'wine of life.' When I asked him if the young men of eighty became impatient with their elders he looked quite shocked and replied that the wisdom of the very old was held in profound respect by those of a younger age, and that the elders maintained complete authority until their deaths.

It had been arranged for us to take the midnight express to Leningrad that evening and there was much speculation as to what we might think of that city. To Muscovites it is, apparently, considered to be rather a naughty place, and certainly a romantic one — rather as we regard Paris. There was much talk of the 'White Nights of Leningrad,' for we were to be there during the season of almost no darkness, and the long late evenings were thought to be especially romantic.

The Moscow station used for the Leningrad trains was built at the same time as the one in Leningrad itself and both are identical. When the Czar was shown the plan for the railway, he produced a ruler and drew a straight line on the map between the two stations, or almost straight, as his thumb got in the way. He ordered the rails to be laid accordingly, quite regardless of any buildings or hills that might stand in the way. The midnight express was shiny and modern, with uniform carriages and a matching engine. Like all Russian trains they were two classes — hard and soft. We travelled soft. The interior decoration of our sleepers, although new, was completely Edwardian. The curtains were of red plush, tables supported brass lamps with red long-fringed lampshades. Comfortable red-upholstered armchairs and carpets. The word red, I was told, meant beautiful, and stemmed from the people's love of that colour, which was why the revolutionaries had chosen a red flag. In my compartment I found a bottle with a message attached which said: 'This is the wine of life which was promised today for Lady Cromer.' Our bunks were soft and the compartment spotlessly clean. The conductor of our carriage was a woman. The next morning I was rudely awakened by this same woman briskly shaking me from my slumber. Our neighbouring compartments were occupied by a Swiss couple who, on reaching our destination, descended from the train ahead of us and found, much to their surprise and pleasure, huge bouquets being thrust into their arms by a group of people on the platform. Their delight, however, swiftly turned to embarrassment when the flowers were snatched back again to be represented to us once the officials on the platform realised their mistake.

The head of the Leningrad branch of the Gosbank resembled Mr Poskonov in many ways. He was, like the latter, much addicted to proverbs. He had all the enthusiasm of a provincial person for his city and, in this case, jealousy of the larger metropolis, made stronger by the fact that up to the Revolution Leningrad (then St Petersburg) had been the capital of Russia.

In the hotel our accommodation was similar to that of Moscow, but the decor, having a French eighteenth century influence, gained in light. The bathroom was equally grand but more decrepit. The main snag in the hotel was the shortage of lifts, which caused a queue and a long wait. The dining room on the fifth floor could be reached, unfortunately, by no other way.

We were told to present ourselves at the Gosbank at ten thirty in the morning where we were shown around. Then a small conference followed (of ten Gosbank officers) to discuss our Leningrad programme, which was done in a most earnest fashion. It was extremely lengthy, and finally they decided to adhere to the original programme. At one point, during an awkward silence, the manager referred to the wishes of Lady Cromer. Coached that morning by Jasper Rootham, I was able to respond in Russian, which produced a burst of clapping. It was really quite amazing how Jasper seemed to know exactly the most appropriate sentence for each day. It was settled that we should visit Peterhof during the course of the morning, but as we were regaled with coffee, biscuits and Russian brandy after the discussion, which typically provoked toasts which had to be drunk, it was not until past mid-day before we set off on the twenty-mile drive to Peterhof.

Peterhof is possibly one of the most attractive of all the palaces, being on the coast of the Gulf of Finland. Besides being a beautiful eighteenth century French château it is also enriched by a magnificent garden containing the famous trick fountains which so amused Peter the Great. Lunch, as we might have guessed, was not on the programme.

In the evening Jasper and I took a walk through the city without an escort which, at the time, was unusual. This elegant and decaying city with its past splendours and streets filled with the atmosphere of a bygone age. The painted classical facades and numerous bridges spanning a lacework of canals. In its heyday and in the winter what magic was manifest. But as we walked and peered through ornate archways, courtyards of indescribable squalor met our eyes: rotting staircases and doorways, no sanitation and walls fast crumbling into dust, and yet within these once-grand homes existed countless overcrowded families. We passed many unused churches topped with colourful domes. One rather larger church had been converted to an atheist museum. It housed books, tracts and other objects proving the non-existence of God.

With the murder of the Czar and the collapse of both Church and Government a vacuum must have occurred, in turn to have been filled by Leninism. In our hotel there was a room on each floor devoted to the works of Lenin; framed portraits and slogans from his teachings hung on the walls; photographs of his person stood on tables. In all the impression of an unusual kind of chapel was given, devoted to his memory.

On our return to the hotel a woman accosted us in English. She had learned our language and, she said, was longing for an opportunity to practise. She spoke extremely well, and was well-read in the english classics. We found it difficult to get rid of her and I wondered if she had, in fact, been intentionally following us for other reasons; but Jasper, who knew Russia well, was convinced that she was quite genuine. In Moscow the British Ambassadress told me that it was perfectly safe for a single woman to wander alone in the city at night. That may not be true today. But it certainly is dangerous for a single female to roam in the dark in either Washington or London.

We were treated to the usual number of courses and many wines at the formal meals which we attended. Always the toast and the speeches. Rowley discovered that he was meant to make at least two, while the subject matter always remained the same: platitudes and praise. The branch manager, who was always present, made a series of speeches, all completely repetitive, but this did not seem to bother anyone. Usually there would be about eleven orations, and as each man got to his feet, so at the same time did poor Ludmilla, whose job it was to translate; the result being that she usually went without her food until Jasper, fortified with brandy, would rise to speak in fluent Russian.

During one of these repasts ownership in Russia was explained. The manager emphatically denied that private property existed, but then added that personal property did. The difference appeared to be based on whether a person was employed by a private individual or not. A citizen of the USSR could own a house, or more than one, enjoy a garden and a car but, on no account employ a person to work for him. Small businesses run by families were permitted, providing no-one was employed who was not a relative. When the businesses prospered and there was a need for other-than relations, then a sharp distinction arose. The business immediately then became private property and was therefore forbidden.

Mr Kudryavtsev sent me a bottle of cognac every morning which he called 'concentrated sun.' During the day he would present me with a box of chocolates or a bunch of flowers; his attentions were endearing. He had not visited Leningrad for a few years although it was his home town. This fact was not passed over by the Gosbank branch. He came in for some teasing. At our last formal meal we, as visitors, were presented with some books, while, to his chagrin, he was given a guide to the city.

We spent our second day in the vast Hermitage viewing some of the huge collection of treasures. It was, after all, the famous Winter Palace, the opulence of which surpassed anything I had ever seen; the extravagant use of precious and semi-precious stones in decoration; solid fat pillars of malachite; table tops and walls of lapis lazuli; gold-leaf lavishly spread; magnificent furniture made, we knew, by the best eighteenth century craftsmen filled the rooms, and were totally ignored by the mob that passed by. It was the materials; the ivory, the gold and semi-precious stones that gave rise to interest, not only from the viewers, but also from the guides.

In place of the throne in the grandest reception room, a huge map of modern Russia adorned the wall, made entirely of precious and semi-precious stones. Not on view, except to special guests, were perfect miniature replicas in real stones of the crown jewels made by Fabergé. Also the Czars' state saddle cloths, embroidered with diamonds the size of hen's eggs. The actual crown jewels were never seen by the public at that time, and formed part of the backing for the rouble.

The next day was spent on more sight-seeing. Czarkoe Selo was having its enormous roof regilded: now called Pushkino, after the poet whose name appeared to be on everyone's lips. The delicately elegant Pavlovsk, built so inappropriately for Catherine's brutish son. And if the summer air in this northern city were any less reviving and beneficial, I do not think we would have enjoyed the full-length ballet of Spartacus as much as we did. The orchestra at the Kirov wore white tie and tails. (The one at the Bolshoi sported open-neck shirts). Spartacus is a long ballet and it was well after eleven-thirty by the time it was over. Night, however, had not fallen. We emerged from the theatre into broad daylight. The sun was still shining and our hosts insisted that we made a tour of the city by the rays of the midnight sun.

Leningrad seemed to be floating in a golden bowl. The

extraordinary clarity and softness of light gave the city a transparency. The strange mixture of dawn and sunset gave an eerie unreality that wrapped the buildings and the silver Neva in a misty dream. These were the romantic nights which excited the poetical mind of the Russian, and this is what they had tried to tell us in Moscow, and now we understood.

The morning of our departure Mr Kudryavtsev and Ludmilla visited the huge cemetery to lay flowers on the monument commemorating the 600,000 souls that had perished from starvation in the seige of Leningrad in the last war. Tears poured down Mr Kudryavtsev's face, for he lived there at the time and knew many of the victims. We heard a great deal about this seige during our stay, although we had not known the extent of the suffering. They, for their part, had absolutely no idea of the privations and injuries England had also sustained. Russian cities had received almost no bombing, and of that inflicted on English towns they were quite ignorant.

We returned to Moscow by air. There were no windows beside our seats. The cabin was also hot, noisy and vibrated. We made an appallingly bad landing and were only too relieved to be on the ground again.

That evening it was our turn to entertain the officers of the Gosbank. We held a dinner in a private room at an hotel and invited the Deputy Foreign Minister, Mr Poskonov, and other high officials, plus Sir Humphrey and Lady Trevelyan. Speeches began, as usual, as soon as we sat down. Almost everyone rose to speak, and at the end, possibly because I was tired of always listening, I got up myself. 'As a humble wife...' I began. This I had never said before, but somehow it seemed fitting, for in Russia a wife, unless she has her own job, is meek and unobtrusive. I knew at once they approved, although there was some surprise, and on Rowley's face utter astonishment. I uttered the usual platitudes, and finished by giving them a toast: 'To the White Nights of Leningrad.' This I immediately felt was wrong, so quickly added, 'and to the Golden Days of Moscow.' They were delighted and kindly told me that it was pure poetry. Mr Poskonov said that I was the first woman that he had ever heard speak at dinner.

By the following evening I sincerely wished I had not.

On our arrival back at the Moscow Hotel, we found various packages: presents from Mr Poskonov. On this visit we had taken some gifts, artificial jewellery for Maya, which we had been told would be most acceptable. And a silver box for her father. Their presents to us were an enamel modern cup, saucer and spoon, a shawl made from a mixture of goats' down and raw silk, very soft and much prized. For Rowley, a travelling case full of vodka and brandy.

The last day of our visit was a blank on our programme and we wondered why. According to Jasper, this was intentional. They had waited to see what sort of persons we were before inviting us into their homes. The day was certainly wrapped in mystery, and it was quite impossible to find out what was in store.

At five o'clock Mr Poskonov, his daughter Maya, Mr Kritsky, her husband, and Ludmilla, arrived to fetch us in two large black cars. Rowley travelled in the first one with Mr Poskonov and the interpreter, Ludmilla; Maya, her husband, Jasper and I in the second. We then embarked on a seemingly-endless drive along a splendid dual-lane road which seemed to go on for ever. One wondered where this important road led and found that, like Winnie the Pooh's footprints, it went in a circle. We had done the circumference of Moscow. Finally we left the highway and bowled along a small dusty road, which provoked excuses from the Kritskys who were, evidently, ashamed of so humble a roadway. Their mortification gave way to humiliation when Mr Poskonov's limousine developed a puncture and had to be abandoned, the result being a squash into the second car. This loss of face was felt deeply. It came as no surprise to us that we passed quite a number of cars whose drivers were dealing with the same problem. Maya and her husband were very impressed to learn that I had a driving licence. In Russia one could only be obtained if the drivers had passed a test in mechanical knowledge and could therefore undertake all repairs themselves, as well as being able to drive. Unquestionably this knowledge was necessary, for I never noticed a garage or filling station during our whole visit.

Eventually our car turned onto a drive and by a lodge where an armed officer stood guard. We continued on through a forest of lofty and magnificent trees, passing occasional, small two-storied houses until we reached a similar one nestling under tall fir trees. This was the Governor's official country dacha. Built of wood and entirely Edwardian in style, it was of very modest proportions. There was some embarrassment when I asked if I could wash my hands. There was only one small bathroom upstairs. It was furnished with one small tap for the basin, a geyser for the bath, and newspaper on a nail for the lavatory. Not a towel or a piece of soap to be seen. There were two bedrooms of rustic simplicity. Downstairs the accommodation consisted of a kitchen, which I was not privileged to see; a living-room, which also served as a dining room, containing a large table, a number of chairs and an upright piano, but no easy chair. The sitting area was an enclosed veranda.

If the house was humble, shabby and down-at-heel, there was no evidence of economy in the dinner provided. We sat down twelve, for some of the party were other high officers of the Gosbank. Course after course appeared, possibly eight or nine. When I took my place at the table I found the number of knives, forks and spoons quite astonishing and inappropriate for the surroundings. Mr Poskonov, seeing that I paused before sitting down, mistook my hesitation and kindly pointed to each utensil I was expected to use for each course. 'It is easy,' he explained through the interpreter. 'You start from the outside and work in.'

It was a sadness not to be able to converse with our host except through someone else. But it is quite surprising how much communication can be made through mime, eye- and hand-talk. We were waited upon by two buxom maids employed, we supposed, by the Bank.

Toasts were drunk and speeches made. To my great consternation Maya rose to her feet and made a very good speech. After all, I had introduced this, and was now hoisted with my own petard. Unprepared I managed to form some stumbling words which no doubt were the same as in Moscow, but by this time so much alcohol had been consumed that the weakest sally was likely to be greeted with a cheer. After this immense meal was over we were shown to the veranda room where another table was laden with cakes, biscuits, fruit and brandy. Later we were taken to a small grass clearing in front of the house where the samovar was steaming. This was pure Chekhov. Before we finally made our departure there was a stroll in the moonlit woods where wild lupins bloomed. Mr Poskonov gathered some wild flowers with the help of some of his cohorts and pressed them into my arms. He slowly kissed my hand, followed by Mr Kudryavtsev with even greater fervour. Before the Revolution hand-kissing was the custom, but with Communism the habit was dismissed as both decadent and a reflection on the inequality of the sexes. Possibly they were carried away by the romantic setting of their woods? A highly emotional people tuned to the natural beauty of their surroundings provoking a charming old-fashioned gallantry.

After this friendly, almost intimate evening, we thought that conceivably our rather distant friendship had become a little closer. We were to be disappointed. At the airport the following day they all assembled to see us off. Gone was the warmth and friendliness of the day before, leaving only coldness and formality. A quick handshake, an impassive face. Maybe the faces were a little too rigid. Did I detect a tear in the eye of Mr Kudryavtsev, or did I imagine it?

The following spring Alexei Poskonov visited us in England, and in return for the wild lupins we were able to show him our woods carpeted with bluebells. He was friendly, and when I welcomed him to our home in Russian, he responded, much to our surprise, in English. 'He does not wish to be outdone by Lady Cromer,' the interpreter imparted.

The last time I met Alexei Poskonov was in Stockholm during the celebrations for the four-hundredth anniversary of the Central Bank of Sweden. At a large but informal lunch party, knowing few other guests, he followed me to a table accompanied by his interpreter. On my other side sat Lou Rasminsky, Governor of the Bank of Canada, whom I knew quite well, opposite Ireland's. Both watched and wondered about the identity of the man to whom I was paying so much attention. Finally Lou, containing his curiosity no longer, asked me in a loud voice who my boyfriend was. So loud was his voice and so curious the others, an immediate silence reigned, while the interpreter translated, to my embarrassment. The information of Mr Poskonov's identity then caused a sensation. The whole table wanted his autograph on the backs of their menu cards. Lou Rasminsky went one better and wrote on his: 'Please pay the bearer one million roubles,' and passed it to Mr Poskonov to sign. As Alexei poised his pen to sign I quickly held his arm. At the same moment the interpreter hurriedly and grimly translated the words. There was a moment of tense and suspicious silence, while it looked as if Mr Poskonov would get up and walk out. Hastening to explain that it was only a harmless joke Mr Poskonov looked me straight in the eye, and then with a guffaw, chucked the offending piece of paper back at Lou. I did not think that East West relations had yet quite reached the point of trust for that sort of teasing. And perhaps it would take many years for that point to be reached.

15

HARD TIMES

During 1964 Reggie Maudling, as Chancellor of the Exchequer, continued to run the economy of Britain in a generous, and even profligate manner. This did not pass unnoticed by the Central Bankers and financial experts in other countries, and slowly their confidence in his policies and capacities began to evaporate. Furthermore, they were unsure of some of his holiday acquaintances abroad.

Rowley, since becoming Governor of the Bank of England, consistently tried to convince the Chancellor in private, and subsequently in public, of the importance of the integrity of the pound. 'I am convinced,' he told the British Bankers, 'that the future prosperity of this country at home and its power in the world abroad depend on the strength of the pound. And the strength of the pound depends on wise and prudent husbandry of our resources.' Those were the days of fixed exchange rates, runs on sterling, and before North Sea oil. Rampant inflation was still distant, but nonetheless, a threat.

Within the previous eighteen years Britain had won a war but gathered no spoils. She had given away an Empire and generously aided new independent countries. Vast welfare programmes were hugely expensive at home, while at the same time the people wished to earn more money and work less hours. Punishing taxation was imposed and the money raised immediately spent. A once-rich country, substantially impoverished, wished to spread largesse on borrowed money. For those who knew the facts it was a bleak scenario.

Rowley's pleas, although fairly well received by the press and public, did nothing to change the expansive policies of Reggie Maudling. The fact that we were hurtling towards a balance of payments crisis deterred him not at all. Expansion and full employment was the cry and, anyway, good politics with an election in view. But it was no way to restore confidence in Britain's currency abroad.

In the meantime the Labour Party, true to its beliefs, produced plans for even greater public expenditure. After many years in opposition they did not possess factual or detailed knowledge (and as is the custom in Britain) of the true state of our financial affairs. Ever heavier taxation was to be imposed with the object of spending more of the people's money for their eventual benefit, as the Labour Party saw it.

The election took place in October and was won by Labour with a narrow majority. Rowley then had the unpleasant duty of informing the new Prime Minister of the real state of our financial position, and also the deleterious consequences of many of his cherished policies which, if carried out, could only damage the pound further. Harold Wilson, understandably, did not relish these warnings.

Many an evening Rowley would call at the private entrance to Number Ten and endure wearisome hours arguing the necessity of holding back certain of Mr Wilson's intended measures, for the Prime Minister was not at all convinced that his dearly-held plans should either be delayed or discarded. Worse, moreover, stricter means of reducing public expenditure might even be needed. Rowley would return dispirited and anxious after these heated Downing Street arguments, in which Harold Wilson was apt to furiously demand who, in fact, governed Britain: himself or the bankers?

In the meantime confidence in sterling rapidly began to dwindle. Labour governments had twice devalued the pound in previous administrations and were reluctant to do so again, especially within a few weeks of gaining power. Rowley himself was apprehensive that a third devaluation under a Labour administration might become inevitable.

When the situation looked grim, Friday was considered usually the worst day of the week on the currency markets, and Friday, November 21st was by no means an exception. Spending the weekend in the country I found that on that Saturday it was necessary to cater for an unexpected army of Bank officials. Summoned by Rowley, they were to put into practice, in my drawing-room, the arrangements for an immediate and unprecedented jump in Bank Rate, in order for this action to be announced on Monday. This was entirely due to the reluctance of the government to act earlier and, conventionally, on a Thursday. And by not stemming the haemorrhage at once, the flow became a flood. People of various nationalities were fast selling pounds in expectation of a forced devaluation caused by lack of faith in sterling and the new government.

The following week an extremely anxious Prime Minister asked Rowley despairingly if there was nothing he could do to hold off the run. Rowley replied that he would see what he could do. He then started a marathon series of telephone calls which continued all through the night. All round the world from Governor to Governor, on an entirely personal basis, he asked for an enormous loan. The largest, I believe, ever given to date. By the end of Thursday, November 27th Rowley had succeeded in raising sufficient funds to ensure the stability of the pound — three billion dollars-worth. An immense sum at that time. The relief to Mr Wilson was enormous, and although he profoundly thanked Rowley personally, he never saw fit to publicly recognise his achievement, possibly for political reasons.

I was, of course, aware of the crisis, since the battle for the pound had, after all, partly taken place within my home, but I had not, naturally, been informed of the details. When Rowley returned from Downing Street, therefore, on that Thursday evening with his Deputy, Leslie O'Brien, looking exhausted, Leslie explained that Rowley had personally enabled Britain to borrow three billion dollars. 'But how simply awful,' I replied, since borrowing and being in debt has never been praiseworthy in my eyes. 'But Esme,' said the amazed Leslie, 'you should be very proud of the Governor.' And indeed I was when the full story came to be told.

With Rowley's personal achievement came an avalanche of publicity, of which one of the more unpleasant side-effects was a series of burglaries, always in the country, culminating in a singularly audacious one: creeping into our bedroom at night and out again with their loot, but at least there was no violence.

Prime Ministers, according to political custom, reward their lieutenants with the fruits of electoral victory by appointing them Ministers, care and attention being given to both their popular position in the Party and their prospective Ministers' preferences. Sometimes the Prime Minister's own position is insecure, and care is taken to see that satisfaction is given to a prominent political personality, even, possibly, at the risk of upsetting another one. Sometimes two leading subordinates might be put in a situation where their very positions versus each other can only be divisive. James Callaghan was appointed Chancellor of the Exchequer and George Brown Secretary of State for Economic Affairs at a time when the realities of our financial position in the world were delicate.

The relationship between the Governor of the Bank, the Chancellor of the Exchequer and Prime Minister is of first importance. The channels between them worked very well, and to have used other channels would have complicated the workings of this relationship. Therefore Rowley kept strictly to past custom. George Brown and the Governor met, in fact, for the first time at a banquet at the Mansion House. George Brown had been placed next to Rowley and was late. When he eventually arrived Rowley proceeded to make some form of friendly greeting, only to be met in return by a brooding silence. After a strained minute or two George Brown turned to Rowley and asked what it felt like to be God? Rowley replied with some relish that he had never applied his mind to that question but, since he had now been asked it, he could only assume that the subject was something to which George Brown must have given constant thought. It transpired that a deep resentment had been created in George Brown's mind due to Rowley's unwillingness to talk to him as freely as he had with the Chancellor. This unfortunate incompatibility led to some amusing, if disagreeable, situations.

At a dinner given in the Italian embassy in honour of the Italian Director of the Budget, Rowley found himself seated opposite the Secretary for Economic Affairs. In the course of the meal George Brown became ever more incensed, and louder became his comments on, in his view, Rowley's unfitness to be Governor of the Bank of England — until it was no longer possible to ignore his accusations. Rowley responded with as much dignity as he could muster and did his best to calm the excited Minister. At this point general conversation ceased, and everyone remained spellbound at the spectacle of a public feud between two such important people, while the much-embarrassed Italian Ambassador tried valiantly to defuse the situation and deflect George from his virulent attack. The Italian Budget Director was seated on my left and during the course of the meal he received a note from George Brown on which was written: 'Beware of Lady Cromer — she is a Mata Hari.' The Italian Budget Director, wholly confused and bewildered, turned to me in amazement and declared: 'Signora, it is a compliment, Mr Brown is jealous and I think he desires to become your lover.' By other meaningful glances it appeared, perhaps fortunately, that George Brown's scene had quite simply been interpreted as a lovers' triangle by the romantic Italians! I did not enlighten him as to the fact that it was the first time George Brown and I had ever met.

There were other embarrassing interludes in public. But when George Brown became Foreign Secretary his attentions were, fortunately, directed towards other matters. Nevertheless, his resentment must have lain deep, for eight years later, during a press interview in Washington while Rowley was serving as British Ambassador, Lord George Brown declared that Lord Cromer must have been the worst ambassador to have been sent to any country in the world. Luckily, by that time, Rowley had established himself securely in the position as one of the most influential diplomats in Washington. George's comments were only to rebound on himself. Earlier, as Lady-in-Waiting at a state banquet, I found that I had been placed next to George Brown. Having reached my place before him, I swiftly turned my place-card over in the hope that the Foreign Secretary would not remember my name. In an ebullient and merry mood, his thoughts far from any Bank of England grievances, he sang lustily throughout the very formal dinner while waving to acquaintances and flirting outrageously. I do not think he discovered my identity, and to add to the incongruity of the scene, I received a very broad wink from the Prime Minister, Harold Wilson, who was seated opposite. Lord George Brown by this time had become a character of world renown. And if some people were embarrassed by his behaviour as Foreign Secretary, visiting dignitaries, and especially their wives, looked forward with excited interest to making his acquaintance. Almost their first words to me on their State Arrival at Victoria Station were: 'Please tell us which is George Brown.'

James Callaghan seemed, fortunately, to have been formed from an entirely different mould. He must, at first, have felt uneasy at the prospect of dealing with someone who, to him, must have appeared a product of the right wing establishment. Rowley, aware of this difficulty, wasted no time in calling on the new Chancellor on his very first day in office, in order to remove any suspicions that Jim might entertain as to his motives. Rowley stated that, as Governor, he saw his duty as being to the government of the day, and would serve them to the best of his ability. And certainly it was not long before Rowley's words were put to the test, and it was shown that he had not been mouthing empty words. If they occasionally had their differences of opinion, as Rowley had had with Reginald Maudling, they seemed to recognise in each other each's feeling of duty and responsibility. Rowley hoped he would find in Jim the seeds of statesmanship; that rare quality seldom found in politicians, to put the interest of the country ahead of personal or partisan advancement.

Harold Wilson and Jim Callaghan wished to recognise the help given to them during the General Election by the *Daily Mirror*, the chairman of which was Cecil King. To do so they had, I believe, offered him a peerage, which he turned down. Instead they wished to appoint him a Director of the Bank of England, which was more to Cecil's taste. Rowley, however, warned that there could be a conflict of interest, but his caveat went unheeded. The Bank itself was surprised and apprehensive, being more accustomed to solid scions of industry, the City or trade unions. Cecil was told by Jim of Rowley's views, but was in no way discouraged, although somewhat peeved — possibly because a directorship of the Bank meant, in the words of one of his children, 'respectability at last.' Cecil King was my father's first cousin. He had been given his job on the *Daily Mirror* by my grandfather. With little personal fortune of his own he had embraced the Labour Party. Within the family he was regarded as somewhat of a maverick, clever but unreliable. Whether the Labour Government ever came to regret disregarding Rowley's advice in view of Cecil's later outburst of criticism of Harold Wilson, history does not relate. But the Bank, on the other hand, came to appreciate Cecil's unusual qualities as he, in turn, did theirs.

It was not possible to reveal to the public the real extent of the damage to the currency during the November crisis for fear of increasing foreign lack of confidence in the pound. After Rowley had borrowed the three billion dollars on his own and the Bank of England's reputation for integrity, it became necessary for the Government to be seen to be following economic policies which could, thereby, continue to justify foreign confidence in the pound. However, in spite of warnings to the Chancellor and to the Prime Minister, nothing was done. They just hoped that the problems would disappear. In the meantime the public, left largely unaware of the true facts, and still believing their country to be a rich one, and more than able to increase their standard of living, as well as lavishing overseas aid, continued to live in happy ignorance.

Rowley, thinking that if he enlightened the people as to the true state of affairs, he might, by doing so, actually help the Government to introduce unpopular measures, but found, instead, that the Government decided to take his words as nothing else but a criticism of themselves — by no means his purpose. He spoke in Edinburgh in February in what became known as his 'Day of Reckoning' speech. In it he said: 'If we continue our affairs in the same manner as before, as if nothing had happened, then the potential danger and threat to our high standard of living is very real. The respite of November in itself no more guarantees our future than Dunkirk presaged victory in 1940.' The Government were furious. The political cartoonists decided that Rowley had now entered the arena of politics and portrayed him as either an Archbishop of Canterbury reading a paraphrased Ten Commandments at a terrified Harold Wilson, or as the skipper of a lifeboat trying to rescue a drunken ship steered by the Prime Minister. The Labour left immediately commenced a 'Cromer must go' campaign, and suggested in Parliament that a Labour Government should not have to struggle against reactionary financial views to implement its policies. His speech was discussed, it was believed, at a Cabinet meeting because of one particular passage in which Rowley suggested that 'those activities which could be deferred, without hardship, should make room for more essentials.'

The press, on the whole, supported Rowley, and pointed out that the Governor of the Bank of England had the right and the duty to speak on the nation's finances, and mentioned that Lord Robens, Chairman of the National Coal Board, had challenged the government's policy on coal production. During this whirlwind of controversy, Rowley remained quite unmoved. As Governor, he saw it above all as his duty.

Two weeks later we were included in a luncheon in honour of the Shah of Persia at Buckingham Palace. The Shah, who knew of the controversy caused by Rowley's speech over which the newspapers portrayed the Prime Minister and the Governor as bitter foes, was most surprised indeed to find that both had been included in the luncheon and, moreover, appeared to be on friendly terms.

Although Rowley's face was well-known to those who read the financial pages, and in the City people would throw him a curious glance, in other fields he would remain happily anonymous. One evening at a party given by Sir Robin Darwin at the Royal College of Art I met a number of artists and found much of mutual interest to talk about. Those were the days of being 'with it' and trendy. 'Square' meant dull and hidebound. The Royal College, characteristically, was full of these modern trendies. Towards the end of the evening they asked me what I did. 'Oh, just a wife,' I replied. 'But what does your husband do?' they wanted to know. 'Oh, nothing that would interest you,' I answered, for fear that they would be scornful of such a really dull profession. These words were to make them all the keener, and on their further insistence I gave in. 'Well, I am afraid he governs the Bank of England.' This was received with a shout of laughter, as I expected. But their spokesman continued: 'Surely you do not think that we would not want anyone not absolutely square to look after our money, do you?' And his friends all heartily agreed. It was a relief to know that they felt that way; also that under their rather wild appearances lay common sense.

During these troublesome weeks Sir Winston Churchill died and with his going it seemed that the glories of Great Britain had also passed away. The end, in fact, of Britain's extraordinary place in world history. In St Paul's, as the voices of thousands swelled in singing the Battle Hymn of the

American Republic, tears were shed both for a great man and the end of a valiant epoch.

That summer in 1965 Sir Alec Douglas-Home resigned as Leader of the Conservative Party. His reasons, we were told, were mainly because of his quite undeserved unpopularity in the press. The 'Grouse Moor' image started in the time of Macmillan and unhappily continued under Alec's leadership, and it was not thought to be a favourable one for the party. Many people were saddened by his selfless action, for it was thought by many, and certainly by those in the City, that with his unquestioned integrity, he might have been the one to lead us out of our present troubles. Elizabeth Douglas-Home replied to my letter of condolence. She wrote: 'I feel melancholy and disillusioned, furious and muddled — but I suppose that I am hopelessly biased.' If it seemed bewildering to her, it certainly did to us. Elizabeth possessed a charm and naturalness not often encountered, and a great warmth of personality. Once at a City dinner she was found in an adjoining room quietly telephoning home to ask her daughter to remove something from the kitchen stove, which she had forgotten to do before leaving to go out. 'Was it a stockpot or stew?' I asked her. 'No, only the washing,' she replied.

With Sir Alec's resignation the Conservative Party decided to hold an election for the first time in its history in order to find a new leader. The two most prominent candidates were Reggie Maudling and Ted Heath. Reggie was far the more popular, and certainly thought himself that he had more than a good chance. He had not, however, reckoned on the effect his reputation as Chancellor had on foreign opinion and, more precisely, on those from whom he had had to borrow so much money. Some of the editors and publishers of various newspapers were aware that this was so. Through family, business and social ties Rowley, at that time, was very well acquainted with most of them. And they were most interested to know what Rowley thought, and also what the overseas financial pundits thought of Maudling. It was becoming increasingly clear that another government must be led by someone un-tarnished by any previously unsuccessful economic policies and someone whom they felt was trustworthy. Rowley told them that, in his opinion, Maudling would not find it easy to win the confidence of overseas bankers. The result of their inquiry changed any thought of supporting Maudling, and on the day before the leadership election the majority of news-papers came out in support of Heath. If the press had in-fluenced the vote, which it may well have done, then Heath won by default.

Edward Heath was an unknown quantity both to us and to most people. We had entertained him twice at the Bank. Though shy and difficult to know, he appeared to contain a depth of sincerity, and an occasional twinkle proclaimed a sense of humour. A pronounced European and a man of determination, shown by his fight to repeal the Price Main-tenance Act: beyond that we knew little. It seemed certain that one day he would become Prime Minister, and whenever that moment would come, we placed our hopes in his ability to lead Britain out of her financial difficulties.

In July Rowley entertained both the Prime Minister and the Chancellor to a large dinner in the Court Room of the Bank of England. This was in order for them to meet leading City personalities. At the time another financial storm had been slowly gathering, due to poor trade returns and the Govern-ment's reluctance to approve necessary measures. So once again the country was plunged into an economic crisis, if not perhaps as serious as the previous November. We now also owed enormous extra sums to other countries. In the words of Lyndon Johnson, 'The state of sterling is hair-raising.' The Labour Government at last realised that problems have to be solved before they disappear, and immediately introduced extensive measures to reduce public expenditure.

On the thirty-first of March 1966 Harold Wilson, who had called an election, won with an increased majority. That evening, watching the election on television, we knew that our immediate future depended on the result, for Rowley's five-year term as Governor was due to end the following June.

It was abundantly clear that Rowley had no inclination to continue serving with a Labour Government under Harold Wilson. Nor, indeed, was it likely that they would want him to stay. Nevertheless it was reputed that ten thousand pounds had been placed with the bookmakers, and the odds on Rowley's reappointment were evens.

The announcement that Rowley would be leaving the Bank was made in April. He was to be succeeded by his Deputy, Leslie O'Brien, which caused a break with tradition. For the last fifty years the Deputy Governor had not become Governor and he was usually appointed with this in mind. Leslie had spent his entire career in the Bank of England and, curiously, had been placed there on the recommendation of Rowley's great-uncle, Lord Revelstoke.

In Parliament, following the announcement of Rowley's departure, a Labour back bencher asked a question: 'In view of the recent changes at the top, can we expect in future that the Bank of England will support Government policy for a change?' The Prime Minister replied that the Bank of England had the right to criticise successive Governments on the question of Government expenditure. 'I heard the present Governor, a few weeks ago, praise this Government for having exercised a tighter grip on Government expenditure.'

In May Rowley made his last speech as Governor. He referred to the Government's policy of giving more importance to overseas aid than to British investment abroad. Amid loud applause he said that: 'it is like landing dental chairs before ammunition during the invasion of North Africa in the last war.'

During our last week at the Bank James Callaghan gave a small dinner party for us at Number Eleven Downing Street. It was a cosy, relaxed evening. Audrey, Jim's nice and intelligent wife, gave us an excellent meal. Jim helped to hand round the vegetables. When he reached me I told him that never in my life had I ever expected to be offered carrots by the Chancellor of the Exchequer. 'Well you never know,' he replied.

We attended a debate in the House of Commons. The Prime Minister was in excellent form and appeared to dominate the House with a pronounced ascendency over the opposition. Later in the week I met Ted Heath who seemed to go to considerable lengths to avoid mentioning Harold Wilson by name.

Rowley celebrated his final day in the Bank of England by giving a large reception in the Court Room for all our friends and acquaintances. It was the first social occasion that had ever been held in the Bank to include both sexes. It was well attended by both political parties. The Prime Minister found time to come with his sweet wife, Mary, and stayed almost to the end. Notably absent was the Leader of the Opposition, Ted Heath.

When the last guest left, Rowley looked around the splendid Court Room and the familiar Parlours for the last time. It was like a captain taking leave of his valiant crew and battle-scarred ship that had successfully forged through tempestuous seas and enemy action for five years. It was an emotional farewell for Rowley.

Shouldering such great responsibilities for five years had taken its toll. Rowley looked far older than he had at the beginning. But those years had also been packed with interest and much enjoyment. It had, we decided, been worthwhile.

One newspaper commented: 'Bankers do not deal in figures [only]; they trust people and, in Lord Cromer, they had a man they were willing to back whatever they may have thought of our Ministers.'

Before Rowley finally left the Bank of England he had seen that every penny that the Bank had borrowed under his stewardship had been repaid.

Years later, when Rowley was installed as Knight of the Garter at Windsor, and took his seat in his stall which, by chance, was next to Harold Wilson's, Rowley turned to Harold and remarked: 'This is until death do us part.'

AMBASSADOR'S WIFE

16

IGNORANCE IS NOT BLISS

In 1971 the human and political climate in Washington was very different from that which we knew ten years previously. Different in a turbulent and uneasy way. Gone was an America confident and proud. Gone the instant warmth of welcome extended unquestioningly to all visitors, and usually accompanied by: 'How do you like our country?' And the pleasure given with the reply: 'Wonderful.' Even if an assurance was needed it was still God's own country and, no doubt, deservedly so.

Now in 1971 this precept was clearly in question, and no-one from the Foreign Office had seen fit to prepare Rowley, the newly-appointed Ambassador, nor me, his Ambassadress, for this complete reversal in attitudes. Returning after an interval of ten years, unadvised and unwary and, furthermore, naively expecting a rather cloyingly effusive press such as we had experienced on our first tour of duty in Washington, instead we plunged innocently into a hotbed of injured national pride; people only too ready to blame their government for past and present ills.

It was the day of 'radical chic' and of being 'with it,' and of the throw-over of past conventions. The nation's youth embraced all kinds of new ideas and social mores. The slightly older harped back to the promise of the Kennedy era. The promise that vanished in the morass of Vietnam. Nevertheless, the ghost of President Kennedy, eight years after his assassination, was tangible. He was still idolised, and it was him that the press repeatedly asked me if I had met, and not, as seemed far more appropriate, President Nixon.

Perhaps, unconsciously, the collective pain of the Democratic Party centred on President Nixon. Blame, like a mother might unconsciously direct towards a surviving, less-loved son, on losing her favourite one.

It was to this scene that our RAF plane unknowingly carried us. Rowley, a Peer of the Realm, an ex-Governor of the Bank of England, an ex-Economic Minister to Washington, and I, a Lady of the Bedchamber to the Queen, evidently carried the wrong credentials, which might have been excused if the Prime Minister thought that they might, conceivably, have been the right ones. The appointment instead, seemed to have annoyed the overwhelmingly Democratic press and their writers. Our predecessors, John Freeman and his wife, were more to their taste, being both left-wing and in the media themselves.

We had not, in the first place, wanted to go to Washington. We had been before, and therefore knew at first hand something about the demands of Diplomatic life, the disruption of family and the temporary severing of interests and obligations.

Rowley had been senior partner in Barings bank, and I was happy in my job as a Lady in Waiting. Also, we had just built a small house on our farm in Kent, and I was busy creating a small garden. It was sad, too, to be parted from our family.

I had always had a premonition that one day Rowley would be offered the Washington embassy. This feeling had come over me on my first visit to Washington in 1947 when we had called to sign our names in the Book. It was a source of amusement for years. We would laugh and say, 'Well, that is something that will not happen because it is the last thing that we would contemplate.' In any case the likelihood of being sent there in that capacity was as remote a possibility as visiting the South Pole.

The reasons leading up to Rowley's appointment may have been diverse. During the 1970 election Rowley appeared on television as a guest of Sir Robin Day. A question was asked about the economy and Rowley replied with complete frankness: 'There is no question that any government that comes to power after this election is going to find a very much more difficult financial situation than the new government in 1964.' We had now had six years of Labour rule, and Harold Wilson chose to fight the election on the health of the economy. Facts, of course, backed up Rowley's assertion. In 1964 our external debt was $168 million. In 1970 it had grown to almost $4000 million. (In current values, about £650m and £11,270m respectively).

The Labour Party claimed that they had turned a deficit of £800 million into a surplus of £500 million. The man in the street may not have understood, or bothered about these dry facts, but the lack of any response at all from the Labour leaders puzzled the journalists. Rowley's small and short intervention became the hinge of opinion. Before, there had been no debate. Now the economy became the issue.

At no time was attention drawn to Rowley's public remarks by the Conservative leader, or thanks given, and certainly Rowley would not have expected any, for he was only uttering the truth, however unpalatable. But the then-Labour leaders immediately decided, on hearing of Rowley's new appointment, that it was the pay-off for his intervention in the election.

Meanwhile Edward Heath, the new Prime Minister and, to a greater degree, Alec Douglas-Home, the new Foreign Secretary, were imploring Rowley to take the job. They told him that there was no-one in the whole Diplomatic Service who was remotely suitable. Another reason that dawned on us much later that may have been in Ted Heath's mind: maybe the Government wished to be rid of so outspoken a person. Be that as it may, our reaction to the offer was absolutely negative. Neither of us wanted to go.

My father, having recently married a Texan, was extremely keen that Rowley should accept, and tried his hardest to

183

persuade me. He did succeed in weakening my resolution. Also, the words 'duty' and 'obligation to your country' kept cropping up with frequency from various directions. Finally, after declining, we accepted this onerous position.

As soon as Rowley's appointment was publicly announced the newspaper reporters gathered. Rowley's brief as ambassador was to help reconcile America to Britain's intention of becoming closer to Europe.

The english newspapers, on the whole, were friendly to Rowley's appointment. But a telegram from the chairman of the Urban District Council of Cromer gave him the most pleasure. It said: 'The people of Cromer send congratulations on your well-deserved appointment and best wishes for the future to you and Lady Cromer.' It was a seaside resort, however, that Rowley had never managed to visit.

On November 5th 1970, Rowley was invited to the Palace for tea with The Queen. Among the subjects discussed, Her Majesty told him that when the Prime Minister told her that he wished to make Rowley Britain's Ambassador to the United States, she had gone quite pink in the face and felt like Queen Victoria that 'we are not amused.' For at one fell swoop she was about to lose one of her personal financial advisers as well as a Lady in Waiting. However, Her Majesty went on to say that in her opinion it was a very good appointment.

Later that month, in Waiting for the Diplomatic Reception at Buckingham Palace I told the Prime Minister that, regretfully, this was my swan-song as a Lady in Waiting. His only reply was that he had just received a long letter from Lady Hartwell in Washington, but he did not reveal any of its contents.

The American delegation, always the largest and led by Ambassador Annenberg and his pretty wife Lee, with hugs and kisses, delightedly introduced me to all his suite. This took place under the eyes of Harold Wilson, who was watching from directly opposite, and who nodded rather coldly as I ran to catch up with The Queen.

On November 20th Rowley dined with a group of civil servants, who told him that the consensus of opinion on the political situation among themselves was that the Heath government was 'the last chance.' That Harold Wilson's group had had it, and that unless all our problems were taken properly in hand we would see a polarisation of left and right. Therefore a strong-arm government would come next, either from the far left or from the right.

For years Rowley had returned from a dining club of senior civil servants (who were by no means all politically right-wing inclined) in a despondent mood, and would tell me how unhappy and despairing they were about the way things in Britain were going — chaotic and inefficient government being the main complaint. They used to shake their heads and sigh. But now the mood had changed. They had a purpose, they agreed. They knew the government would try, and they hoped it would not be too late to resolve the country's plight.

That same month I was expected to visit the Ministry of Works situated near Southwark Bridge to see an official in order to discuss the British Embassy Residence in Washington. An appointment was made, and Rowley told me more than once beforehand that on no account was I to ask for much redecoration to be done, on the grounds of economy. After all, one had to practise what one preached about government spending. It was known too, he said, that most ambassadresses the world over bullied their Ministries unmercifully into redecorating their respective embassies, and that the poor civil servants had a very difficult task restraining them.

I reassured Rowley that in my case they would have no cause for complaint, as I had absolutely no intention of re-doing the embassy. In fact the thought of choosing and finding endless colour schemes, materials &c was less than enchanting and not something that I had ever enjoyed doing. Besides, after making a difficult choice I had often found that the material I selected had been discontinued or was unobtainable. It had been an exhausting and frustrating experience in our private homes on other occasions. In any case we had managed to live with a dreadful colour scheme for two years the last time we lived in Washington.

At the Ministry I was shown into an office where three neatly-dressed gentlemen greeted me warmly and showed, with pride, various mock-ups of the schemes they had recently carried out in some rooms at the embassy. They all seemed very nice, if unimaginative. But when I stated that I had no intention of altering anything they seemed surprised and not a little disappointed. One remarked hopefully that he felt certain that once I was installed I would want to change something, but to please remember that money was tight and not to do too much. I replied, with some asperity, that I knew only too well about extravagant government spending, having lived in the Bank of England.

I asked one of the three gentlemen whether they employed an outside professional decorator, and he replied: 'We are all decorators,' after which he opened a door and ushered me into a large room where, stacked on all sides, were large samples of material, carpets, brocades, silks, satins and chintz. It was a veritable Aladdin's cave, and they seemed enormously proud of it and assured me that any sample chosen was always obtainable and, if necessary, could be specially ordered. They became somewhat disappointed when it appeared that I did not want anything different, so to please them I asked them to cover one stool and make two small table covers.

It seemed to me wholly understandable that the various ambassadresses might go rather wild and make extravagant orders. After all, here were three charming decorators trying to please, with thousands of pieces of material at their command — showing so much riches for the least possible effort, and above all, with no bills to pay.

It was only after Rowley's appointment had been announced publicly that the Foreign Office told him that the embassy was in urgent need of repair, and that we should

10th January, 1942: I leave
the Ritz with my father.

I arrive at St Dunstan's in the West, Fleet Street.

A Captain in the Grenadier Guards called The Viscount Errington.

No icing on the Wedding Cake. Sugar rations would not stretch.

Overdressed at the Albert Hall with Queen Mary and Princess Margaret.

Our lucky find: our Long Island cottage.

Thinned down by wartime rations.

Fun in the Great Blizzard, New York, for Lana and Evelyn.

Winston Churchill opens Carnival Parade at Westerham with me and Christopher Soames.

Success with Jersey cow.

Photo opposite: **Dressed up for the Coronation.** *Photo: Daily Mail.*

...owley arrives at the Bank ... **England.** *Photo: Bank of England.*

The Nawab's Court.

Unless we went first in the convoy we were caked in dust.

Rowley sinks under a welcoming garland of flowers from Pathan chiefs.

Rowley and Reggie Maudling. Some doubts?

I was told not to mention prison to President de Valera.

Rowley in the Governor's Parlour. *Photo: Bank of England.*

A Governor's wife's perk: watching Charlie Chaplin direct a film.

Flying away to show unconcern for the wobbly pound. *Photo: David Newell-Smith.*

Rowley presents his credentials. *Photo: Paul Popper Ltd.*

Discussion Group: Rowley, Burke Trend, President Nixon and Henry Kissinger.

Photo right (from left to right): **Henry Kissinger, Rowley Cromer, Bill Rogers, Burke Trend, Robert Armstrong, Walter Annenberg, Prime Minister Heath, President Nixon, Alec Douglas-Home, Denis Greenhill at Camp David.**

Rowley crowns the Azalea Queen (Sarah Rippon): NATO's festival. *Photo: AP.*

Dinner with Cap Weinberger at the Folger Library.

Dining Room, British Embassy, Washington
Photo: Vivian Baring.

Programme for British Embassy Players' Music Hall.

The poised, sophisticated Lorraine Sherman Cooper.

"SIXTY GLORIOUS YEARS"

In Joyful Celebration of The Diamond Jubilee of Her Gracious Majesty

QUEEN VICTORIA

THE BRITISH EMBASSY PLAYERS
Present MUSIC HALL
June 13th to the 24th, 1897
*The British Embassy in Washington in the District of Columbia
United States of America*

Holding Uncle Leicester's 1st Edition of Chaucer at Folger Library.

Lana orders her supper.

Prime Minister Heath's arrival at The White House.

I was asked for 40 paintings by an impossible deadline. *Photo: Vivian Baring.*

move into an hotel for six months on our arrival in Washington. On hearing this unwelcome news, Rowley said: 'Well, if I had been told that before this, it would have been the absolute deciding factor in my decision not to go.' As it was, he refused to allow any alterations until the end of our tour of duty. By that time the plumbing had seized up.

A number of farewell parties were given for us by kind friends. One of the most memorable was at Penshurst given by the De L'Isles. Amongst ice and freezing fog we slithered out to dinner at less than ten miles an hour from our farm to noble Penshurst, where a warm welcome awaited us. Bill De L'Isle advised me on the desirability of keeping time for oneself, and also the need to discriminate between the important and importunate. He spoke with the experience of an ex-Governor of Australia.

After dinner we played charades. Lady De L'Isle's team included Lord Cornwallis, a most distinguished and greatly-loved Lord Lieutenant of Kent who, at the age of eighty, removed the upper part of his clothing, donned a bathing cap belonging to our hostess, and pretended he was taking a bath amidst gales of laughter. Our side, led by Lord De L'Isle utterly failed to guess the word which, one should have known, was Washington.

Hardy Amies most generously offered to give me a couture dress. He told me that he always offered one to new ambassadresses to Washington. This was very welcome news, since there was no dress allowance forthcoming from government sources, nor tax relief either. And it was essential to provide oneself with a large and varied wardrobe. Hardy invited me to view on my own a part of his Spring Collection and afterwards to give me lunch. It was indeed very nice to be spoiled in this manner. Our conversation ranged widely, and included his present success with men's clothes in Japan. He showed me a well-cut man's suit earlier in the day accompanied by the remark: 'Isn't it pretty?' He also told me of his lack of success in America which was caused by the American unions, who were very difficult to deal with. They also did not understand that lapels should be properly finished, and considered that it involved too much unnecessarily-concentrated work.

Lunch at Number Ten was not in our honour. 'A New Year's party for friends,' Ted Heath said. By Ted's place was a gavel which he banged at various intervals. First for Grace by the vicar of St Margaret's, than The Loyal Toast and, lastly, for a neat speech in which he brought in almost all the names of the people present. He told us that the only people he was leaving out were those that had either been running, or were about to run for Number Ten.

Ted was leaving for Singapore the next day to attend the Commonwealth Prime Ministers' conference. I suggested that the Republics within the Commonwealth should, in all conscience, leave. He laughed. There was some discussion between him and Sir Denis Blundell, High Commissioner of New Zealand, about whether the Queen, as Head of the Commonwealth, should be in Singapore.

Singapore, being a republic, seemed to make the situation a contrary one. Evidently the Governor General of Canada was planning official visits to some European countries. This provoked the thought as to what his status would be. He represents the Queen in Canada. Abroad, was he also representing Canada? Also, I learned that the Governor of Australia was about to make an official visit to New Zealand. This apparently created a precedent, and we all wondered where it might lead to.

Christopher Chataway, who was among the guests, told me that he had been at Oxford with Catherine Freeman (the lady whose shoes I was about to put on) and also, that they had worked together on a television programme called Panorama. He told me that her first husband, Charles Wheeler, had been the BBC's representative in Delhi when her second husband was appointed High Commissioner to India. For reasons of tact the BBC then re-posted Charles as their representative in

Washington where, subsequently, the Freemans caught up with him when John Freeman was appointed ambassador there. But this time Charles Wheeler stayed. Maybe it was thought that Washington was large enough to hold them both?

Early in January Rowley started working in the Foreign Office. His room was small, poky and could only be reached by a fire-escape. So very different from the one he had used at the Treasury before leaving for Washington the first time. That had been princely by comparison. Nor did his first impression of the efficiency of the Foreign Office compare at all favourably with the Treasury.

Some of the remarks and suggestions that I received from friends and acquaintances were notably strange and their advice even more so, and hardly ensured much enthusiasm for what lay ahead.

'You do realise that all the British ambassadors' wives have returned quite mad?' and 'How lovely to be going to live in that gorgeous Lutyens building, even if the kitchen is a mile from the dining room.' And again, 'Of course, you must not on any account go out of the front door except to climb into a locked car.' One began to feel less and less secure. 'Nancy put on an act of extreme eccentricity in order to spare herself from overwork, and has never been quite the same since.' And one Foreign Service wife went so far as to say: 'When I was in Washington I spent as much time as I could digging for rubies down the Cowie Valley in the Smokies, and I advise you to do the same.'

I was also getting tired of people saying: 'I do think that you are brave.' 'I do hope that you will not be hijacked, kidnapped or blown-up.' This was only too real, as there had been an attempt to blow up the Minister of Employment only the week before, and the British Ambassador to Uruguay was still missing after being kidnapped.

January 10th 1971 was our twenty-ninth wedding anniversary. The years had flown, and yet the lives we had led twenty-nine years before seemed to be those of quite different people. It was, to me, a very happy day, if a hard-working one. All our three children were with us, which was quite a rare event: our son-in-law, two grandchildren and a house-guest. I cooked a big lunch, played with the children, produced a large tea. The sun shone all day, and everyone was in a happy mood. I was weary by the end, but full of gratitude for such a perfect day. The older boys had built a bonfire. Rowley wrote his Pilgrim speech, while the grandchildren and I fed the pigs and played hide-and-seek in the afternoon. After the grand-children and their parents had gone I cooked a three-course dinner.

John Freeman, on a visit to London, kindly spared time to dine in order to brief us about the domestic side of the embassy, and other relevant matters. I was glad of the oppor-tunity and somewhat fascinated to meet him after viewing his weekly 'Face to Face' programme on television, which had been masterly. True, that in some cases they were insensitive, such as when he reduced Gilbert Harding to tears in pursuing rather too far Harding's devotion to his dead mother. How-ever, to my surprise, he proved to be cosy and most helpful.

John Freeman told us that our domestic staff in the embassy consisted of eleven resident staff and an army of daily cleaners. We also made the sorry discovery that it fell on us to find, engage and supervise the staff. Evidently the Paris Embassy has always had the distinction of a Comptroller to undertake these responsibilities, because it is historically the most senior of our embassies — in spite of the fact that the Washington Embassy is not only the largest but the busiest, and also the most important.

There were some vacancies on the domestic staff. One of the Freeman housemaids had suddenly gone berserk. She had been discovered stark naked running down Massachusetts Avenue, and was subsequently found to have been on heroin for a month. There was also a vacancy in the kitchen and another in the pantry.

It was difficult to know where to start finding help. To

advertise might mean undesirable applicants, possibly spies. Fortunately, a nice young man presented himself for the pantry job. He was a friend of one of the other footmen. Our gardener's son, aged nineteen, wanted to come as a trainee cook and a new housemaid was found by a London agency.

The chef wished to stay on, and we were at least glad of that: that is to say until the very sophisticated Mrs John Sherman Cooper called me up. Lorraine had been an old friend for many years. Her husband was still a distinguished and well-known Senator. She was also considered to be one of Washington's most elegant hostesses. 'You must find a new cook,' she told me and, not mincing matters, continued: 'The food at your embassy is foul, possibly nutritious, but on second thoughts, not even that.' Rowley and I pondered with some shock over this unwelcome news, and hoped that it might be no more that a case of the Freemans not bothering and, maybe, we might be able to improve it. Possibly if there were a spark we could blow on it and then, who knows, perhaps a good fire might result.

At any rate, the Freemans' social secretary said that she would like to stay on and we were very glad to hear that. But she very much wanted a job with a publisher in London, and left almost immediately.

We finally heard that our departure was to take place on February 3rd by VC10 from Brize Norton by courtesy of the RAF. This was only because BOAC could not find their way to fly us direct to Washington on any day that week, although Pan Am said that they would be delighted to, as it would be good publicity for them. (Maybe, but hardly for us, as it would be certain to give rise to remarks of being unpatriotic!)

We took off on one of those really beautiful, mild and sunny winter days from the depths of the Cotswold countryside. Our two sons saw us off, and I do not think I was ever so sorry to be leaving anywhere before, and felt very depressed as we soared upwards into the blue.

After almost eight hours flying time, and a mistaken attempt to land without a runway, we arrived at Andrews Air Force Base through low cloud and amidst freezing rain.

The Minister and his wife, Sir Guy and Lady Millard, accompanied us in two Rolls-Royces to the airport lounge where, ranged in a long line, quite unexpectedly, stood most of the Commonwealth ambassadors. After being greeted by them, we encountered another long line, this time of senior British embassy officials.

When all the greetings were over, we were shown into another room, and were startled to find ourselves at a press conference. Rowley answered their questions adroitly, but they were made especially difficult, due to the fact that Rolls-Royce had just gone bankrupt. There was also some interest in the reason why we had landed at the prestigious Andrews Air Force Base. The press had assumed it to be a precaution against hijacking, since no other ambassador had landed there to begin his term in Washington. 'What a problem there would have been had he found himself in Cuba,' Colonel Toye (Acting Military Attaché) remarked as our aircraft came in to land. When asked about using military aircraft, Rowley replied: 'Although it was a first time, one of my predecessors, the 1st Earl of Halifax, had, in fact, arrived in a battleship.'

Our arrival at the Embassy Residence was worthy of many an old film portraying the arrival of a new heir and his bride to their recently-inherited stately home. On the steps, up to the front door, were ranged the entire domestic staff, led by the butler, who presented the chef, footmen, maids &c strictly in accordance with their seniority.

The hall, although a long way from the kitchen, smelled unpleasantly of poor food. A quick peep around the reception rooms showed us how unsuitably the furniture had been arranged. About two-dozen vases and baskets of flowers had arrived from kind friends, from quite small posies to vast arrangements, but we were never able to find out who had sent what, because all the cards had been removed, and then placed in rows upon a tray. Well-meant, perhaps, but it did not proclaim a good start.

Exhausted, we sat down to a light meal, which only too unhappily confirmed exactly the warning that Lorraine Cooper had given us, for it was quite inedible.

The next day I set about re-arranging all the furniture in the reception rooms. If I have a flair for that kind of thing it is entirely due to my mother who could have easily followed a successful career as an interior decorator. The butler and footman were delighted with the change, for I found that they took a lively interest in and cared about how the embassy looked. The old negro floor cleaner, who had polished the marble floors for years, looked at me with a grin and said approvingly: 'This is a big improvement. Last time it was just a juke-box.'

A tour of the extensive domestic offices came next, and again much disapproval was registered by the domestic staff, this time over John Freeman's decision to move the Queen's portrait from the front hall to the servants' dining room.

The portrait of The Queen as a pretty young sovereign had been painted by an American artist. It was at once photographic and sugary, but it was also a good likeness, with a sweet and compassionate expression. The butler informed me, with a triumphant air, that no sooner had the Freemans departed, than he had given orders for the picture to be immediately restored to the front hall. In the hall, instead of The Queen's picture, the Freemans had placed a sculpture by Barbara Hepworth, an abstract phallic symbol, people thought. The butler did not know where to put it and, moreover, did not consider this example of modern art suitable to the dignity of the embassy. He was not altogether satisfied, either, when we found an alcove in the garden where, although conspicuous, the Lutyens brickwork walls and neo-Georgian grandeur made it look out-of-place. We discovered later, and before security became so strict, that cars would drive through the gates of the embassy and round by the front door, where they would halt for a moment while the occupants could see and admire the Queen's portrait, lit up and most effective in the distance.

The British Embassy Residence is far the largest and most imposing in Washington and is, we discovered, held in great esteem, even affection, by the Americans themselves. They seemed to possess a proprietary attitude and interest towards it. One felt it was more theirs than ours. Joe Alsop, the writer, told me that once Lutyens had designed the grand portico and staircase he lost interest in the rest, which may explain the extreme inconvenience of the building. It was also rumoured that the grand portico was originally designed to face Massachusetts Avenue and not, as it does, overlook the garden. Certainly Lutyens never visited the site for at that time he was occupied in constructing New Delhi. It was possible that the local builders misread the plans, Joe suggested.

In London we generally view the Diplomatic Corps, and certainly their embassies, with respect, and would never, unless the ambassador or his wife are close friends, dream of imposing on the hospitality of their Residences (which are, in any case, a fractional part of their own countries and, therefore, extra-territorial). Before we left England an elderly Washingtonian had called me up on the telephone. Lily Guest was known to be a formidable lady; her manner was direct and quite abrupt and she was, it is true, known to be a familiar at the British Embassy, having been friendly with many a former ambassadress. However, this did not really give her the right to say on the telephone that 'I am taking the Embassy over,' and to give me a date in the following February on which she intended to do so. 'But,' I attempted to explain, 'that is the date on which our luggage is due to arrive so it is really not at all convenient.' Whatever I said, however, did not seem to make the slightest difference. Mrs Guest was adamant. It was, she told me, to be a charity in aid of the Incurables, and that it had already been arranged. I told her that, all the same, I would have to ask Rowley, but her only reply was: 'It is too late as it has already been fixed.' Ten years earlier we had entertained her to dinner at our house on S Street and I had not, until that moment, heard from her since.

Rowley was most put out when he heard, and told me that it was not at all the correct procedure in the Diplomatic Service, besides being extremely inconvenient. He said that no ambassador ever makes commitments for his successor, who always arrives with a new and clean sheet; and for that matter, there could be Ministers and other important people staying, or meetings and lunches to be arranged on that same day, for all one knew. He decided to send Mrs Guest a polite, though firm, telegram putting it off, or so he thought.

Before we left the shores of England we had been told that a small piece had been printed about 'the thoughtless and uncharitable Cromers' trying to prevent the charity for the Incurables taking place. This was our first hint of difficulties to come with the press in Washington.

On February 8th Rowley was conducted by the Chief of Protocol to the White House to present his credentials to the President. He was driven in a car from the Mayflower Cab Company, hired by the White House, from which flew the Union Jack and the Stars and Stripes on each front wing. Sandwiched between a motor-cycle escort they tore down Massachusetts Avenue leaving me behind, for it is not the custom, as it is in London, for wives to accompany their husbands.

At the White House a guard of honour lined the drive and Herald Trumpeters played Rule Britannia as Rowley alighted from his car. President Nixon was very friendly and, as Rowley took his leave, joked, 'I hope that you will lecture Arthur Burns (the then Chairman of the Federal Reserve) and John Connally (the Secretary of the Treasury) on financial affairs.'

The presentation of Rowley's credentials had been hurried forward so that we could attend the Diplomatic Reception at the White House that same evening. The French ambassador was somewhat peeved when he learned of this, for he had waited some five weeks to present his credentials whereas

Rowley had waited but four days.

The Diplomatic Reception was the first that had been held for two years and it was the last for President Nixon. The traffic congestion near the White House was such that our arrival was somewhat late, and after the President had begun his address to the Diplomatic Corps in the ballroom. Unlike in London, only the ambassadors and their wives are invited, and no other members of their embassies. All over the ballroom, small white cards pinned to the floor resembled a huge flower bed filled with white daisies. Each represented a different country, and on each stood an ambassador.

After the President had ended his speech, he and Mrs Nixon withdrew. Then the ambassadors were lined up in order of precedence, which meant according to the length of stay. As we were the most junior, having been the very last to present credentials, we discovered our place at the end of the queue — or almost at the end of the queue, for behind us, to our confusion, was an elderly couple dressed in national costume. They told us that they represented Lithuania which, of course, did not officially exist. There were others as well who, sadly, represented the thought and not the fact of countries long since absorbed by mightier neighbours. We wondered if this was due to the various ethnic minorities living in the United States.

We all advanced slowly from the ballroom through the red and green drawing rooms to where the President and Mrs Nixon stood to receive their guests, both being lit up by spotlights. Directly opposite them and behind a cordon stood a packed crowd of newspaper reporters busy with their notebooks and pencils. After shaking hands we continued through to the State dining-room, which was hot and very crowded. The general talk was about the two new portraits of President and Mrs Kennedy which were considered to be controversial, particularly as John F Kennedy was portrayed with his head bowed down and looked, so people said, as if he had just been shot.

Three days later Rowley was involved in his first official public duty when he had to sign a treaty with the President and the Russian Ambassador on behalf of Britain to stop dumping radioactive material at the bottom of the oceans; while I went to a benefit lunch for the Heart Association where, to my embarrassment, the newspaper photographers immediately pounced and insisted on taking a picture of Mrs Nixon and me. And then, further adding to my discomfiture, told Mrs Nixon to move away as they wanted one of me alone. Mrs Nixon, however, showed no displeasure. Instead she gave me a sweet smile and hopped out of the way. But it seemed to me that the photographers showed a want of respect to their First Lady.

Our Information Counsellor, who had only been in post for two days, informed Rowley that, apart from the Ambassador's own press conference, there was quite a large number of women who were anxious to interview me, and that therefore I must hold a press conference myself. This was totally unexpected and almost too dreadful to contemplate, so I did my level best to avoid such an unwelcome trial, but with little success, and pressure was brought to bear. 'There is no way of refusing the journalists' requests,' I was firmly told. Unwisely I thought of another method of facing the press. Could I not invite half of them to tea one day, and the other half the next? I was prompted by a deep fear of public speaking, of getting up in front of a sea of faces and collapsing with stage fright. The Information Counsellor thought this was a good idea and did not realise the pitfalls any more than I. Unhappily, those young and pretty faces were the spearhead of a relatively new phase in journalism: that of 'search and destroy.' He also arranged for the tea parties to take place two days apart.

The first tea party went extremely well. There was, after all, not much to say. After family, clothes, hobbies and various female topics, all that could be said had been said. The next day, to my surprise, appeared many columns of quite flattering reporting on all the women's pages of all the chief news-papers of the United States. One headline amused us. It said: 'From Cattle Breeder to Queen's Aide.'

Two days later came the second tea party. Had one had a little more time to think, or been long enough in Washington to have studied the newspapers, it would have been obvious that a quicksand lay ahead. Publicity breeds publicity until the subject becomes stale, and that had not happened yet. The new group arrived, bringing with them a flavour of depriva-tion, of having been done out of fresh news for the women's pages, for the day between the tea parties had seen the publication of all there really was to be said. So a new slant was needed, and an awkwardness hung in the air. Questions on being a Lady in Waiting, already answered before with a few unimportant facts, now took on a new sharpness and intrusiveness, and was centred on the Queen. 'What is her bedroom like?' 'Have you seen her wardrobe?' I told them as nicely as I could that I was unable to talk about such things. They all looked somewhat aggrieved and I felt sorry for them, especially as one rather nice older lady held up a large clipping from the *New York Times* and, rather mournful, remarked that it seemed to cover everything.

On my writing desk was a photograph of our elder son, Evelyn, dressed in combat uniform and taken when he was a war correspondent in Vietnam for the *Bangkok World*. Unfor-tunately the subject then turned in that direction. 'What do you think of the Vietnam war?' I answered them, in all truth, that I knew nothing about it. Next they asked me if I had been to South-East Asia to see my son, to which I answered, 'Yes,' and somewhere within a rather light-hearted conversation a pretty young blonde with a soft voice asked me what my chief impressions had been, to which I unguardedly replied that I had been struck by the strong accent put on face by the Chinese and the Far Eastern peoples: that to them it really seemed more important than life. This remark, unexpectedly, proved to be dynamite. To the present time, it must seem somewhat odd that so well-known a fact could have caused a sensation at all. But it most certainly did. And it took me a long time to live it down, if I ever did during the rest of my time in America. The pretty young blonde next asked if I thought the United States should hasten out of Vietnam, and I replied that I really did not know, and then added with a smile that I hoped that the USA would not lose face.

The next day the headline of a small piece of a news page in the *Washington Post* read: 'It is a long and terrible war, but saving face means so much more to the Asians than life. Life means nothing, but nothing, to them.' This indeed was dynamite and gave a few words out of an hour-long talk a wholly-new and dangerous meaning. To me it was as unexpected and as painful as being stung by a hornet. A political writer, Mary McGrory, picked up this item and made much of it. 'Is this the view from Queen Elizabeth's bedchamber where she served? Is it the view of Her Majesty's Government? Is it the view of Lord Cromer?' She went on: 'East of Suez, in Commonwealth nations, this may cause hackles to rise. Labour back-benchers will certainly be on their feet asking for explanations.' There was much more besides.

The Embassy Information Officer rushed out an explanation; 'Lady Cromer intended to convey, on withdrawal from Vietnam, that she supported President Nixon's policy, and that it seemed to her a mistake to scuttle immediately from Vietnam without regard to the consequences.' It was, moreover, open to the North Vietnamese to make peace wherever and whenever they wanted to. Instead, for reasons of face, they appeared to be determined to humiliate America in war, rather than make peace. Lines in the Chancery buzzed. Mary McGrory's column was syndicated throughout the United States, with the result that I received angry and abusive letters from all over the country for many weeks afterwards. Admittedly, among them were some letters supporting what were considered to be my views, but in reality I had none at all.

All this did nothing to mitigate the already-alarming initiation into the rigours of ambassadorial life. To say the least, I felt that I had let Rowley down, and everyone else, for that matter, and began to shed weight at an alarming rate. The culmination of this distressing time came when a Labour Member of Parliament raised the issue in the House of Commons by asking the Foreign Secretary, Sir Alec Douglas-Home, if he would recall Lord Cromer. It seemed that I had sunk to the lowest ebb, and certainly wished that we had never agreed to embark on what seemed an ill-starred venture. Then, shortly after, a small ray of sunshine pierced the gloom. My telephone rang. It was Mrs Nixon's social secretary. She said that Mrs Nixon particularly wanted me to know that she and the President drank my health and said 'Well done, Lady Cromer.' It was the beginning of a close and trusting relationship with the President and his administration and ourselves.

It was also the start of occurrences that later became commonplace. A small bomb had exploded in the Capitol, followed by a telephone call to the Chancery to say that another had been placed in the Embassy Residence and it was timed to go off that night as a gesture against the British Embassy's present stand on the Vietnam war. Clearly our present position was not one for anyone of a nervous disposition. It also brought home the state of hysteria in America at that time.

Lorraine Sherman Cooper was a highly respected Washington personality, and an excellent hostess, at whose table the most influential people in the land would often be found. Also, her long experience of the ways of the capital was profound. Lorraine looked like some beautiful, exotic bird with her long neck, narrow nose and slanting eyes, framed by jet-black hair. She was slim and chic, and was complemented by her extremely elegant home to which I was bidden for lunch.

Lorraine, perturbed by the bad press that I had received, and being an old friend of my father, telephoned him in England. He, possibly not fully understanding the uproar, told her that, after all, I had not wanted to come in the first place. This did not make things any better, and amazed and rather shocked her. She had invited no-one else but me and, I am sure, the invitation was most kindly meant, but the prospect was none the less daunting for all that. A faint mention of the then-famous Cooper-Church Amendment had just reached my ears. This had taken place in Congress before our arrival. It was, I believe, to do with prohibiting US military activities in Cambodia and represented the first limitation ever voted on the President's powers as Commander in Chief during a war situation. John Cooper was a Republican liberal and Frank Church a Democrat.

Lorraine had always been deeply interested in politics, and I guessed she thought that I held some strong views from what she had read in the newspapers. One of the most poised of women, she was also thoughtful of others. Our lunch, however, was awkward. She warned me, fairly sternly, that if I made another public gaffe it would be the end. By that, I took it to mean that pressure would be brought to have Rowley recalled. During her homily, and feeling very small, I wondered how on earth I would manage to get through three years without being misquoted or, for that matter, quoted. To be gagged for so long a time seemed like a term of imprisonment. It was a truly worrying situation. From then on, after every party or public appearance, I was never certain what I might read in the newspapers the following day.

During these first weeks we were extremely busy on the social front. Three old and cherished friends from our previous tour of duty, Mrs Edward Macauley, Mrs Marquis Childs and Mrs Gerard Smith jointly held a very special dinner-dance in our honour at the exclusive F Street Club. They had gathered together as many amusing and influential people as it was possible to muster, and it was a glittering and very successful party and gave us great cheer and encouragement at a very difficult time. Without the friendships we had made during our previous stay in Washington life would have been very much worse.

There were other parties in our honour, given almost every night, and on each occasion we continually met new people. Being shy and lacking confidence, it became a real trial to be the subject of forthright curiosity and, in some cases, even hostility. Sometimes, quite unexpectedly, total strangers would suddenly and gushingly rush up and congratulate me for speaking out as they thought I had. Either way, it was a false position to find oneself in, and from then on I began to entertain a fellow feeling for President Nixon. He seemed to be doing what he thought was right in the face of extreme personal vindictiveness on the part of the press in Washington and, after all, he must have known the global facts better than anyone, however unpleasant. It all went to show how highly volatile the mood was in America at the time. The slightest spark producing wild reactions.

Courtesy Calls were new to me for they had not been part of our duties during our previous post in Washington. They were, evidently, a more senior diplomatic convention and involved visits from and to other Ambassadresses. It was the custom for the new arrivals to call first on the senior Ambassadress who would, after an interval, return the call. In some cases this curious practice would become doubly embarrassing and difficult if neither of us could find a common language and had, therefore, to mime as best one could, punctuated by uncomfortable silences.

The visits usually took place in the morning around eleven o'clock, and when they called on me there was a prescribed ritual. First an appointment would be made via the social secretaries. On arrival the visiting ambassadress would be met at the front door by the butler, who would show her to the top of the grand staircase where she would be handed over to the social secretary who would, in turn, escort her to the drawing-room where she would be greeted by me at the door. I would then ask her what she preferred in the way of refreshments while the first footman hovered before carrying the order to the pantry.

Rowley decided, since he believed firmly in Europe, that we should start with the Common Market embassies, and then move on to the Old Commonwealth, followed by India and Pakistan, Africa and some others, including Russia and Ireland. The Diplomatic Corps had grown from about a dozen embassies to one hundred and fourteen in fifty years and, moreover, was to add another twenty during the three years of our tour of duty. Therefore it was not necessary or practicable to call upon them all.

The Doyen was customarily the first to be called upon. At that time he was the Ambassador of Nicaragua. The Sevilla-Sacasas had been in Washington for many years and were liked and respected. It was an important position for a small country. His wife, to my great relief, proved to be friendly and motherly, and was clearly very used to Courtesy Calls. At that time most of the ambassadresses were agog to meet the newcomer who had exploded onto the scene with a diplomatic gaffe, their interest possibly the keener since she was not a professional diplomat's wife. Some of them told me afterwards that they had expected to meet a pushing, abrasive woman holding strong views, and were most surprised to find, instead, a timid and rather scared soul.

The French Embassy, smelling of expensive perfume, exuded a certain chic and a casual polite efficiency. The Ambassadress, petite and bird-like, was not enjoying good health, nor Washington either, as became increasingly evident during my visit. She told me, with a weary air, that the wife of an Ambassador to Washington should be under twenty-five years of age and possess good health and stamina. 'Older than that, and one is past it,' she said.

The Italian Embassy evoked Italy from the moment of entry. Large and gloomy, with heavy Italian antique furniture, a whiff of pasta cooking, and two grand pianos in the drawing-room, and I could have been back in my school in Florence. The Italian Ambassadress, a tall grey lady, spoke without drawing breath, and seemed a little distraite. Julia

Ortona and her husband, however, were much loved and an undoubted success. They both enthused, smiled and charmed, were extremely intelligent and gifted as well.

The Belgian Embassy, pretty, with original panelling, Aubusson carpets and eighteenth-century furniture, proved rather surprisingly to be the most elegant. I was regaled with pastries and coffee, served with silent care by a Philipino. The Ambassadress was forthcoming. She kept, she said, an indoor staff of eight, composed of six different nationalities. The main problem of having so mixed a staff was food. The Philipinos and Haitians liked rice, the Portuguese and Spaniards preferred it cooked in a different manner, while the German and Danish taste was towards potatoes and meat. It was some comfort to me to know that, at least, I was spared problems of that order.

These visits began to seem like a mini-tour of the world. The Canadian Embassy, small and comfortable, had no distinguishing features, but the Ambassadress, a French-Canadian, Madame Cadieux, was a distinctive personality and held decided opinions. Undoubtedly intelligent, she informed me that she thought that the Western world was veering away from socialism, while it seemed to me, on the contrary, that at that time, America appeared to be rushing towards it.

The German Embassy was modern and bright. The Ambassadress short, chunky and mini-skirted. Wearing white boots, she sported an urchin haircut, and bounced into the room where I waited for her. I never discovered if there was any diplomatic significance in being shown into an empty room. This particular German lady offered me endless cups of tea accompanied by stodgy cakes, while I found myself face to face with a photograph of General Dayan of Israel, which surprised me. Tel Aviv had, she imparted, been their last posting, and she made a special point of saying how much she admired the Israelis. Tall, disciplined and military, they had really been quite different to what she had expected. The conversation did not take at all the course which I would have anticipated, for she went on to talk of the cruelty of nations.

The Iranian Ambassador told Rowley that his country spent millions of dollars a year sending students to American universities, from which they returned as Communists, and those that they sent to Russia, which cost much less, returned as anti-Communists.

The Russian Embassy Rowley and I visited together. A heavy and gloomy building containing ponderous furniture with a dismal decor, but with a smiling, urbane Ambassador of obvious intelligence whose eyes gave notice of a sense of humour. His wife, a good-looking, comfortable lady, was also most agreeable. Anatoliy Dobrynin emanated an air of importance far greater than one would have expected, and we felt certain that here was no minion of the Kremlin, but someone held in high esteem. He and his wife were also very friendly towards us.

17

PRIVACY NO LONGER AN OPTION

On March 7th we attended a 'Worship Service' by invitation of President and Mrs Nixon at the White House, which proved to be an unexpectedly pleasant occasion. The ballroom was full of sun and gentle organ music, with prayers led by both Catholic and Episcopalian clergy; two hymns, sung beautifully by a Baptist, and the sermon delivered by the Chief Rabbi of Washington. We were given seats in the front row close by the President who, in his turn, gave a short and most polished address.

The Rabbi talked about sin. It was interesting, and to us most revealing. He declared that Rousseau took 'the sting out of sin' in the mistaken belief that all men were good; that this idea had, once again, caught credence. Therefore the time had come for all men to look into their hearts and divide within them the good from the bad. His sermon provoked a good deal of thought. How wise and how tactful the Rabbi was, and yet the gist of it was no different from what we had heard in our childhood. So unlike those sermons generally given at that time and subsequently; which seemed to have everything to do with social welfare and little to do with the power of good and evil.

After the service was over the President, Mrs Nixon, the Rabbi and the Baptist singer received the guests. The President took my hand and held it first in his right and then in his left, and with a warm smile said that he hoped to see us at a more intimate gathering. I mentioned to the Rabbi that his sermon was one of the best that I had ever listened to. Overhearing, the President spun round and simply remarked: 'She comes from England.'

Refreshments were served in the dining-room where we found ourselves by a friendly group of high officials in the administration whom we were glad to have the opportunity of meeting; and just as I was enjoying our chatting a swarm of women unexpectedly fell upon me. They were the ladies of the press, and there appeared to be no means of escape. They remarked on my clothes and then asked how I felt over the bad press that I had been given. Feeling somewhat fed-up I asked them whether they had noticed that all those that had been so critical had, in fact, been Irish. This produced a laugh and I could uneasily hear others a bit further away muttering, 'What did she say?'

Oh dear! Had I put my foot in it again? The next day there was, inevitably, some mention of my remark on the women's page of the *Washington Post* which roused an unexpected reply in the shape of a St Patrick's Day card from an anonymous Irish person who wished me well and then went on to explain that a number of Irish names were taken by Polish and Ukrainian immigrants. That evening at seven thirty the third footman, Peter, knocked on my bedroom door to ask if he could fasten my windows, for a telephone call had been received from the IRA with a kidnap warning.

Dr Henry Kissinger was considered to be the 'eminence grise' of the administration, an appellation he seemed to enjoy. A German-Jewish immigrant of enormous intelligence, and a professor with a taste for being seen with pretty girls, he had come straight from the cloisters of a university onto the world stage. He was, undoubtedly, the most sought-after personage in Washington, both by the diplomatic corps, the press, and possibly the world. For two evenings in succession I was fortunate enough to be placed at his side at dinner. This proved to be a pleasure for he possessed a most engaging sense of humour and, disarmingly, laughed mostly at himself. He told me that however difficult his life might be at that time, just think how much, for ever afterwards, he would enjoy boring other people by talking about it!

Henry recounted an amusing incident when President Mobutu of Zaire had come over on an official visit, as was then customary, to ask for loans and gifts. His line was to impress on the administration in Washington the need to keep Communism away from his borders. In particular he needed some naval vessels for this purpose, as well as funds. He was duly granted his request. After leaving Washington Mobutu went on to Los Angeles to visit Disneyland, which so enchanted him that he instantly ordered a Boeing 707 to bring over his family from Africa in order that they should also share in the fun of Disney's masterpiece. Later, when President Mobutu went on to New York, he was entertained royally by the Mayor who arranged for some of the City's fire boats to give a display in his honour. Mobutu was so impressed by this spectacle that he decided to cancel his order for the naval vessels and order some fire boats instead!

Rowley and I had by now been in Washington five weeks and we had been much impressed by the judgement, common sense and capability of those in the administration that we had so far met. It was true that some of them were attracted to, and by, the press and therefore were constantly in the newspapers, such as Henry Kissinger and Elliot Richardson, but there were others too who, although given little publicity and even less credit, also wielded much influence, and were important and capable men, and who later returned to high office in future administrations.

At the end of the first month there was not quite enough money to pay the household bills, and an urgent request for an increase in the Frai was sent to London. British ambassadors, although abroad, have to pay full UK tax on their salaries, which at that time, in spite of a Conservative government, was exceedingly harsh.

The Frai is the diplomatic term for the expenses in the

actual running of the Residence and, in our first month, we had attended far more meals out than in, and moreover not yet plunged into the heavy entertaining that would be necessary. The question too of the quality of the food had to be solved, and although I had made a beginning it was not very successful. The chopped garlic which over-flavoured every dish had been eliminated. (This ingredient, in any case, has to be used with much discretion in the heavy social life of diplomats). Words were spoken about the over- or under-doses of salt and pepper, and gravy made up from tins of powder. So giving one little or no surprise and a great deal of relief, the chef sought me out to give in his notice. But not before I had asked him from curiosity where he had worked before taking up his employment at the Embassy. His answer: 'With an important dog-food company' caused me great difficulty in suppressing a laugh, especially as it was said with an air of important condescension.

The staff were jubilant at the thought of a change particularly when they heard that the new chef was to be a Frenchman who had worked at the Connaught Hotel in London (and of whom we had come to hear from an english friend). Once installed, the difference was astonishing. No longer did bad cooking smells invade the public rooms. Instead, an occasional whiff of something delectable could be inhaled in the back passages. The bills also shrank, and yet the food was abundant and delicious. At first, the new chef, from ignorance or a desire to excel, presented me with a menu of ten courses. The first footman, on seeing this gargantuan list, remarked that 'the chef must think that he is at the court of King Louis XIV!' With tact, I reduced the courses to five. Beyond that, for the time being, it seemed discouraging to go.

Sensibly, the usual American lunch consists of three courses and, sometimes, very much less, as on one occasion when we lunched at the home of a quite senior State Department official where we were offered an organic meal consisting solely of a salad composed of raw spinach and chopped tomatoes, followed by cheese and biscuits, then apples and coffee.

In addition to the every-day entertaining, such as dinners and lunches, there were various bodies to which I was expected to belong. Firstly, within the Embassy itself, the wives of the huge Chancery staff met regularly for coffee mornings. These I was familiar with from our previous tour. There were also the American International Groups to which, this time, I was elevated to that of Number One. If the senior group was a privilege to belong to, it never had the relaxed enthusiasm of Group Two, of which I had been a member the first time, and which treated me with kindness and sympathy, and even went so far as to give a special luncheon in my honour. There was also the Commonwealth Wives Association which met monthly for tea, talk and entertainment, and often, when attending these, I wondered what we really had in common other than language. Besides these social gatherings there were other groups from all over the United States who would request, by means of the Consuls, an invitation to the Embassy during their visit to the capital city. These would range from catfish farmers from Georgia to other and equally unusual groups from other States.

The Embassy boasted a tennis court which had, through the years, been the scene of many a diplomatic coup by means of an imparted confidence. It was also used by the extensive Embassy personnel who always asked in advance, although many Washingtonians did not. Possibly at some time they had been given permission to use it by an ambassador, and never thought fit to renew it with successive ones. One was never quite sure who would be using the court. One day, not long after the *Washington Post* had been so hostile, we discovered to our amazement its publisher, Kay Graham, in full play on the court. Difficult though it was, swallowing my pride, I walked over to the court and, after waiting for the set to finish, asked her and her partner to join us for tea which, I am certain, was the last thing they wished to do, but could not very well refuse.

Advice still flowed in from friends and acquaintances on how I should 'handle myself.' It was often conflicting. One person would tell me to be modern and informal. Another would say that I should be dignified and well-dressed at all times. Then again, that I must keep abreast of the times and wear frayed jeans, which were then much in vogue. The embassy wives themselves liked to give helpful hints (and their husbands also) on whom they thought we should entertain. Bewildering pressure came from all sides, and somehow one had to try to rise above it all.

Interest had to be shown too in the activities of the embassy wives, which at that time was 'Frontier Nursing.' This involvement had great appeal, and since it had been started by an english woman their interest was, apparently, welcome and needed. But I often wondered where exactly the 'frontier' was meant to be. Kentucky and West Virginia was rather vaguely mentioned. There was also, of course, the American Red Cross, and we all gave time for that.

One morning I received a letter from an organisation called 'The Daughters of the British Empire,' and with the same post came another from 'The Daughters of the American Revolution.' Both wanted my support. The first was an invitation to be their president, which position seemed to fall to the wife of successive British ambassadors automatically. At lunch that day I mentioned these two letters to Sir Isaiah Berlin. He was astonished that there should even be a society called 'Daughters of the British Empire,' and jokingly told me on no account to join, as he felt sure that it must be a subversive movement. In fact it was an association which successfully ran old people's homes for people of British descent in different parts of the United States. I did attempt to persuade them to change their name to a more modern 'British Heritage' but to no avail.

The Daughters of the American Revolution wrote to say that they were holding a big luncheon and hoped the British, Spanish and French Ambassadresses would attend, 'that is to

211

say, those countries who took part one way or another in our struggle.' I decided to accept, even if that meant that I would be the sole representative of the losing side. In the event the luncheon proved to be extremely popular.

A huge gathering filled the enormous ballroom at the Shoreham Hotel, and when all were assembled the guests were told to rise and dedicate themselves afresh to the National Flag. As the French and Spanish ambassadresses were present I quickly glanced at them for a cue, and found that they had indeed risen to their feet, but rather than looking at the Flag, they both lowered their eyes to the floor, so I did likewise. There then followed a small military parade led by fife and drum band dressed in eighteenth century costume and playing, to my surprise, Rowley's old regimental tune 'The British Grenadiers.'

The three ambassadresses were seated at the top table, raised above the others, with senior members of The Daughters of the Revolution. The first course was already laid before us, and just as I began to eat, a formidable lady came up to insist that I accompany her to the VIP lounge where, somewhat to my surprise, was a photographer from *The Star* newspaper who simply wished for a photograph. It seemed that a photo call took precedence over all, for when I managed to return to the luncheon table, introductions had commenced. These introductions took the form of the chairman calling the name of every member of the top table who would, in turn, stand and bow, to varying degrees of applause. It was always rather an embarrassing procedure. On this occasion I found, on my return, some puzzled expressions, only to discover, to my dismay, that the Lady President, not having noticed my absence, had gone on to introduce an invisible person on an empty chair. Maybe she thought that I was making a small protest. If she did, no-one saw fit to say anything. As it was, the photograph was never published, The Daughters of the Revolution being regarded, so I was informed, as an antediluvian affair and of little current interest.

Most members were clearly middle-aged and therefore anti-pathetic to the radical youth whose readership journalists seemed to be most keen to favour.

After our arrival in Washington it became evident that Mrs Lily Guest and the secretary of the Incurables had decided to ignore Rowley's cable, and had carried on printing their publicity leaflets and making their arrangements just as if we had given our approval. There was really nothing we could do but fume and submit to their intransigence. In the event the tiresomeness was manifold and it caused great disruption in the running of the Embassy. Firstly, druggets had to be laid to protect the marble floors from being injured by thousands of shoes. Then ropes put up to keep the crowds within bounds. The domestic staff would get upset while all our bibelots, valuable objects, china and other movable items had to be listed and carefully packed away due to voracious souvenir hunters. The fact that the whole exercise gave a wonderful opportunity for a robber or anarchist to case the joint was another hazard. Anyone with the price of a ticket could enter. Sixteen of the embassy wives, and sixteen wives of Senators and Congressmen stood on a shift system for hours at various strategic points. There were also six armed guards keeping an eye open for any untoward moves or suspicious behaviour.

The footmen in their livery of tailcoats, brass buttons and lapels embroidered with crowns, came in for the most atten-tion and admiration from the women. But, above all, it was the grandeur that pleased them; the huge portraits of kings and queens on the staircase, and most of all that of George IV. One of the footmen played the Land of Hope and Glory on the hi-fi in the ballroom which gave an appropriate atmos-phere. There were moments of humour to lighten the after-noon. One couple were heard discussing the significance of ER in gold on the backs of the dining-room chairs, 'They stand, you know, for Esme and Rowley.' Some had come in buses from hundreds of miles away and none asked for their money back. Four thousand five hundred people poured through and a large sum was raised for the worthy charity. But we were all very glad when it was over and hoped for a long interval before the next invasion.

With all the scares and alarms of bombs and kidnaps, I began to wonder just how secure the Embassy was. The mock-Georgian sash windows were secured with only the usual small fastener. The fence between Massachusetts Avenue and the Embassy garden was fairly low. It seemed to me a very easy matter to gain illicit entry. Therefore I challenged the security people that, given sneakers, a pair of trousers and a knife, I could gain entry from the Avenue in a matter of seconds. This had the desired effect and from then on floodlights played on the Embassy walls all night.

Later that month my telephone rang. 'A Mrs Kennedy would like to speak to you.' For a moment I wondered who it could be. Then to my astonishment an elderly, metallic nasal voice spoke. It asked me if I would be so kind as to answer some questions as 'I am writing a tiny bit of my autobiography.' It became apparent that it was Mrs Rose Kennedy on the line, the venerable mother of JFK. 'Do you know what the feathered headdress is called that is worn at Court?' 'The Prince of Wales's feathers,' I replied, without any certainty, and hurried to explain that both Courts and Court dress had been discontinued since the beginning of World War II. 'Do the men still wear velvet breeches?' she continued to enquire, and went on to tell me that when her husband had been Ambassador at the Court of St James's, he had caused a stir by refusing to wear Court dress. I stopped myself from saying that to my knowledge no American Ambassador, on a point of principle, had ever worn velvet knee breeches. She then asked me 'if you have ever carried the Queen's purse, as a Lady in Waiting?' I began to wonder what she might ask next but, after a pause, and changing her tack, she wanted to know whether I had met any of her children. I told her that I had known Kathleen (I had shared a bedroom

214

with her in New York in the war and found her to be charming). That did not seem to be of any interest. She wanted to know if I had known Jack. I said that I had met him, but did not go on to reveal what a very poor impression he had made!

In 1939 Jack had been invited by my father to stay with us in the country for a dance. It was my first grown-up ball, and he sat by my side at dinner. In those days there was a rule that every young man asked both his hostess and his two dinner partners to dance. This was a kindly-meant rule and a saver for any new or shy young girl. Jack Kennedy did neither, and on reaching the dance floor sped off after some other girl of his choice.

Mrs Kennedy thanked me for my help and I apologised for my ignorance of Court life before the war. 'I forgot,' she said, 'that you are much younger than I am,' and rang off. Strangely she did not ask if I had met Edward Kennedy, who actually lived in Washington and whom we had just encountered the week before.

April in Washington is pink and white. A springtime blossoming that transforms a rather brown drab city of muddy waters and creeks into a magical mixture of pink petals and white buds. Almost overnight avenues of flowering cherries compete with copses of magnolias, the previously bare branches newly-clothed in startling raiment. It is the moment to visit this suddenly very beautiful city. The white marble public buildings glisten among the sea of pink blossom and young green. From my bedroom window in the Embassy a solitary minaret, belonging to the Mosque, stood above a mass of flowering cherries, and that is all that could be seen of the city. Only the blare of traffic from Massachusetts Avenue and the shriek of police cars crashing on one's ears served as a rude reminder that all was not peace and tranquillity.

This is the time of year when America likes to transform a pretty girl into a Queen. She becomes the Cherry Blossom Queen, or a Magnolia, or even an Azalea crowned head.

Sometimes the honour falls to foreign countries and an attractive girl of well-known parentage is asked instead.

The Azalea Festival in Norfolk, Virginia, is a big event, and in 1971 the organizers decided to ask Arabella Churchill (Sir Winston's grand-daughter) to be their Queen, and some months earlier they did so and she accepted. Now, with the Festival almost upon us, Arabella changed her mind; her reason was, so she said, that she had not known at the time of her acceptance that the Azalea Festival was sponsored by NATO and, in particular, the American Navy. The organizers were horrified and most displeased, and naturally looked to the Embassy for relief. Arabella then made things worse by taking the opportunity to air her views by means of the media. She decided to tell the world that she was quite unable to undertake this duty as she was, she said, a pacifist and considered NATO to be the 'final curtain.' This statement shattered the Admiral in command in Virginia, and he could scarcely believe that Winston Churchill, the great war leader who believed, above all, in peace through strength, could have had such a grand-daughter: one holding such opposite views; besides letting everyone down.

Mrs McCain Smith from the White House telephoned to say how upset they were, for the President's daughter and son-in-law (President Eisenhower's grandson) were also taking part in the festivities. Messages were sent to London asking for a substitute, for both the Chancery and the Foreign Office were most concerned. But nothing was forthcoming. We racked our brains before settling on Emma Soames to save the family's honour, but to no avail. It seemed that as time was so short, most girls were committed to some other engagement and would not be able or were not prepared to change their plans. Consternation filled the Embassy. It seemed to be a storm in a teacup, but it was causing quite a stir and giving grave offence at a sensitive time.

The matter became known in Westminster and even came to the notice of the Cabinet. Geoffrey Rippon, known at that time as 'Mr Europe' because it was his duty to try and obtain admission for Britain to join the 'Conmart' (as the Americans called it), had a daughter who, evidently, was willing to come. There was great relief all round, tempered with some doubt, for we could not help wondering about her looks. Her father was known to be no oil painting, and the name Rippon meant nothing in America. Fortunately, however, our misgivings proved to be groundless. Sarah Rippon, a vision of youthful blonde beauty, stunned us all. Moreover she was in her second year at Oxford University and therefore possessed brains as well. Besides being astute she was also thoughtful. The relief in the Embassy was enormous, not least to Rowley. Sarah charmed everyone she met and made, it was generally agreed, the best Azalea Queen that the festival had ever known. She delivered eight or nine short speeches within four days, and modestly confided in me that she had pretended to the young naval cadets that she was studying at a secretarial college, in case they might be put off by her blue-stocking achievements. This considerate young girl managed to completely restore any lack of faith in the British.

The actual event took place in a leafy grove before rows of seats, and Rowley crowned her Queen in a tender fatherly manner to the strains of the 'Land of Hope and Glory,' while the Union Jack fluttered above their heads in the cloudless sky. It was all unexpectedly touching and handkerchieves were removed from pockets to mop away any stray tears. Everyone was delighted and, undoubtedly, the ending of this unfortunate incident was a very happy one.

We had now been in Washington two months. It seemed more like two years for we had packed so much into a little time. We exchanged impressions on the general scene and our positions in it. The discovery that my life was truly public, in the sense that there was no privacy, was disconcerting. A typewritten paper was produced daily by my nice new social secretary and circulated to at least twelve different people every day in order to monitor my every movement. There were other discoveries too. Truck-loads of paper were brought to the Embassy from Consulates and other British offices throughout the United States to be thrown into huge incinerators. This was known as the disposal of confidential garbage.

Ambassadors, it seemed, were a separate species conditioned by their job — eager and ingratiating, never uttering a tactless word, nor sharing a heated argument, unless the subject was bland and probably banal as well. Never, of course, the faintest hint given of any criticism of or about the country they are accredited to. But in the seclusion of their Chanceries at the close of day, they would be able to give ample vent to their feelings, and caustic telegrams and reports full of wit and merciless criticism would pour through to their respective governments — not unlike repressed and outwardly subdued persons committing all to their secret diaries, which in turn possibly acts as an important safety valve. But for the wives, no such outlet for bottled-up opinions was so readily available.

My new social secretary, Torie Legge-Bourke, was only twenty years of age and without any previous experience. With Hannah's sudden departure it was difficult to find a suitable replacement in so short a time, and we could not contemplate much of a delay. Fortunately we came to hear from a goddaughter of Rowley's that a close friend of hers was keen to come. We were pleased, as I already knew that she was good with people and also, evidently, had an excellent scholastic record.

At the end of April we heard that Harold and Mary Wilson would be in Washington on their way to Texas, and would be stopping at the Embassy to refresh themselves. For some weeks past *The Sunday Times* had been serialising Harold Wilson's memoirs, and the Sunday before his arrival had featured the acrimonious controversy between Harold as Prime Minister and Rowley as Governor of the Bank of England concerning the sterling troubles of six years previously. Mary Wilson, whom I have always liked and admired, required breakfast, while Harold went to the White House to take his with the President.

Torie had been told to let me know when either or both of the Wilsons arrived so that I could be at hand to greet them. Good manners, to say the least, required that, but I had not reckoned with a nice girl's protective inclinations. After breakfasting upstairs I discovered to my horror that the Wilsons were holding a press conference on the terrace, and that Torie had seen fit to close the curtains of my sitting-room which gave on to the seated group outside. Furthermore the curtains could not be drawn back for fear of their movement drawing unwarranted attention; so waiting with some trepidation in a darkened room, I wondered which eagle-eyed reporter had noticed this curiosity. My fears proved to be groundless, fortunately, and the wait rather a long one. Finally Torie came to tell me that the press had left, and to my dismay the Wilsons as well. All I could do was send a message via Rowley's secretary apologising for my want of manners, to which Wilson is reputed to have replied: 'Tell her that I think she is one of the most beautiful women in England.'

Ever since our arrival, Rowley had been working on President Nixon to get Congress to agree to guarantee loans for the Tristar Airbus, in order to save Rolls-Royce engines. The result of Harold Wilson's breakfast with the President was to give Wilson full credit in the press for this. Yet again his mastery of the art of front page publicity managed, not for the first time, to get in first, whereas the credit should have gone to a Minister — Aviation or Defence.

The United States being so large a country, it is almost impossible to cover it and keep near to the administration at one and the same time. British Ambassadors appeared therefore to fall into one of two categories: the professional diplomats who consider it their duty to visit as many States as possible during their term in office in order to make Britain and British goods known throughout the length and breadth of the land; and this view had its undoubted uses. The other category, the political appointee, such as Rowley, found it of more value to keep in close contact with the administration. And, in fact, whenever he did venture deeper into the country and visit some of the other large American cities, Rowley would inevitably be pursued by a telephone call from one of the President's Cabinet. 'What in the hell are you doing in the sticks?' would boom Connally (Secretary of the Treasury), or, 'Not in the boondocks again, for heaven's sake,' would be another. So it was that Rowley felt his place to be at the centre of affairs. After all, that was where the action was.

We did, nevertheless, make some visits to other parts of the United States. New York hardly counted, being just a short hop away by aeroplane, and many were the functions and dinners we attended there. New Yorkers tended to look down on their capital city, considering it to be rather provincial, but we infinitely preferred it, having lived in both.

The first city we chose to visit was Chicago, which involved two days of unremitting activity. Our programmes were completely arranged by the British Consul General in Chicago and a member of the Chancery. Being a new experience, we did not like to change any part of the programme, nor did we feel competent to do so.

On arrival we were both immediately and unexpectedly swept off to separate luncheon parties. The Consul General's wife, a lady brimming with self-confidence, without any explanation rushed me off to a banquet composed mainly of women whom, without warning, I was expected to address. Wrapped in a shock of nerves, I tremblingly declined. This was fortunately taken for bashfulness. Sitting next to me was George Ball, an ex-Deputy Secretary of State under Lyndon Johnson who was, comfortingly, an old acquaintance. He seemed to be sympathetic and understood my predicament. Under his encouragement I was emboldened to rise and make a few remarks. Suddenly inspired, I mentioned that as in ancient times all roads led to Rome, so in modern times all railroads led to Chicago. This banality I mistakenly thought to be a compliment, but it was unfortunately out of date. For at that time most Chicagoans had become ashamed of their extensive rail junctions and sidings which, in their view, disfigured their city and which were at the time fast being replaced. The people at the luncheon were warm and friendly, as indeed were all we met at every function. In response to endless similar questions my answer was the same: 'What a beautiful city I consider Chicago to be.' The local newspapers, however, were disappointed. 'Lady Cromer is carefully trying not to be controversial and keeps repeating gushingly, "What a lovely city Chicago is!"'

Each day huge afternoon receptions were held, dinners, visits to old-people's homes, and other worthy institutions. Always people, people, new people, shaking hands with glad smiles. Standing until one's knees refused to bend when, at last, the chance came to sit down. Our faces ached from smiling, arms from being shaken. Always the same question: 'What do you think of Chicago?' Yet I had hardly seen the city. Only the people. Very nice people, full of life and vitality. Moreover, they exuded a decided confidence in themselves which made a refreshing change from Washington.

After a visit to Philadelphia to open the Franklin Institute's Exhibition on Light, by cutting a ribbon with a laser beam (a very new device at the time) we were back in Washington in time for the grand preview of the Kennedy Center for the Performing Arts, which had been breathlessly anticipated for months.

The decision that Washington should have a cultural centre had been taken some fifteen years previously by President Eisenhower's administration. Before that there was no opera house, decent concert hall or theatre. Washington was a cultural desert and people simply went to New York instead. On a previous tour of duty ten years earlier there had been much talk and speculation on the size, shape and location of such a complex. Since then the original concept had, somehow, been transformed into a grand memorial to President Kennedy. The real need for some kind of cultural centre in Washington had got lost in the passion for producing this Memorial. Many people now stated that it was wrong to spend millions of dollars on marble and stone as, surely, Kennedy would have wished the money to go to the poor and starving. The original idea had melted into the emotional sands of time obscuring any credit that the Republican administrations might have honestly claimed.

The money was raised by public subscription and government loans to build the huge white marble edifice that resulted. It was classical and yet modern, and certainly in my opinion a very fine structure. The ground was donated by the Government but unfortunately was in the direct flight path of National Airport. To counteract the noise an extra million or so dollars had to be spent erecting a terrace on which trees could be planted to act as a sound barrier. Much later some wit described the building as 'looking like the box that Watergate came in.'

This particular preview was intended by the organizers to honour those countries which had presented gifts. Tickets for the public cost one hundred dollars each, and three thousand five hundred people from all over the United States decided to buy them.

Some of the gifts were princely in the extreme. Those from France took the shape of huge and costly crystal chandeliers which ranged down the gigantic foyer as far as the eye could see. The Italians had almost beggared themselves donating vast quantities of marble. The purses of many countries were stretched wide in response to invitations to participate. It could have been, in part, recognition for the generous financial help America had given so many countries for so long. Asked a number of times what the British intended to give, and being quite unable to reply, we at last discovered that it was to be a piece of sculpture by Barbara Hepworth, which proved to be dwarfed by its surroundings, and incomprehen-

222

sible to most. It was also a tardy arrival.

The vast interior had mainly been decorated in red and white. The opera house, in red plush relieved only by the sparkle of a great chandelier, was described as a jewel box by some, and looked like a sore throat to others.

Various people held dinner parties at large round tables in the huge lobby. The tables covered in flowered cotton cloths, specially imported from Paris, looked attractive. Our host and hostess, Marquis and Jane Childs, were old and valued friends, and among their choice of guests were Henry Kissinger and Laurance Rockefeller who conversed animatedly about the US Congress decision to halt production of supersonic transport planes, which evidently caused much satisfaction to the Canadians who, it was remarked, could become the providers of the chief international airport for North America. Henry Kissinger was, as usual, enjoying the limelight, the reporters and the attention.

Rowley and I had been given special tickets and instructions to go to the Presidential Suite after dinner was over. The lobby and hall by that time was a squashed mass of jostling people, and nobody we could find seemed to have the faintest idea as to where the Presidential Suite could be found. Finally we were directed up a staircase to a room where, to our astonishment, Mrs Rose Kennedy was receiving the guests.

Mrs Kennedy was dressed to kill. An abundance of black hair piled on her head was crowned by a huge diamond brooch as long black simulated eyelashes fluttered beneath. Her dress was a mass of pink organdie ruffles, her manner animated while her eyes glittered and sparkled in evident pleasure. She was, it seemed, enjoying her position to the full. One could not but admire her fortitude. She was, after all, over eighty years of age and had led a life packed with drama, riches and tragedy. It was not the time or place to mention our telephone conversation, nor did our names or position spark any interest.

The only other guests in the room were other ambassadors

and their spouses, who giggled and whispered and agreed, in hushed tones, that the whole affair was most peculiar. After a little time had elapsed we were told to form a procession before descending the staircase to the sound of distant trumpets. One ambassadress whispered loudly that she had not realised 'we were the performing arts.' A military band then struck up and led the procession, while a US Marine took each ambassadress by the arm as we, in turn, made our entrance to rather weak applause. Later we discovered that Mrs Mamie Eisenhower had also been expected to receive with Mrs Kennedy but, whether from confusion or policy, she chose to remain at her table in the foyer.

From the political point of view the evening was interesting. All the Kennedy family repaired to the opera house where pop groups played modern music. The Nixon administration kept strictly to the foyer where the music was traditional, while outside fireworks blazed. Henry Kissinger kept announcing that it was his birthday to myriads of reporters, as Hubert Humphrey did likewise. It was the second that year for Henry, so people said. President Nixon had another engagement as did Mrs Jackie Kennedy Onassis. Senator Ted Kennedy, on the other hand, made as much out of the occasion as he could.

Six weeks later Bill Blair, The Director of the Kennedy Center, told me that more than seventy-nine of the specially imported French tablecloths had been pinched. And that the quantity of large crystal drops that had been taken from the chandeliers were numerous; people had even been spotted climbing onto each others' backs to remove pieces from these colossal chandeliers, each piece being almost a foot square. Somehow they had been secreted away in the general crush. Eighty-two pieces in all had disappeared. One lady, caught red-handed, excused herself by saying, 'And why shouldn't I? I am a tax-payer.'

That same week two Cabinet Ministers arrived to stay, Peter Walker and Robert Carr. Peter brought his young wife with him as she had never before had the opportunity to visit

Washington. Mrs Walker had already made known her wishes as to how to occupy her time. Although pregnant she indefatigably drove around Washington to look at the customary handsome public buildings and monuments, returning to announce that as she had now seen the best of the city she would now like to see the worst. This request caused consternation all round, but growing ever more determined with each word of discouragement, Mrs Walker finally set off with one of the most experienced Embassy drivers, Rowley's personal diplomatic secretary and all doors firmly locked. She later referred to it as her 'tour of the ghetto.' She did, however, admit that perhaps it was not the most accurate description since the city, being overwhelmingly black, possessed a relatively small white section.

The black areas of Washington were and are indeed unruly. When I later visited the National Hospital for treatment which lay beyond the white enclave I would be accompanied by an armed guard to see me safely through the black districts. The evening newspaper ran a weekly toll of rapes. There had been four hundred and fifteen cases in ten months. Peter, our third footman, on his first day off after arriving from England had mistakenly caught a bus going in the wrong direction. On waiting for a returning bus he was set upon by four black youngsters at the point of a knife who stole all he had: his money, his new overcoat and his prized signet ring. They would have taken his trousers too, he told us, if he had not begged for mercy. The youngest, Peter said, looked no more than nine or ten years old. The poor young man was in a state of shock for weeks.

Peter Walker, who had been made Minister for the Environment, a new Ministry formed by Ted Heath from the old Ministry of Works plus some other Departments, told me that on discussing the new name, Ted had suggested, rather quaintly, that it should be called the Department of Living. That lasted only until someone quipped, 'Well, that would mean that Peter Walker will be Minister for Life.'

18

THE QUEEN'S BIRTHDAY PARTY

The Queen's birthday was regarded as one of the main events of the year by Washington officials and residents alike, as well as the Embassy staff. It was expensive and caused a great deal of time and trouble. Since then, for various reasons, it has been discontinued.

Meetings chaired by the Ambassadress would take place at regular intervals with various officials, caterers and the domestic staff, so that every detail and contingency could be discussed and organised. Some unlooked-for benefits came in its train, for any much-needed maintenance of the house, both inside and out, and which had been delayed indefinitely, would at once be given priority if the words 'Queen's Birthday' were declared loudly a few times.

The day itself was a marathon and required great stamina. By the second week of June the temperature would soar; the humidity likewise. There would be two separate Garden Parties in the Embassy Residence: one in the morning for those working in British Government Agencies, besides the Embassy and Military Mission. Eight hundred would be invited and usually seven hundred would turn up. A queue would form from early in the day outside the front door, and then, in single file, guests would pour in at great speed to shake hands with the Ambassador and his wife. This fast-moving line would cause vertigo. To overcome this giddy feeling it was necessary to place oneself at an angle. This had the calming effect of greeting people who were coming towards one instead of flicking past.

At eleven fifteen precisely the Ambassador and his wife would enter the garden. On one occasion a lady, overcome with excitement, exclaimed loudly: 'Oh, a twenty-one gun salute,' as she heard the first of a series of back-fires issuing from Massachusetts Avenue. The Ambassador, standing on the steps, would make a short speech, raise his glass, and with the assembled throng, drink the Queen's health in champagne. A great quantity of food would be consumed, which seemed rather odd since the event took place before lunch, and the temperature usually reached around ninety-two degrees in the shade. As soon as possible Rowley and I would disappear, for otherwise we would be in danger of having our hands shaken once again by the departing guests.

The garden plants were tuned to bloom for the second week in June in order to provide a blaze of flowers for the Birthday. A riot of mainly roses, supported by cyclamens, geraniums and bougainvillaea, but by the middle of July the intense heat finished off most of them, leaving a cooling green.

The second Garden Party would start at five thirty, and was the more important. During the weeks leading up to this event, flowers, books, plants and other inducements would arrive from young and old. These presents were from anxious people worried that either they might be overlooked, left off the guest list by a new Ambassador, or dropped for some other reason. The telephone would ring unceasingly by callers demanding an invitation, and it was the thankless and delicate task of the social secretary to exercise the greatest tact, and employing her most dulcet tones, managed to put them off without causing the slightest offence. A balancing act which Torie Legge-Bourke did unflinchingly and extremely well.

British visitors or residents without an official connection were not invited. This was a rather unkind rule for those that treasured their national loyalty; the reason was probably purely economy. But why anyone should want to sit in a traffic jam for an hour or so before being admitted to a humid, noisy and crowded garden with the temperature in the nineties, dressed moreover to the nines, with gloves, hats and formal dresses, was beyond my comprehension. The men, too, in dark suits and collars and ties; although in earlier days it must have been worse when tailcoats and waistcoats were the expected attire.

In the garden the men would mop their brows, while the ladies' make-up would run in the heat, and inside the Embassy itself there was no respite, for at that time it was not air-conditioned. To mitigate the discomfort, we had fast electric fans placed along the halls and passages, and as we greeted the guests, had one placed close to us. That first year I wore a full-skirted short chiffon dress by Hardy Amies. The skirt billowed out in the current of air created by the whirring blades, 'A very dramatic effect, and Lady Cromer thought it out with that in view,' was the printed remark, but for which I could really take no credit.

Sixty loaves of bread were consumed and a million strawberries.

The Queen's Birthday Party the following year was an uncertain affair, for the Duke of Windsor had died but three days previously. The question then arose as to whether we should hold it or not. After much consternation, Buckingham Palace was consulted. The reply came back that the Queen wished everything to continue as normal. However, as the Duke was married to an American and lived for much of the year there, we thought that some sort of mourning would be appropriate. I managed to dig out a black and white outfit I had worn for some years and hastily redecorated a white hat with black. The shops had been closed for three days due to a national holiday so I was left with the forlorn hope that the women's page reporters would hold off from unkind remarks. It was, of course, too much to expect, even after a year and a half.

That year the black Mayor of Washington and his wife, Mrs Walter Washington, attended the Queen's Birthday Party and, to my astonishment, greeted me on arrival with the words: 'You have done so much for our city.' On reflection I realised that his remark clearly encompassed the entire embassy. This statement was accompanied by a warm embrace, and I looked round hopefully to see if this moment was being recorded by the ever-present reporters. Disappointingly it was not. Instead I observed a group of them talking suspiciously together, and wondered what they might be up to. I did not have to wait long, for on being introduced to a Mr Kleindienst, who insisted on kissing my hand, the photographers went into action. Unknown to me the, by now, more experienced Information Counsellor had warned Rowley of a plot to photograph him with Mr Kleindienst and Rowley took evasive action by sticking closely to George Meany whenever a photographer hovered. George Meany was the powerful head of the most powerful union, the AFL-CIO and, therefore, no political mischief could be made out of that. Poor Mr Kleindienst was the Acting Attorney General, who at that very time, was having the utmost difficulty getting his appointment confirmed in the Senate. The usual dirty work and washing was being brought up to besmirch the poor man's reputation.

An old friend from ten years earlier, Gene McCarthy, was there with his wife, Abigail. They embraced me affectionately, but this happy greeting, too, did not stir the camera shutters. Gene had previously been the Democratic candidate for the Presidency and was considered to have been rather left-wing. He was certainly the darling of the university students. The press, however, were, it seemed, determined to forge an image of Rowley and me as far-right characters who only consorted with rather dubious members of Nixon's entourage.

To be so concerned with one's public image was at once vain and oversensitive, but there was a certain importance in being seen in a reasonable light: important for the Embassy and for Britain. Although we entertained many and encountered even more, in so vast a country it was impossible to get across without the help of the media.

During the second year's Queen's Birthday Party the footmen, unknown to us, who had played their patriotic records with such success for the Charitable Tours, thought it would be fitting to play them again at the morning party for the British. The Military had arrived in uniform, as was customary, and that year wore black armbands out of respect for the Duke of Windsor. The footmen's favourite record was from a military tattoo, which included the National Anthem. It took some moments before Rowley and I became conscious that the rapidly-moving receiving line had come to a halt, and that all the Navy, Army, and Air Force officers and their wives were rigidly standing to attention, while those already in the garden were doing the same, while trying to conceal their champagne glasses. Hearing the distant strains of 'God Save the Queen' issuing from the ballroom, I hurriedly found a footman who was enjoying what he considered an appropriate spectacle and told him to swiftly turn it off. What our morning guests thought of this unusual departure we never discovered for no-one ever liked to mention it.

The day after our first year's Queen's Birthday Party we flew to London to celebrate our son Vivian's twenty-first birthday. We held a cocktail party in the House of Lords and then went on to Annabel's for dinner with a party of his young friends, where we opened the family's last bottle of Napoleon 1912 brandy.

The next evening we dined with the Queen at Windsor and listened afterwards to a 'Quiet Entertainment.' This was Lord David Cecil reading extracts from Alice in Wonderland and Hans Andersen's Nightingale, interspersed with renditions on the harp by Dr Osian Ellis. Both were remarkable, composed and fluent. Princess Anne was keen to hear news of my social secretary, later to become her Lady in Waiting; Princess Alexandra to hear news of our elder son in Bangkok. Princess Margaret wanted our views on the Embassy. And the Duke of Edinburgh to see the bathroom which, I told him, had been specially decorated the year before for his last visit of one night. Its main feature was a most luxurious long-haired white carpet which, he said, he never noticed.

We returned to Washington within a week to find yet another bomb scare by the IRA and also the scandal of the Pentagon Papers.

The Pentagon Papers were a series of secret documents which had been published in the *New York Times* and the *Washington Post*. The Deputy Secretary of Defense dined with us on June 20th and he was later due, he told us, to wrestle with this problem all day. 'It will go to the Supreme Court,' he said, and when it did the verdict was six to three in favour of Daniel Ellsberg, who had been the person who had given the papers to the press. The Supreme Court seemed to divide on party lines, that is to say, they seemed loyal to whatever administration had appointed them in the first place.

The next evening Supreme Court Justice Byron White, one of those who had voted in favour of Daniel Ellsberg, came to dine. Dean Acheson was also one of the guests. At one time Secretary of State, he was possibly the most distinguished and skilful Secretary that America had known. He had served in a Democratic administration and was himself a member of that party. I asked him his views on the Pentagon Papers affair and why the judges voted as they did. He explained that throughout American history recourse to the Supreme Court on various Constitutional matters had occurred with great frequency. Furthermore, although the judges were political appointees, they were considered to be above politics once in the Supreme Court on the premise that as their careers could not go any further, they owed nothing to anybody and, therefore, should be wholly objective and good patriots. Nevertheless Dean Acheson gave me the distinct impression that he was not entirely in favour of the papers being given to the press and understood the diplomatic implications of the judges' majority decision. Surprisingly there is no Official Secrets Act in America, nor is anyone asked to take an oath of secrecy on taking office.

Dean Acheson had been criticised for a remark he had made

some years previously when he declared that 'Britain has lost an Empire but not yet found a role.' This remark was greatly resented in Britain, possibly because of its obvious truth, and he was condemned as anti-British, when in fact the opposite was the truth. I asked him what he considered Britain's future role to be, and he replied: 'It is quite obvious that the role of Britain is now in the Common Market. She must become a part of Europe.'

The Russian Ambassador was clearly delighted with the American discomfiture over the Pentagon Papers. That much he made quite clear when he lunched privately with us on July 1st. On that occasion he told Rowley that the Russians found the English more difficult to deal with than any other member of Western Europe. Mrs Dobrynin confined herself to asking questions about the Royal Family and whether I thought the Queen would abdicate like Queen Whilhelmina of The Netherlands had done.

That week at a dinner party given by Henry Kissinger, a relaxed summer affair, we noticed Bob McNamara dancing robustly with an air of somewhat forced gaiety. It had been he who had originally ordered the Pentagon Papers to be written. Joe Alsop wrote in his column that 'If the American academic world were not a noisome swamp of modish decay, the scholars who compiled the Pentagon Papers would be drummed out of their Universities.'

This whole affair showed clearly which was the wind had started to blow, an ill wind that was eventually to lead to Watergate.

The season in Newport, Rhode Island, an exclusive summer resort, begins with Independence Day and ends Labor Day. The socially ambitious would compete with each other in inviting prominent people, especially for the opening dance, which would take place during the Independence Day weekend. The dance that year was being given by our host, Wiley Buchanan, who had been Chief of Protocol under President Eisenhower, and whom we had known well on our previous duty in Washington when we each had daughters to bring out. The Buchanans were not a Newport family, having been in possession of a Newport house for only eight years. I felt a distinct undercurrent of disapproval that they should be so conspicuously hospitable, for when a Washington/Newport resident asked me whom we were staying with, and I told her that it was the Buchanans, she replied: 'Good Lord! They are already having the Italian Ambassador, and now the British too.' She was aghast. 'They are very rich,' she added. With sudden curiosity I asked her how he had made his money. 'He is an oil squirt,' she replied with evident disapproval.

The Buchanan house was spacious and comfortable. Both Wiley and his pretty wife, Ruth, were excellent hosts. Rather quaintly, the walls were covered with paintings by Ruth Buchanan and her friends, mixed haphazardly with original French Impressionists. The pride of place was touchingly given to the works of Mrs Buchanan, while a fairly well-known Toulouse-Lautrec was almost hidden behind a door.

The Buchanans employed a staff of four which did not, however, include a cook. Domestic labour was almost impossible to find, and many arrived for the summer to find themselves staff-less. Lunch, fortunately, presented no problems at all, as all and sundry repaired to the Beach Club for sustenance from a running buffet.

The heyday of Newport was at the turn of the century when the fabulously wealthy, such as the Vanderbilts, erected what they modestly described as their 'Summer Cottages.' These lay mainly in a row along Belleville Avenue, and were faithfully copied from French châteaux, German schlosses, English or Scottish castles, in some cases transported across the ocean piece by piece. The peculiar thing about them was that they were built side by side, and each occupied barely an acre. In all, they represent a strange and bizarre sight. From my window in the Buchanans' house I could see, just over the hedge, a complete replica of Petit Trianon.

Our host, we discovered, was a leading light in the organisation for the preservation of these extraordinary houses. They had been allowed to decay, as had those in England, until some enterprising persons woke up to the realisation that they were not only special, but a part of their national heritage. The marbles imported from Italy, the richness of the carving, the painted ceilings where gold leaf abounded, had all been the work of imported European labour. The extravagance of taste at a period noted for its over-embellishment is almost unimaginable. As is also the sheer, unashamed vulgarity. And yet they were only occupied for two months in a year.

The Elms, a French château built within ten yards of the street, had belonged to a coal millionaire. The only remaining member of his family had died aged ninety a short time before our visit. She had been bedridden for many years, and her bedroom still clung to a sad atmosphere of bygone memories. The large bedroom, originally sumptuous, had been allowed to fall into a sorry state of repair. The silk coverings on the walls hung in dirty threads, the curtains were in tatters. She had, we were told, begged for some redecoration, but to no avail, and had lingered on and on, while the splendour of her surroundings declined from year to year, to end in dreary squalor.

The wife of another millionaire, clearly a martinet, had a curious gadget installed in her bathroom. It was something that neither of us had ever seen before: a clock with some thirty or forty buttons, each marked with the office of various members of her enormous domestic staff. Once a button was pressed the clock would immediately start, timing how long it took before the bells were answered.

Each evening we dined out in formal evening clothes at smaller, by past standards, Newport homes. Smaller they may have been and without extravagant decoration, but they nevertheless were full of rare and valuable possessions. One elderly couple, with five cars, had simplified the number plates by using just their initials followed by number 1, for their best car, down to number 5 for their station-wagon. It was somehow reassuring that a flash of the old extravagance could still be seen. The talk at the dinner parties was mainly of the passing of the good old days and the rapid change of only the previous five years; the time, now past, when Americans admired riches, and delighted in seeing fine houses and large automobiles — when they were proud to meet millionaires and hoped to attain that same distinction for themselves. One Newport person remarked how sad it was that no-one really liked to be seen in a large or expensive automobile in case he received a shaken fist or screams of abuse. That person added that he considered that the young generation was hopeless, and he rested his hopes on the next. They, he said confidently, would be certain to react against their delinquent parents.

On our return to Washington we were entertained by Henry Kissinger. It was a private party held in a friend's garden, and the guests were a strange mixture: mainly newspaper commentators and film stars. The garden was dimly lit with just one candle on each table. One man grabbed my hand in the dark and said: 'The name is Frank Sinatra.' I thought it was a joke, but it was not.

The Dutch Ambassador at another party told me that neither he nor the French, Italian or German ambassadors hardly ever saw Dr Kissinger, and did Rowley? I replied, 'Quite often,' and thought it best not to mention the darkened party in the garden where I had dimly spotted the Israeli and Indian ambassadors. At that time, most probably, their countries were of greater interest to Henry.

The weekend of July 10th found the Embassy alive with police. Trotskyites had threatened to make trouble all over Washington. They had been behind the first Vietnam Veterans demo the previous May, 'The Tidy One,' as it was known.

The sofa in my sitting-room was also found to be alive with insects, something one does not usually expect to find, and certainly never in England. But in the hot, humid climate of a Washington summer they flourished, and they were not something that the english head-housemaid was used to look-

235

ing for. It was the season too for cockroaches, which appeared to eat anything, and a careful watch had to be kept.

On July 14th we held a Newcomers' Party for those who had taken up their jobs in the Embassy in the last six months. They amounted to one hundred and thirty, which gives an indication as to how large the Embassy staff was. Torie Legge-Bourke had cleverly devised a system where the new ones wore labels with the names written in red ink, and the longer-serving ones in blue. The party went well and, to our surprise, we found that rather more alcohol was consumed than would have been the case with the equivalent number of Americans.

The domestic household were soon to take their summer vacation, with the exception of the French chef, who elected to stay in Washington, for reasons best known to himself. The first footman decided to leave and found a job as butler with the Averell Harrimans. This was a usual practice, for after a prescribed time in the Embassy they were permitted by the authorities to find employment in the United States where they were much better paid. Therefore we found that with that and other reasons of home-sickness &c, the turnover of domestic staff was very high. One member of the domestic staff who had worked in the Residence for years was called Ivor. One morning I mistakenly addressed him as Ivan, which caused a rather shocked reaction, although nothing was said. Feeling that something should be done, I reported the incident to Rowley. He did, indeed, turn out to be Russian, and his name had been Ivan, but we were assured by Security that he was all right!

Torie Legge-Bourke had had her pictures in the newspapers as a possible bride for Prince Charles, which caused some excitement among the staff. Her father was, at the time, chairman of the 1922 Committee in the House of Commons, and had publicly emerged as an anti-marketeer, but fortunately the American press made nothing of that.

Solly Zuckerman was a house guest and also Professor

Bondi when we held our last dinner party of the summer. We sat down twenty-four at table, which was more or less our average number, and we entertained an average mixture of guests, among whom were the German Ambassador and his wife. The evening went well from the start, and to add piquancy, Rowley was told that Secretary of State Bill Rogers would ring at ten o'clock to impart some important information. Also the President would be appearing on television at ten thirty to make an announcement. A television was immediately installed in the drawing-room, and there was much speculation during dinner as to what it all might mean. Solly guessed correctly.

When the expected call came through from the Secretary in California, Rowley took the German Ambassador with him to the telephone and they both spoke to the Secretary of State, sending telegrams immediately afterwards to their respective governments. On their return to the drawing-room neither would, tantalisingly, tell the eagerly waiting company anything, so we had to wait another twenty-five minutes for the President to tell us on the television. The German Ambassador only remarked on the fact that it must have been the first time in history that the German Ambassador had sent his government a telegram from a British Embassy.

When President Nixon did appear on television it was to announce that he would be visiting China within nine months, and that Henry Kissinger had been to Peking, when all the world thought that he had been confined to bed with a stomach upset. This was, indeed, a momentous breakthrough and a triumph for the President.

Ray Kline, who was head of the Intelligence Section of the State Department, was one of our guests. He had lived in both Hong Kong and Taiwan for some years and knew the Chinese mentality rather well. He voiced the hope that America would not become too euphoric over the impending meeting and would keep guarded reservations. A couple of weeks after this dinner party, Ray invited Rowley to lunch, in the course of which Ray mentioned that as Rowley saw Henry Kissinger fairly frequently, perhaps he would be so kind as to keep him informed as to Henry's thinking in general diplomatic development. Ray Kline was insistent in his request, and although Rowley did not want to disappoint him, he had in the end to say that it was not really appropriate for the British Ambassador to be an intelligence gathering agent between the President's National Security Advisor and the State Department. It showed, I thought, the measure of trust put on Rowley as well as the lack of communication between the State Department and the White House.

Before we left for our summer holidays we dined very informally with Senator and Mrs Mike Monroney who were old friends from our previous sojourn. It was a relaxed party with everyone seated around the swimming pool in Georgetown talking freely about current events in the knowledge that we were all friends. Gene Carusi, who was another old friend, and I, found ourselves in complete agreement over President Nixon's Vietnam policy of slow withdrawal with as much honour as could be salvaged from an unfortunate affair. We also found common ground in thinking that once America had gone into Vietnam, she should have waged a more intelligent war. It was at just that point that Clark Clifford joined us by the pool. Clark, a man of enormous charm, had been President Johnson's Secretary of Defense. A friendly argument began with Clifford announcing that he was exceedingly suspicious of Nixon's motives, and was certain that he wished to prolong the war indefinitely. Gene replied that he thought that idea absurd. Originally Clark Clifford had been a fervent hawk and had then done a U-turn and then become a rabid dove, like so many others.

Gene asked Clark what he thought of Nixon's surprise announcement about his impending meeting with Chou en Lai in nine months time in Peking and Clark replied: 'He should get out at once,' and that he did not believe that Nixon wished to make any agreements with the Chinese, 'and,' he added, 'he just wants to go on with the war.' At that I intervened to say that I was certain that nothing could be hurried with the Chinese, that these things took time, and that an ungainly rush to meet Chou or Mao might be interpreted as meekness and certainly weakness. Clark responded with a question, 'Well, how do you think we should get out of Vietnam?' and I replied, 'With all due respect, I think you should leave in the same manner as you came in, by degrees.' Later in the evening Clark reappeared and announced that he would bet Gene, Dorothy Macauley and me that Nixon would have over forty-thousand military personnel in Vietnam this time next year. We all took him on but, afterwards, I realised that we should have specified combat troops, so we eventually lost the bet.

The following summer I received a letter from Clark written clearly with his tongue in his cheek. In it he said: 'It is my sad duty to inform you that on 17th July 1972 there were forty-seven thousand one hundred and sixty-five American Military personnel in South Vietnam. You will recall that the famous wager we entered into involved the figure of forty-thousand. That figure was exceeded by more than seven thousand.' With ill-concealed delight he went on to write that he would take us all out to lunch with the money he had won, and ended 'with this gentle reminder, my affectionate regard and my high esteem.' It was a polished letter from a charming man — but one who, I could not help thinking, would have been far better placed as an Ambassador of importance than a Secretary of Defense during an undeclared war in which his country was engaged.

Clark Clifford told me at the same dinner that when Harold Wilson dined at the White House during the Presidency of Lyndon Johnson, Wilson made a speech condemning the Americans for their involvement in Vietnam and that the large audience froze in dismay at his remarks, and that from then on President Johnson and his administration thoroughly disliked him. I replied that no doubt Harold Wilson was thinking of a wider audience for, although elastic, he was no fool.

We took our annual holiday in the summer to avoid the overbearing heat. As one inhabitant put it: 'Washington in the summer smells like a damp basement.' It was not just the heat, but the intense humidity that got people down. Holidays, however, were not sacred to men in public office.

For some time we had been beset with trying and sad family problems and once back in England we did our best to try to solve them. This was hardly restful. We spent two weeks in our small villa in the South of France, but while there, a dollar crisis erupted. The telephone rang early one morning at three o'clock. John Connally, the Secretary of the American Treasury, was on the other end wishing to describe his measures to sustain his currency to Rowley who patiently listened while standing shivering on the cold tile floor. It was hard, too, to overcome the shock of being woken up so early from a deep sleep. It was a strange repeat of many years before when, in the same place, sterling had caused just such a rude awaking. The consequence of Connally's call meant that Rowley had to leave promptly for London to see the Prime Minister. He was able to return for just a few more days rest before returning to London for further consultations.

With sad farewells, we returned to Washington the third week in September to be greeted as usual with yet another bomb threat to make us feel at home. During our leave the Peruvian pot boy, a good worker and popular with the staff, was murdered in a Washington cafe. A knife had been plunged through his heart by an angry Puerto Rican. This tragic event plainly upset the household. The vacancy in the pantry had also to be filled.

Apart from the security risk of advertising, any mention of British Embassy footmen sent the British Labour Party into a frenzy of indignation. There had already, soon after our arrival, been a question in the House of Commons from a Labour member asking how many footmen Lord Cromer needed to employ. The idea that an Earl must be rich and waited upon by countless footmen and handmaidens was either a political tease or showed how out-of-date the Labour members were. In fact, the number of domestic places in the Embassy had always remained the same, and were no different from the number serving the Labour Party appointee, John Freeman. It seemed to me a pity that no-one questioned the number of footmen that the Labour envoys required.

Another Peruvian was found to take the place of the murdered one. And a young Welshman applied for the vacant post of footman. It may seem strange that we should worry over a large household being short of one or two employees, but when it happened the others were wont to complain of overwork, and we were compelled to curtail the entertaining from the scale expected.

19

AN UNEXPECTED DUTY

Rowley and I flew back to Washington independently on different days. On my aeroplane, a Jumbo, I found Pierre-Paul Schweitzer, then head of the International Monetary Fund. In those days the Jumbos provided an upstairs bar where the first-class passengers could wander for a drink, and where Pierre-Paul and I repaired to enjoy an aperitif. He disclosed that he was returning from a Group of Ten meeting in London which John Connally had also attended, and where the latter had been very outspoken.

John Connally was a popular Governor of Texas. He had been a victim, too, of Oswald's gun, having been wounded by one of the bullets that killed Kennedy. He was sitting beside the driver of Kennedy's car when the assassination took place. Tall, good-looking, shrewd, if lacking in sophistication, John Connally appeared to be a tough Texan. But his directness and bluntness did not go down well with the polite and wise financial leaders of Europe. The Europeans had, evidently, been rather taken aback and Pierre-Paul remarked to me that 'if anything could have brought England closer to the Common Market it was John Connally.' He had, it seemed, turned to Tony Barber (then Britain's Chancellor of the Exchequer) and told him bluntly that Tony was in no position to say anything to America after the way Britain had managed its affairs in the past. This was by virtue of Tony having added the UK's voice to others' in trying to persuade the US to lower its ten per cent tariff on imported goods.

242

All the world's financial leaders were now descending on Washington for the World Bank and IMF meeting. Tony Barber, Leslie O'Brien (Governor of the Bank of England), his wife, and a Treasury Minister, Terence Higgins, stayed at the Embassy. Through many years we had attended those meetings, but this time, instead of a central, Rowley had only a peripheral role: that of giving hospitality. He was, of course, acquainted with almost all the leading personalities, and for that reason decided to give a large buffet dinner one evening in the Embassy. It was not unlike those we had given for the same meeting so many years earlier, only larger.

One hundred and seventy people were seated at round tables covered in yellow cloths with white candles and pink, white and yellow flower arrangements in the centres. The effect was a happy one. A musician had been engaged to play as the guests arrived, and he continued until the noise generated drowned his playing. The men, naturally, outnumbered the women, by about five to one.

John Connally sat on my right. He seemed a bit put out as he said he had understood from Rowley that it was to be only a small and relaxed party. However it did not take long before he succumbed to the general cheer and informality, helped enormously by Araminta Aldington, who sat on his other side. I knew she would surprise and charm him with her originality and intelligence and I was not disappointed. Connally possessed a keen sense of humour and, before long, I heard hearty laughter. Araminta is a noted breeder of Jacob sheep and she did not lose the opportunity to promote them. John was highly amused, as he said that in spite of all his preaching throughout the past three weeks on cutting US imports from Europe he had been sold, while dining at the British Embassy, a new sort of animal from England which he had never before heard of, and which, it seemed, the United States could not do without.

Peter Flanigan, a White House adviser, who sat on my other side, divulged that John Connally was, in truth, both nervous and scared to be amidst the world financial experts, and that this was his first World Bank meeting. It was a pity, Peter said, that John had not yet attended one abroad which took place every third year, for the very strangeness of the foreign host country tended to bring the participants together. They suffered, as in India, from 'Delhi belly,' or as in Vienna enjoyed the delights, or in the East savoured the exotic entertainments, all of which tended to put everyone at ease, with shared jokes and experiences. Tony Barber had evidently delivered a good speech at the morning meeting, and that evening he made a big hit with the American ladies, one going so far as to describe him to me as 'that truly delicious Mr Barber.'

The next evening John Connally gave a dinner for seven of the Finance Ministers. I was told the following morning that he had explained his choice of guests during a short speech. The British Chancellor had been chosen because of our close culture and history; the Indian because they still remained friends in spite of having the largest Communist Party in Western Europe; the Mexican because Texas was the common border; the Austrian because of particularly enjoying a holiday there; the Australian as he owned a ranch and would like to buy another; and, lastly, the German as he had a pretty wife. The dinner was evidently a great success and all the guests felt that they now knew Connally better. 'He was a rough dealer,' but knew what he wanted and was always prepared to do a deal.

John Connally was a Democrat, and it was widely thought that he would have become President, or certainly won the Democratic nomination had he not, in good faith and to his credit, wanted to give support to the Nixon administration when it was at a low ebb because of Vietnam, so announcing his conversion to the Republican Party. It was a brave, sincere, and gallant gesture, and by making it he also ended a spectacularly promising career.

Shortly after the Bankers' meeting Rowley had to dash off to San Francisco for British Week. These weeks were a feature which took place somewhat frequently all over the country.

They were purely promotional for British exports and in some cases they were considered important enough for a member of the Royal Family to attend.

In Washington it was decreed that the Eisenhower Theater at the Kennedy Center should have a public opening in October by the President himself. But the Kennedy family, presumably not wishing to be left out, had shrewdly booked the theatre for a Kennedy Foundation benefit the evening prior to the official opening. Their event was bound to attract the maximum publicity, publicity being an important element in American life, and the Kennedy family in any case moved continually in the limelight, encouraged in every way by the liberal press.

The Director of the Kennedy Center, himself a Kennedy supporter, wittingly or unwittingly allowed the Kennedys to go ahead with their arrangements. It was only when the White House came to hear of it a short time before the actual event that they, quite understandably, raised an objection. The Director, Bill Blair, in consequence, hit on the tactful idea of moving the Kennedy benefit to the already-opened Concert Hall where, as he artfully pointed out to them, more money could be raised as it had a larger seating capacity. The Kennedys reluctantly agreed and Bill Blair, as he ruefully stated afterwards, received recriminations from both sides. As it came to pass, the Kennedy evening did, as expected, receive the maximum publicity, and the Presidential opening rather less than it deserved.

A little later that month Senator Ted Kennedy saw fit to make a blistering speech attacking British policy in Northern Ireland, the result of which caused him to receive an extremely bad press in Britain. His speech was at best unhelpful, and certainly seemed anti-British and was aimed, it seemed, for political reasons at various constituencies. It was also inaccurate and showed ignorance of our history. He was, however, stung by the bad press he received in Britain into writing a letter to the London *Times* suggesting that he had been criticised purely because the British possessed 'a guilty conscience over the Irish problem.'

In the opinion polls at that time Ted Kennedy was rated first choice as Democratic candidate for President. This was a worrying prospect for Britain and a puzzle also. The subject of 'Chappaquiddick,' a sordid and sorry episode of only two years standing, seemed forgotten, and any mention of it by a foreigner quite often produced surprise. It was evidently thought strange that anyone outside America should know of it at all, let alone the fact that it had been of interest the world over.

In discussing morality we discovered a fundamental difference between the American and English interpretation. In England, if a public person (such as Jack Profumo) offended society rules and became involved in an unsavoury episode, he was forgiven providing he subsequently led a quiet life out of the public gaze, and certainly did not tell the rest of the world what to do. In America, however, a scandal appeared not to preclude that person from continuing in public life and, moreover, to run an office actively engaged in raking up any disreputable events in the careers of political opponents about to be confirmed by the Senate for public office.

The end of October found us in Columbus, Ohio, for one of the usual promotions: this time a British Fortnight sponsored by a store the size of Harrods with, we learned, four times the turnover. The Governor of Ohio kindly invited us to stay at his official residence. Governor Gilligan, as his name suggests, was of Irish ancestry, and charming. With the Northern Irish troubles much in the foreground it seemed somewhat strange that he should have asked the British Ambassador. Until, that is, the reason became quite clear. Practical considerations were paramount. The owners of the huge store were enormously rich and their influence may have had something to do with our invitation. In any case our presence gave the Governor the opportunity to invite them for dinner, and at his small dinner party he also included his personal political fund-raiser, and the talk at dinner centred on money. Were donations in order?

The Governor told us that he had not paid any attention to the many threatening telephone calls he had received about our visit. He enjoyed talking about Northern Ireland, although our understanding of the situation markedly differed. Nevertheless it was all most good-humoured.

We sat down to a dinner of many courses, served by several well-trained black domestics who were also looking after our needs upstairs. It was just as we were retiring to bed that Governor Gilligan remarked on the fact that his obedient and well-trained staff were all 'trusties.' He then disclosed that each one was a murderer, and that the excellent butler had, in his time, killed six people. He reassured us that they did not actually sleep in the house, but were brought there each day by police truck from the State Penitentiary. The butler, he added, was a nice young man as long as he remained sober. One drink and he was apt to become homicidal. As a tray of whisky and gin had been placed in our bedroom we were somewhat perturbed and hoped that we would survive the visit. Later on we learned that employing 'trusties' seemed to be a universal perk for Governors. In Ohio's case the trusties received twenty dollars a month for their services. They clearly seemed to enjoy the work, while at the same time providing cheap and necessary labour.

The British Fortnight opened promptly at nine o'clock the following morning. Rowley attempted to make a speech in the presence of twelve marching men playing bagpipes who were followed by the Town Crier shouting 'Great Great Britain.' Later the Governor waited to receive us in his official office and then showed us around the State Capitol, in the dome of which were inscribed the names of all the Presidents of the United States provided by Ohio. The Governor pointed to them with pride, in spite of the sad fact that, out of eight, three of them had been assassinated. Governor Gilligan also carefully arranged that at no time were any photographs taken of himself with the British Ambassador, an unusual omission in America.

From Ohio we flew to Kentucky for Rowley to address the English Speaking Union in Louisville. The ESU are a very active body throughout the USA and, more often than not, a dinner or reception was held by them for us wherever we travelled. Lorraine Sherman Cooper, the wife of the State's senior Senator, was at the airport to meet us. This was a very nice gesture and we were comforted and pleased to see a familiar and friendly face. The contrast between rural Kentucky and the exotic and elegant Lorraine seemed rather extreme, but we learned that she was as popular in Kentucky as she certainly was in Washington.

Soon after our return to Washington the Russians celebrated their National Day, in commemoration of the glorious October Revolution. They held the customary huge reception, usually very well attended, due to a certain extent to the obvious popularity of the Ambassador, Anatoliy Dobrynin. He and his wife stood by the drawing-room on the first floor to receive the exceptionally long line of guests, and there was nothing to suggest that this party would be any different from any other. National Day parties took place at the rate of at least two a week, but no-one ever contemplated attending them all. Most ambassadors quickly learned to make an 'acte de presence' by slipping in and out with great rapidity. On this occasion a sudden uproar exploded. Two young Americans leapt up the huge staircase and, with the speed of lizards catching a fly, clipped themselves with handcuffs to an ornamental railing behind the reception line, at the same time shouting loudly and continually: 'Free Soviet Jews. Out with Soviet spies.' It seemed that ours was not the only embassy beset with protesters. The Russian officials showed complete sang-froid, as no-one batted an eyelid as the queuing guests moved stolidly on to shake hands with the receiving line of senior Russians. The Ambassador himself, however, moved quietly into the dining-room with Henry Kissinger.

Members of the Special Diplomatic Protection Corps were sent for and two smartly-uniformed but inexperienced young blacks appeared. The uniforms were impressive but their ability was not, and it fast became apparent that they could not cope. It was not until some time later, when the ordinary police arrived with hacksaws, that the demonstrators could be removed from the railings, arrested, re-handcuffed and led away.

Rowley was indignant, on behalf of a fellow-Ambassador, that his hospitality had been violated. But I thought their audacity commendable, and decided that it would be so much better if the IRA were to demonstrate likewise; that is to say, in an open manner, rather than by a ruthless shot in the back, or a bomb in the post without warning.

The YWCA, founded by the British, is a large organisation in the United States and a special service was held for them in the Cathedral in Washington to which we were bidden. The cathedral had been festooned with gas balloons and on each was inscribed the words 'Come Alive.' This was evidently to stress the underlying theme which was to combat racialism. The service itself was regularly interrupted by the sound of sharp reports as the balloons exploded in the warmth of the over-heated cathedral. The Dean (Sayer) held the string of a monstrously large balloon as he led the procession of clergy carrying smaller ones. He explained at the start of the service that all the balloons represented prayers and would be re-leased heavenward during the service. That the balloons, once released, soared upwards to become stuck on the ceiling fazed him not at all. He told us also that when we came to the Lord's Prayer we were to say it out loud, each in his own language. The effect of that was an indistinct babble. The sermon, delivered by a woman, was political in the extreme, and seemed to be lacking in any religious sentiment at all. Rather quixotically, she reminded the congregation, of whom about half were black, that in spite of being of different races, we were all middle-class! This preacher was, we were both told, the president of a major religious movement in the USA.

The Dean told us that at one point during the service the congregation was to rise and shout 'Come Alive' and rush from their pews and embrace each other. When the moment came, one white lady in front of us, overcome with emotion, tearfully embraced all within reach. It did not seem to me that the blacks and whites were rushing with any great enthusiasm into each others' arms, but I did observe a small white man leaning down and trying to look inconspicuous as a large black lady in a big white hat looked devouringly at him as she advanced in his direction. I was not, however, able to witness the conclusion as Rowley, taking advantage of the confusion whispered: 'Quick, it's time we left.' The service had, after all, already lasted some fifty-five minutes. On our way out a white lady stepped in our way and with an air of solemnity, mournfully declared: 'Come Alive.'

Two old friends, Ronnie and Heather Grierson were just about to enter the cathedral as we were leaving. They had decided to visit the cathedral for romantic and sentimental reasons and were somewhat taken aback when a complete stranger shouted at them 'Come Alive,' and were not a little put out.

Ronnie Grierson was visiting Washington as President of the New Philharmonic Orchestra and it was to be the first english one to play at the Kennedy Center. There was some concern, for the orchestra had become somewhat depleted due to the leading flautist being mugged in New York. He sustained a badly lacerated mouth. Two others had been battered in Boston, and one had been taken for a ride by a bogus taxi driver who robbed him of all he had and left the poor musician stranded.

The next day Rowley had lunch with Henry Kissinger at the White House in order to talk over the world monetary situation. They were constantly interrupted in their conversation by messages from the President on how to phrase the impending announcement of new troop withdrawals from

Vietnam. The State Department had not yet been told of the announcement and Rowley learned that an Assistant Secretary was only just on his way to be given the news.

That evening we dined with the Fulbrights. Senator Fulbright and his nice wife Betty had been friends since our previous tour. Bill was still, and had been for many years, an outstanding Chairman of the Foreign Relations Committee in the Senate, and in his time a most influential and highly respected statesman. Now we found a sadly changed man. Despondent and aggrieved, he appeared to be obsessed by the Vietnam war and talked constantly of it. He made it clear that he felt deeply that all present ills could be blamed on the Vietnam conflict. The wasted sums spent on the war could, he felt, be far better spent on welfare. He spoke, unsurprisingly, with the then-conventional wisdom that a nation's wealth, raised by taxation, should be spent on welfare and ever more welfare — a rejection, it seemed, of the old belief; in a man standing or falling by his own efforts — which had originally made America great. Like England after the second world war, they seemed to be turning in on themselves with the wish to cushion the young, to tax and to improve the lot of the multitude. But at what expense to individual enterprise, I wondered. Bill Fulbright equally deplored the huge sums being spent on space exploration for the same reasons. Did he not think, I asked, and in the perspective of centuries, that it was wonderful that in our brief lives we had been privileged to see a man actually walking on the moon? An American man: and was that not something to be proud of? Was that not worth more than ephemeral welfare? There was a pregnant pause after my lengthy questioning before Bill launched into a tirade against the power of the Unions, and the fact that unemployment pay was large enough to deaden the desire to work. 'We have become lazy,' he said.

Rowley and I had been in Washington nine and a half months, but still kind friends were giving dinners in our honour 'to welcome us back,' they said.

251

We celebrated Thanksgiving at a small family dinner with the President's chief speech writer, Bill Safire. He and his pretty english wife wanted us to enjoy the experience of turkey with sweet potatoes and marshmallow stuffing. It was delicious and we would have done it more justice if we had not already been fed due to the unexpected arrival of a Minister and a secretarial error. These mistakes happen occasionally, and now and again we would find ourselves having to try and consume two lunches or dinners one after the other. During our very pleasant dinner with the Safires, Bill told me that President Nixon's appearance on television caused great problems with make-up. His upper lip and chin could be seen to be perspiring despite all attempts to cover them and after trying every make of deodorant. Bill Safire continued that before a press conference as many as eighty-six probable questions would be prepared by his staff. The President would then look at them all, and sometimes pencil in his answers in a black book. And yet out of eighty-six possible questions only about eight would be asked. Bill felt sure that this black book would eventually become a valuable historical document.

We dined the following week at the French Embassy to meet Monsieur Beaumarchais who had been appointed Ambassador-Designate to Britain. Although the dinner was in his honour, and his name and new appointment so described on the invitations, we were told on arrival by Monsieur Lucet, the French Ambassador, that on no account were we to speak to Monsieur Beaumarchais of his new appointment. Even stranger was Monsieur Beaumarchais' behaviour at dinner. Placed next to me, he turned his back, and it was only after Monsieur Lucet noticed and caught his eye that Beaumarchais turned. But instead of employing a little polite small talk, for it was our first encounter, he regaled me with a torrent of anti-Common Market remarks, the gist of which appeared to be that he considered the Market quite large enough already and that it therefore did not need to include Britain. He was anyway, it seemed, convinced that the majority of people in

England were against it. Not being able to mention the next step in Beaumarchais' career, I was left wondering why a man of his persuasion should, at that time, be sent as France's representative to Britain. Monsieur Lucet, who clearly found him to be at least difficult, told me that although Beaumarchais could speak fluent english, he insisted on speaking through an interpreter when he called on various members of the American administration, thereby making a very poor impression. Monsieur Lucet was somewhat embarrassed, and in explanation Beaumarchais told him, with some condescension, that he had been told by President Pompidou to speak only in French to American officials.

In New York in December we lunched at the United Nations with the UK and the US representatives, Sir Colin Crowe and George Bush and their wives. We were interested to meet George as we had known his parents, Senator and Mrs Prescott Bush, during our previous time in Washington when they had been extremely nice to us.

The United Nations itself came as something of a surprise. Expecting to find a dull and rather dead place, on the contrary it resembled a bee-hive, alive with the drone of myriads of scurrying people chatting excitedly in various tongues. At lunch Colin Crowe and George Bush spoke only to each other and at great pace, exchanging anecdotes and news items with much eagerness. Neither was in the least interested in talking to the women or Rowley. Barbara Bush was cheerful, warm and nice, and at once one knew her to be a genuine person. The United Nations, however, seemed to be a world of its own, an amusing and gregarious club. Colin Crowe remarked as we left that he had to deal with all the countries in the world, whereas Rowley had only one. But Rowley had the last word on the subject when he said in the car: 'The United Nations strikes one as being like an airport terminal, but where nothing ever lands or takes off!'

That evening, as often in America, spouses were separated. The husbands go to one dinner, their wives to another, and all in full evening dress. This particular event was called 'The Ends of the Earth Dinner' and was reputed to have been founded by Rudyard Kipling. Possibly Rowley's dinner was more useful than mine because towards the end of the evening I was asked what occupation my husband followed and, in any case, I had been taken for a Bostonian. The evening had been arranged by the New York Consul. His wife, an American, was in a state of embarrassment for, she explained, when told to come in full evening dress, she told the organizer that as she did not possess any jewellery. She would borrow some from the Queen. Her remark was taken seriously by the organizer and so the distressed Consul's wife, thinking that it would get back to the Queen, asked me to send her abject apologies.

We hurried back to Washington early the next morning in order to attend Secretary Connally's Brunch Party. This Rowley felt had to be attended at all costs, because word had reached him that the Texan was incensed over a speech that Rowley had made some weeks earlier to the bankers in New York. Rowley had spoken the truth, which is seldom popular, and less so with politicians. The European and Wall Street bankers had been impressed and complimentary but Connally, it appeared, was not, although what part of the speech he had taken exception to was not known. I asked a White House advisor how Rowley should tackle Connally over this difficulty and he was kind enough to give me a useful hint. 'It is never profitable,' he asserted, 'to apologise to a Texan, or to humble oneself. They like a fight, and enjoy crossing swords, so get the better of them and they will admire you.' He continued: 'Be tough. They despise any signs of weakness.' His advice proved to be invaluable.

On arrival at the Connally's hotel apartment we found it full of other Texans, and were greeted warmly by a delightful Nellie Connally and frostily by our host. Taking to heart the good advice we had been given, Rowley managed to think up something which might be appreciated without appearing to appease. In a three-cornered conversation Connally announced that Rowley was becoming 'meaner and meaner.' 'Keener and keener, is what he really means,' Rowley butted in, and went on to say: 'I have been dealing with money all my life and have never found a coin that did not ring true unless it had two sides.' Connally threw back his head with a loud laugh, and all was then warmth and friendship. He embraced me as we left. So it seemed that all was forgiven.

Christmas at the Embassy is no wit less busy than in other times or places, even if one is spared stuffing the turkey and stirring the pudding. Besides, a Christmas party was expected to be held by the Ambassador's wife for the Embassy children. I managed to limit the number by stipulating that their ages must not be less than three or more than seven, which reduced the number to seventy-five, and that seemed to me quite large enough. As it was, seventy-five presents had to be purchased from our personal pocket and wrapped in Christmas paper. Seventy-five balloons to be blown up, and the most jovial and rotund guard persuaded to dress up as Father Christmas. Then a puppet show for entertainment, the ballroom decorated and a large tea prepared.

The butler informed me, to my surprise, that we would not need any tables, nor covers or napkins. And, against my better judgement, I gave in. 'We have always pinned sheets onto the dining-room floor and given the children paper mugs and plates. They help themselves to food from a side-table and then squat on the floor.' This arrangement seemed extraordinary to me, resembling more of a picnic than a party, and I wondered uneasily what the nannies might think, little party dresses all crushed and creased on the floor. In the event I need not have worried, for no nannies appeared, nor mothers either. The children were simply dumped at the door, to be cared for by Torie and myself. Eating on the floor was completely to their taste, and presented a friendly informality. The butler looked rather smug, and I had to concede that he had been entirely right. This party was a far cry from those I had given in London when the parties had, in truth, possibly been more for the nannies who admired or criticised each others' charges, as they sat sedately at tables, all carefully dressed in their best clothes.

Our two young grandchildren, Ashley and Tamara, both within the prescribed age, were spending Christmas with us, and stood at the top of the grand staircase in some bewilderment as the hordes of little strangers poured in. Apart from members of our own family, the Governor of the Bank of England and the Chancellor of the Exchequer were also staying at the Embassy, for a Group of Ten meeting was taking place. Neither had come with their wives, being, as it was, so close to Christmas.

That day brought home the fact that an Ambassadress's job encompassed more than trying to be a gracious hostess and running a stately Residence. A few minutes before the children were due to arrive, and still busy tying the last bunch of balloons to the walls, the butler interrupted my activities to tell me to hasten to the front hall as the Governor of the Bank of England had just returned looking awful. I hurried down the staircase to find Leslie O'Brien as grey as granite and in a state of collapse. He was trembling like an aspen leaf and felt as cold as ice. Immediately I realised that he was feverish and must be put to bed at once and the doctor sent for. From that time on it took a super-human effort to keep abreast, indeed a step ahead, of seventy-five noisy children and a very sick man.

While I was quietly watching the puppet show with the children, the butler once again glided up to tell me that I was needed. Upstairs I found an almost insensible Governor, and a grave-looking doctor who informed me that his patient was suffering from a sudden attack of erysipelas. Leslie's temperature had reached a hundred and four and the seat of his infection was centred on his upper leg. The doctor solemnly informed me that it was absolutely essential for hot compresses to be applied to his leg every three hours to check the infection from reaching his heart. After this instruction he left, saying that he would do his best to engage a day and night nurse. But there was no time to be wasted. Quickly marshalling a kettle, basin, towels, rubber gloves and other requirements, I performed the first treatment in front of the butler and one of the footmen. I stripped poor Leslie of his pyjamas thinking, as I did so, of the formality of our first meeting when Rowley had been the new Governor and Leslie the Chief Cashier of the Bank of England. I asked the butler and footman to watch how the compresses were applied so that the pantry staff could take it in turns on a rota system throughout the night, or until a night nurse arrived.

The compresses, I was told, had to be left on for twenty minutes. Having laid the first one on, and removing my rubber gloves and apron, I rushed downstairs and found on reaching the ballroom a host of squalling children needing comfort, and beyond even the cheerful care of young Torie. Somehow, as children do, they had sensed that something was wrong, without understanding why, and this made them restless. The puppet show was over and by this time it was necessary to shepherd some of them to the cloakrooms. So Torie and I, taking half a dozen children at a time, helped them to the lavatories. Between the shuttle service the Governor's compresses needed removing. But before I could reach his bedroom the butler sidled up once again. This time he was to inform me, to my horror, that as the disease that the Governor was suffering from was infectious, neither he nor his footmen could possibly be expected to endanger themselves, nor had they any intention of touching the Governor or performing any treatment. I was aghast, and then realised that in the last resort it was to the boss or his wife that these responsibilities always lay. It was for them to take whatever risk there might be.

Up and down the stairs I went, comforting infants and ministering to Leslie. On one trip along the upstairs passage I passed our son Vivian who had just returned from his studies. He looked extremely surprised to see me tripping along in an apron and holding a steaming basin and towels. 'I thought you were holding a children's party,' he said. 'The Governor's got erysipelas,' I gasped breathlessly. Vivian misheard and gave me a horrified look, which for years afterwards caused us much merriment. Poor Leslie! In my fear of the illness taking a terrible turn I placed far-too-hot towels on his leg. So ill, he could not remonstrate. Scalding they must have been, but they did the trick.

At six-thirty Rowley returned to the Embassy, and it took him a little while to comprehend the situation. 'But I thought you were holding a children's party! And now you are telling me that you are nursing... who did you say?' I slowly and quietly explained what had occurred and that throughout the night he, as well as I, would have to take it in turns to administer the compresses. Rowley was both taken aback and concerned.

The doctor informed me before he left that he knew of someone who had died from the disease in the White House, but I would have felt better had he left me in ignorance. This news did however give further urgency to the situation. Finally, at 11.30 pm the night nurse arrived, a large comfortable black woman. From then on, day and night, nurses alternated, as did their colour. Leslie told me later that he found that the black ones were the better nurses. He also said that he never thought he would ever see the day when I would be doing such things to him.

The week before Christmas was chosen for a top-level meeting between President Nixon and Prime Minister Heath in Bermuda. Rowley left with the Chancellor while the Governor still languished in bed.

Walter Annenberg, one of the most popular ambassadors to Britain, arrived to spend the night at the Embassy before continuing on to Bermuda. With Torie and me as company, we spent a most entertaining evening, for Walter's colourful means of expression and original choice of words were spellbinding. He was in great form and kept us continually laughing. One of his favourite remarks 'completely boresome.' Like all very wealthy men, he had his own rather quaint idea of extravagance. He noticed that Torie was extinguishing her cigarettes when only half-smoked and told her that it was wasteful. Torie replied that it did not matter as they were the Embassy's. This shocked Walter even more. 'Then, my dear, you should think of posterity.' Walter then told us of an eminent english visitor to Lyndon Johnson's ranch in Texas earlier that year and remarked, 'That man Johnson would entertain a rattlesnake for want of company.' He then related to us how, when he first met Lord George Brown at a party, George had truculently told him: 'You have been here six months and have not yet done me the courtesy of inviting me to dinner.' This statement astonished Walter, who thought the English were a very polite people, and embarrassed those other members of the Labour Party who were present.

The day after Christmas Madame Mwila of Zambia called on a Courtesy visit. She told me that her numerous offspring found it very difficult to make themselves understood in American schools although they spoke perfect english.

The New Year began with another reception for newcomers — two hundred and fifty since our last party in July. On 10th January we celebrated our thirtieth wedding anniversary by holding a dinner-dance for old and new friends who came from far and wide. It was a moving occasion for us, for friends whom we had first made when we lived in America as far back as 1947 made an effort to be with us. Rowley made a touching speech, mentioning that our first meeting had taken place in a London taxi, and a toast was proposed by Jack Morgan (J P Morgan II) who was our neighbour in Long Island twenty-five years before. It was a happy climax to end our first year at the Embassy.

20

CAESARS TO ASTRONAUTS

In the middle of January 1972 we headed out west for California and Nevada. It is safe to use the word 'out' when going west from the eastern seaboard of America, but not if one is going to America from England. The word 'over' is preferred; the reason, one can only guess, may have something to do with colonial times. At any rate the word 'out' gives offence.

Walter Annenberg kindly arranged for us to dine with the Governor of California, Ronald Reagan and his wife Nancy, in Sacramento. This involved a two-hour drive both ways over rather uninteresting country, of which the only landmark resting in my memory is that of a cafe proclaiming 'Topless Bar' in lights, while placed in a singularly sparse bit of country.

The Governor's mansion was a temporary one, an ordinary comfortable home making no claim whatever to ostentation. The evening, too, was unpretentious. We were given an excellent dinner by our kind and hospitable hosts and with no other guests but the Annenbergs and our Consul-General for San Francisco. Ronald Reagan I did not find easy to talk to. Well-mannered and attractive, he was a commanding figure and treated with evident respect by Walter. The talk centred on the coming Presidential election. This was not unusual, for election talk in America starts quite two years before the actual day. Reagan remarked that if Teddy Kennedy should run he would see to it that slogans all over America would ask the simple question, accompanied by the face of Kennedy,

'Who will cross this bridge into the future with me?' This would have been a devastating reminder of Chappaquiddick. Mrs Reagan seemed gentle and quiet, looked very beautiful and, like her husband, effected an informal charm.

Our visit to Los Angeles was unremarkable, and by no means as interesting as the one we had made ten years before, when film studios and film stars had been on our itinerary. This time it was the Consul-General and the customary receptions, mainly for business people, for Los Angeles is an enormous and industrial city. From there we made the short flight to Las Vegas.

Our intention to visit Las Vegas caused surprise from some of our American friends and not a little comment although, curiously, our impending visit was never mentioned in the press. 'You do not mean that you are really going to Las Vegas? How awful!' an elderly political columnist said. 'What for?' he continued. 'It is a dreadful place.' And he seemed embarrassed that such a spot should exist in his country and that we should be so tactless as to wish to visit it. However, one sophisticated young man described it to me as 'the heart and real culture of America,' and with a wry smile he added: 'Everything else is imported from other lands.' 'That Mecca of materialism,' another person said. All these remarks did nothing to lessen our curiosity.

As our aeroplane came in to land in Las Vegas we noticed from the windows a gaudy cluster of coloured lights in an inky blackness, like a huge, sparkling jewel on a black velvet dress. As our plane flew lower, we noticed a number of police cars with their roof lights flashing, parked close to the runway, and assumed that it had something to do with the hijacking that had taken place that very morning, and which had been widely reported. However we were mistaken. For instead, to our astonishment, they were waiting for us.

Led by the Chief of Police, we stepped into a large black limousine, with three police cars leading the way and outriders by our side. With lights flashing and sirens screaming we made

261

our entrance into Las Vegas.

Our stay was a very short one, to last only one night, but it proved to be one of the most memorable nights we ever spent. We were put up at Caesar's Palace, where we were given the largest suite in the hotel. Cavernous, the sitting-room could easily have contained two-hundred people. Violent, the colour scheme was a shock: a mixture of orange, puce and imperial purple, each fighting for supremacy and none succeeding. On various tables stood huge baskets of flowers and fruit. Two bedrooms on either side presented a choice. One decorated purely in scarlet boasted a vast bed, the other in muted tones had twin beds. Two bathrooms and a cloakroom completed our accommodation. Our son's lodging was almost as magnificent but, tantalisingly, this overwhelming luxury was barely used, for there was no time to sleep.

We had had no warning of, or programme for the evening we were to spend. We had, in fact, no other plan than to stay in the hotel, whose lobby, like all the others, was full of gambling machines and gamblers. It was only when we were changing for dinner that a message from Rowley's secretary informed us that the Manager and his wife would call for us at eight thirty. This we found wholly mystifying. The manager and his wife stayed in our suite making desultory conversation over some drinks while constantly looking at their watches. After half an hour, to our relief, they mentioned something about dinner and insisted on escorting us, our son, and Rowley's secretary to a private elevator in which we soared to the top floor. None of us had the remotest idea where we were heading and supposed it to be towards one of the hotel dining-rooms. Instead, however, we found ourselves alighting in a marble hall, which proved to be the entrance to the hotel owner's penthouse. The owner, a spare, short, middle-aged man, welcomed us warmly, and introduced us to his fiancée, a pretty young girl, whose hair was elaborately dressed as Cleopatra in the film of that name. And as we were walking towards his drawing-room, I glimpsed through an open door an enormous bed, completely upholstered in silver fox, bed-back and cover. In the drawing-room a man quietly and steadily played a piano. A bar, big enough for a saloon, lined one wall, and a table in the middle was laden with shrimps and canapés. We were served by busty girls dressed as Roman centurions in mini-tunics.

Our host was clearly very proud of his accommodation and asked if we would like to be shown round, which invitation I accepted with alacrity, as I wanted to take another look at the bedroom to prove that my eyes had not deceived me. I was told with pride by his fiancée that sixty skins had gone into its making. Enjoying the bizarre, I felt that the evening was full of promise. Outside the apartment the roof garden sported a private sixty-foot swimming pool. After a while other guests arrived. A movie producer and his girl-friend, the owner of a local newspaper and his lady, while hotel personnel stood unobtrusively on one side, alert for a question or a command.

Mr Perleman, our host, was both charming and forthcoming. He told me that he owned hotels and businesses in Las Vegas and Miami and was, clearly, an extremely successful man. He had started life with nothing and lived in a slum, being of poor immigrant parents. But, he said, he had never felt poor as there were always others poorer than himself. He had scrimped and saved and done odd jobs until he had earned enough money to buy himself a hot-dog stand, whence he never looked back.

It was the classic American success story, and possibly because of it, Mr Perleman was unquestionably right-wing. Not so his publishing friend, who had inherited his business. Their dialogue was interesting. 'There are too many poor,' declared the publisher, 'and we must share and give them all we can in welfare.' 'Certainly not,' replied Mr Perleman, repeating that he never considered himself poor, even as a slum child, and that it had never occurred to him that there were both rich and poor until he moved out of the slums and started to mix with rich people. Moreover, he informed us all, he had enjoyed a perfectly happy childhood. These remarks made me realise that whether one felt rich or poor depended entirely on whom one was with. The publisher shook his head vigorously. He held very different views. He had been spared the struggle from the lower rungs of the ladder but he had increased the fortune that had been left to him by buying Las Vegas real estate. He drove around with pride in a white Rolls-Royce and did not see anything contradictory in that.

'It is a great honour to have the British Ambassador in Las Vegas,' we were told frequently, and were then informed that the Russian Ambassador had been twice, and that he had gone down very well, but they found his wife formidable. Anatoliy Dobrynin looked a little sheepish when next we saw him and told him where we had been.

It was not until sixteen years later that I was to hear again the clatter of one-arm bandits in a hotel lobby, and that was in Moscow at the Cosmos Hotel.

At about ten-thirty Mr Perleman took us all down to the Bacchanal. This was the largest of the many restaurants in the hotel. We passed the Noshareum and then a door marked Caesars which puzzled until we passed one called Cleopatras. Both gave a glimpse of marble and imperial purple within.

At the Bacchanal we were shown to a large square table, the centre of which was a mass of flowers, and on one side was a line of telephones manned by some sober-suited gentlemen who, judging by the comments made, were monitoring the gamblers, possibly in case a big coup might be in the making. I was placed between Mr Perleman and the publisher who continued their argument. Astonishingly, Mr Perleman began to quote Plato. He was, he told me, an ardent admirer of the Greek philosopher. I wondered if maybe he had only recently had the time or the inclination to study the classics. At any rate, he managed to cap anything that the publisher had to say by besting him with an apt quotation from Plato, much to the latter's bewilderment. The talk contrasted wonderfully with the scene as we were waited on by various oriental beauties dressed in scraps of wispy chiffon and assisted by more mini-skirted centurions.

In between many delicious courses, artistes were brought to our table to entertain us. These artistes were well-known stars who were performing in the hotel cabaret for vast fees. Before dining we were asked if we would prefer to see a Star Show or a Spectacle, and we opted for the Spectacle, not realising that Caesar's Palace only liked to specialise in Star Shows. Nevertheless, after a short consultation with his officials, Mr Perleman waved his magic wand, and after dinner we all set off in the publisher's white Rolls-Royce plus other grand and vast automobiles, for the Stardust Hotel which, judging by the deference shown to Mr Perleman, we concluded also belonged to him. The Spectacle proved to be an even more lavish version of the Paris Lido brought over specially from France.

Later we were taken further into the city where the neon lights shone even brighter, and certainly gave credence to Las Vegas' boast of turning night into shining day. Finally, at three o'clock in the morning, we returned to Caesar's Palace where, as in all the Las Vegas hotels, the front lobbies, full of all kinds of gambling tables, were still loud with the noise of one-arm bandits, and thronged with eager punters. We felt that we had to have a go, but it was far more fascinating to watch these hordes of earnest people trying to make their fortunes, some with suitcases of coins by their sides, and most likely, about to lose their savings.

So late, sleep was not easy to come by, so rising again at eight o'clock, and curious to see the hotel lobby at that hour, I discovered no difference from a few hours earlier. The place was still full of people, and some, I was told, had been up all night. If they achieved a win on the machines, they still continued until their pockets were empty. There were never any clocks in the gambling rooms, in order not to remind anyone of the time.

As we flew back to Washington, sleepless and weary, we all

agreed that the visit had been more worthwhile than anything we had anticipated. It was certainly something different to anything we had ever seen. We wondered also how much the hotel had cost us, but we were never to find out, for unknowingly, we had been the guests of Las Vegas, and very spoiled ones at that.

We were welcomed back to the Embassy in the customary fashion, only this time with a slight difference. Warnings had been received from the Security Police that fifty Irishmen had boarded the Metroliner express from New York, with the intention of demonstrating outside the Embassy. Their non-arrival sparked the suspicion that, after all, some wayside bar had luckily proved to be a greater attraction. Or perhaps they were hatching a different plot? More likely it was a hoax. We never found out.

The following day I hosted a party to launch Jaeger's new Spring Collection. It was very well attended and as Jaeger naturally wished for the maximum publicity the women's page writers arrived in force. I forlornly hoped that by this time they would lay off me, but that was too much to hope for. 'This is the first time for a year that Lady Cromer has been seen in public, not since her blooper about Vietnam, she has been living in monastic splendour behind the Embassy walls.' One could not win.

It was by then more than a year since we had arrived, and looking back through the months, it seemed a very full one, and by no means uninteresting. Crime in Washington seemed to be getting worse. The Brazilian Ambassador, our next-door neighbour had been mugged while walking in his own small garden after dark. He had been on his way home from his Chancery close by.

We were cheered to hear that Mrs Longworth said how much she had enjoyed our Anniversary Party, and that it had been like the good old days. We touchingly received a bottle of 1942 Bordeaux, the year of our wedding. Our financial situation had, however, worsened. We made the unpleasant discovery that the Foreign Office expects its ambassadors to spend half of their annual gross personal salary on entertainment to compensate for their and their family's upkeep. The job was fast becoming an unendurable drain on our pockets. It was so unlike working for the Treasury, when we managed to actually return home with a saving. One could not help wondering why the British government did not purchase a smaller and more economic building as an Embassy which, surely, would have been more appropriate to our position in the present world. After all, when Lutyens designed the edifice it had, as Britain's Embassy, also represented a quarter of the earth's landed surface.

Mrs Nicholas Longworth was the most highly regarded grande dame in Washington. Not a great hostess by any means, but possessing a high intelligence and a caustic and penetrating wit. The daughter of the 'Great Teddy' Theodore Roosevelt and widow of a Speaker of the House of Representatives, she had, at various times, finished off a promising career with a simple remark, such as that when she declared that Thomas Dewey 'looked like the little man on top of the wedding cake.' He was running as the Republican Presidential candidate.

Henry Kissinger was at that time portrayed in the press as a womanising swinger. He mentioned to Rowley that the girls whom he had occasionally taken out before he came to Washington must be wondering what they had missed when they read the newspapers.

The London Symphony Orchestra had been engaged to hold a concert at the Kennedy Center that month. The conductor was to be André Previn, and Rowley received a message from the Prime Minister to the effect that he would be glad if the Embassy would extend him hospitality. Ted Heath had, evidently, conducted the LSO himself on one occasion the previous year. Without an inkling of the vexation it was going to cause we despatched with pleasure the invita-

267

tions to Mr Previn, the orchestra manager and the leading instrumentalist to a dinner in their honour. Their reply, however, was not quite what we expected. It was to the disappointing and rather surprising effect that Mr Previn and the manager, being democratic, did not like to be separated from the other members of the orchestra. Either we must invite all one hundred and thirty members or none at all.

Feeling less than hospitable, we nevertheless felt obliged to entertain them, and the only possible solution seemed to be a reception for the entire orchestra in the large round room in the Chancery, after which we hoped that the conductor and manager might like to attend a small dinner in the Residence with some leading members of Congress. This arrangement was, we understood, agreed to, providing one or two leading musicians could be included, and to this we concurred. As time was getting short we asked the other guests who were known to be musical and were eager to meet Previn. But a day later another message arrived, saying that, after all, Mr Previn would be unable to dine, nor could he attend the reception. By this time, we were ardently wishing that we had never started this particular hospitality effort for which, in any case, the funds would come out of our badly-stretched pockets.

Quite by chance, at a luncheon I attended the next day, I discovered that Mrs Yehudi Menuhin was also a guest. I took the opportunity to pour out our woes regarding the LSO and she was most sympathetic, comfortingly telling me that it was not worth worrying about. The next day another communication arrived from the leader of the orchestra saying that, after all, Mr Previn would attend the reception but not the dinner, so the dinner was cancelled.

At the reception the wife of the orchestra's manager buttonholed Rowley and lectured him on the importance of democracy, and how necessary it was in an orchestra. Having earlier received a programme of the concert, Rowley spotted that no member of the orchestra had been named other than the conductor, so he was able to ask her if she thought that was democratic. Her answer was bewildering. 'The omission,' she explained, 'was entirely due to a photograph of the Queen that had to be printed.' As there was no picture of the Queen in the programme Rowley was mystified.

André Previn himself dispensed great charm, and seemed to be oblivious of all the inconvenience he had caused. He told me that he was a great friend of Ted Heath's and that he would send me a recording of Ted conducting the LSO which, however, never arrived.

At the beginning of February 1972 in Londonderry, a Civil Rights march took place, although illegal (marches at the time had been banned by the Stormont government at the behest of the Catholics). The paratroopers intervened. They were accused, in the resulting mêlée, of killing sixteen civilians and wounding some others. The reaction to this incident was an even greater wave of anti-British feeling than usual amongst those of Irish descent in the United States. That same week the Scots Guards band were due to hold a concert at the Kennedy Center. The English Speaking Union decided to use the occasion as an evening out for their members, and had booked almost half the concert hall. They invited the Canadian, Australian and New Zealand Ambassadors. The chairman of the ESU had been lent the President's box and Rowley was invited to take the salute.

Security arrangements for the evening were even tighter than usual. After dining with the committee of the ESU we were given a police escort and outriders, who rushed us to the Kennedy Center by means of the basement, passing as we went a number of pickets waving banners marked IRA. We were then escorted by very serious-looking armed guards to the front of the President's box.

The concert hall was packed. As the lights began to dim, two men stood up in the gallery waving the flags of Eire and shouting slogans. One, with a raincoat over his arm, caused further consternation, for in one interminable second we all wondered if it concealed a gun. Then, after a silent pause, the audience of more than two-thousand five-hundred shouted in unison: 'Boo,' and continued to shout 'Boo' until the two men, struggling, were forcibly evicted, the result of which caused a loud burst of clapping which deafened our ears and cheered our hearts.

The lights, which had been turned up, dimmed again, only to return to their full brilliance as a voice asked everyone to please disperse and clear the hall due to a bomb threat. All who were in our box repaired to the President's ante-room, including one of the President's Counsellors who was hosting the box, and who busied himself distributing champagne. Ironically his name was Peter Flanigan. His wife, Brigid, was also of Irish ancestry. A journalist, who was with us, remarked jokingly that 'surely the White House could have sent an Ehrlichman or a Haldeman (known as the Berlin Wall) instead of an Irishman. However both Peter and his wife were pro-English and close friends of ours.

The enormous Kennedy Center lobby was worth seeing, and from a balcony near the President's box we could observe an extraordinary sight. All two-thousand five-hundred people stood shoulder to shoulder like a field of ripe corn. A pin could not have been pushed between them. Like statues they stoically stood, unruffled, immobile and making no sound. It was uncanny and impressive. In the meantime the security dogs took twenty minutes to sniff out the auditorium, and fortunately found nothing.

The concert eventually began, and would have been most enjoyable if, when the brass symbols met with a crash, or the big drum was beaten, I had not nervously jumped, looking to see if Rowley was still sitting upright. During the interval Rowley, out of politeness, asked the Canadian Ambassador, who was senior to him, if he would not mind if he (Rowley) took the salute at the finish of the performance. 'My dear colleague,' the Canadian Ambassador replied, 'I would not get up there on that stage in front of all these people in these circumstances for anything in the world.' But Rowley, however, had no choice, and for his pains received an ovation from this extraordinary audience.

An englishman, Edward Russell, telephoned the Irish Ambassador to protest. He told him that 'the Irish are demonstrating and threatening a bomb, and we have been kicked out of the concert hall.' The Ambassador, who had been dragged from the dinner table, replied that he was sure that they were American citizens who were doing it. 'No doubt they are,' Russell replied, 'but I think you should know that two-thousand Americans are mad at the Irish.' The Ambassador closed the conversation by saying that he would send his Information Officer down to investigate. The audience, we discovered, were mainly of Scottish descent, and they had absolutely no intention of being intimidated by anyone or anything, certainly not the Irish. At an earlier performance in New York after an Irishman had stood up and shouted something rude, two burly Americans of Scottish descent, sitting in the row in front, turned round abruptly and with two swift blows knocked his front teeth out.

The Today Programme, which is televised at 7.30 am, regarded as peak hour on American television, asked Rowley to appear, and he accepted, for he thought that it might present an opportunity to explain the dilemma of Northern Ireland. To try and explain that Ulster is an integral part of the UK, much as Alaska or Hawaii is to America. It was not an easy task, but he did the best he could. Nevertheless, Americans of all shades of opinion kept describing our troubles in Northern Ireland as our Vietnam. I was a bit nervous over Rowley's television appearance as it came just after the British Embassy in Dublin had been burned down. However, the only visible consequence was a demonstration organised outside the Embassy the next day on behalf of the IRA. To our surprise, half of the protesters were black. It was our first encounter with 'rent a mob.'

A rumour reached the Embassy that a prominent article

271

compiled by a female Washington writer in harness with an english journalist was being written to 'put down the Cromers.' The American writer had been supplying erroneous information which the Englishman, taught to confirm his facts, sought to verify. He called up the Information Department at the Embassy to ask if it were true that the Cromers had been deficient in their entertaining, as he had been told they had barely done any at all. Luckily my social secretary had kept a daily tally of exactly how many people had enjoyed our hospitality and in what manner. It proved that our entertaining was considerably more extensive than that provided by the Freemans, which came as no surprise to us, having received that impression from those domestics that had served us both. This news was received with disappointment and, fortunately, put an end to any such article.

One of my great-uncles had been a noted bibliophile, Sir Leicester Harmsworth. He had quietly amassed a book collection of great distinction which, after his death, had taken many years to disperse. The famous, indeed probably the only Shakespearean library in the world is the Folger. It is one of the treasures of Washington, like the National Gallery, and at one time the Folger had purchased a great number of my uncle's rare books. It was for that reason that the Board of the Folger invited me to become chairman of the First Council of Friends. I decided, however, that it was more practicable to be a working member of the Council, and subsequently much enjoyed many a working lunch and being involved with this fine Institution; and, moreover, bringing it into contact for the first time with the British Embassy, eventually leaving a legacy of interest to our successors. Sir Peter Ramsbotham, Rowley's successor as Ambassador, even went to the length of presenting the funds raised for his leaving present to the Folger to finance a special Ramsbotham lecture. Later Lady (Oliver) Wright was to act on the stage of the Shakespearean theatre (a perfect replica of the Globe) — which was an integral part of the Folger. No mention of my work or involvement at the

Folger ever entered the columns of any newspaper.

By March Courtesy Calls from new ambassadresses were becoming more frequent as the turnover became greater. Also new embassies were being created for new countries. The Indonesian Ambassadress called one morning and proudly declared to me her husband, a doctor of medicine by profession, had been chosen for the most senior job, over and above the heads of his three brothers, who were professional diplomats, and were at that time serving as ambassadors in Poland, Holland and Switzerland. The reason for the good doctor's eminence, she imparted, was simply that he was a trusted friend of the President.

John and Nellie Connally gave a dinner at their apartment in the Sheraton Park Hotel to which we were bidden. John was in excellent form, and very much pleased with a speech that he had given the day before in which he had described himself as 'the bully boy of the manicured playing fields of International Finance.' The Vice President, Spiro Agnew and his wife, were also present at the dinner, and John gave all his guests a bottle of prohibition whisky labelled 'Medicinal Spirits Only. To be taken for reasons of health.' After dinner we watched the President on television who talked about 'bussing,' then a very hot topic. Children were being taken many miles across the city for no other reason than to keep a racial balance. The President was practical and sensible. And the rest of the company, which included the Chief Justice of the Supreme Court, Warren Burger, all agreed on the stupidities of 'bussing.'

The Vice President's apartment was immediately below that of the Secretary of the Treasury. It seemed odd that such a rich country could not extend better dwellings to its chief officials. The Vice President was eventually given a former Admiral's house within a guarded complex, which must have been a great improvement; while Rowley and I, in our turn, moved into the vacated Vice President's flat when we left the Embassy Residence due to decoration. We then discovered

273

that all Spiro Agnew's windows were made of bullet-proof glass.

That April in 1972, we were still attending dinner parties in our honour to 'welcome us back' — this, one year and two months after our arrival. Maybe, we wondered, with some misgivings, these welcoming parties would even overlap those farewell parties, when the time came. That month the International Midwives were meeting in the US and a British delegation of one hundred and fifty had, clearly, to be entertained at a reception at the Embassy. It was expected of us.

At the International Group lunch that month, Mrs Sally Reston, wife of Scottie Reston, the well-known columnist, decided to show her slides from photographs taken on a recent trip to China. One of the features was a close-up of a large notice outside the Shanghai Bund Club. Left untouched, it proclaimed in english, 'No dogs or Chinese admitted.' Embarrassed in front of the Russian Ambassadress I murmured to her that in England dogs always came first. She remained impassive, if slightly baffled.

Senator Fulbright dined and seemed to be still wholly engrossed with Vietnam. The subject possessed his mind, and his opinions appeared to coincide with those of the Russians, and not with my own view of American long-term interests. At that time even Paul Volcker (then Under-Secretary for Monetary Affairs and subsequently Chairman of the Federal Reserve) thought that revolution was not unlikely in the United States, and that it should be kept at bay by welfare and yet more welfare. He told me at a dinner party that the dollar had not been devalued but gold revalued, and I asked him who he thought he was kidding, even if, on the surface, it did make devaluation sound more respectable. After all this was old and common ground to us. In the years to come Paul Volcker came to play a very different tune. I never found that Americans minded one talking directly or voicing opinions openly in private conversation. Plain talk was, at least, honest talk.

That spring we flew to Texas — to Houston in particular, and stayed in a suite at the Warwick Hotel. The walls of the drawing-room were clothed in priceless carved panelling brought over from France. It had originally decorated a room in the Palace of Versailles, according to a plaque, the date 1685. Could we really be sitting within four walls of wood which might have enclosed the Sun King and yet be in Texas? The idea was preposterous. The history of how this priceless panelling had travelled so far through time and territory was not revealed, but that the panelling was genuine was beyond doubt. The other curiosity in the hotel was on the menu: Scampi Méditerrané, the recipe for which, the menu disclosed, was brought back by an Earl of Warwick from the Crusades. This was somewhat harder to swallow than the dish itself.

Houston lies near the coast of Texas, and would certainly have been considered a hardship post before the advent of air-conditioning. Some said that it was air-conditioning that turned Houston into a city. It was fairly warm during our visit, hovering around seventy-five fahrenheit but, we were told, that was much cooler than usual. The climate and weather, however, seemed superfluous, for we only inhaled fresh air for a moment or two between car and front-door during our entire stay. There was, it is true, a park outside our hotel, but a park without paths and no sign of people. The windows of every building remained shut, and we were never beyond the vibration of an air-conditioning plant. The country is flat, the horizons huge and the sky a magnificent dome. We were kept busy with the customary civic and English Speaking Union events. The Consul-General's reception surprised me. Expecting to meet tall Texans, the guests instead seemed of uniform shortness, accounted-for perhaps by finding that almost all of the people were birds of passage and few permanent residents. One of them did admit that he had been conceived in Texas, but then confessed that he had been born in Liverpool.

275

The highlight of our stay was undoubtedly a visit to NASA and to the home of an astronaut. We were kindly given lunch by Colonel Dave Scott and his wife. Colonel Scott was the person who drove the Moon Buggy across the lunar landscape. All the other guests were either astronauts or scientists and by the end of lunch we knew a great deal more than we did at the beginning. The senior scientist, a genius, who looked no older than eighteen, dropped gems of information which were certainly new to us then. The Moon, he said, was older than the Earth, and is warm inside, and not boiling like our own planet. Furthermore the warmth is constant and quite the opposite to its surface, which varies 300°F daily. He also stated that the moon rocks are much richer in minerals than those of the Earth, and when powdered and mixed with those of the soil of the Earth, the growth of plants becomes very much faster. We also learned that it was discovered that the human is extraordinarily adaptable to almost any condition.

I wondered why those who reached the Moon had not been given a small piece of Moon rock, but none of them, when asked, seemed to think that it was in any way his due. More modest people would have been hard to find, each was so normal and nice. And yet there did seem to be an undefinable difference between them and us, an apartness, distant and detached. Without arrogance of any sort; and yet one felt humble in their presence. The scientists came from a different mould, eager and ready to talk, to answer and to enthuse. They were very much of this world. Colonel Scott told us that his seven year-old son was quite uninterested in astronauts or space travel, and was apt to regard it all as a great bore. His father disappeared to his office as far as he knew, and all the child was interested in was eventually becoming a cowboy.

We were prevented from driving to Dallas from Houston by the police. There might be bandits or kidnappers lying in wait, so they said. How wild was Texas, we wondered? It would have been interesting to see something of the countryside. Maybe the authorities were being over-cautious. Without causing a bother it was best, we decided, to go quietly by aeroplane.

We preferred Dallas. The wide horizons remained as flat, but it seemed a smaller, if taller city. The people younger, politer and a shade more sophisticated. In Houston, those we had met appeared to be a little critical that we had chosen to stay but three days, whereas in Dallas they seemed to think that three days were quite enough. There is, nevertheless, the usual competitive feeling between the two cities that one finds so often around the world. Montreal and Toronto, Leeds and Newcastle, to name a few.

Mayor Wes Wise of Dallas gave me the Key to the City instead of Rowley. 'It is,' he said, 'to demonstrate that the City of Dallas really appreciates women.' One dinner given by a rich and prominent couple was held in their spacious bungalow. This home, although comfortable, was quite unadorned, other than a by a quantity of famous French Impressionist paintings hanging from the walls, and piles of pre-Columbian art lying in dusty heaps in corners. The paintings gazed at each other in rooms almost bare, like in a museum.

While driving through Dallas we looked at the location of Kennedy's assassination, and were astonished to find that the building which housed the sniper was situated in such an obvious and unusually commanding position: one which proclaimed its strategic importance, giving the gunman plenty of time to aim as the Presidential motorcade came towards him, and minutes, not moments, to get away. What also seemed strange was the smallness of the city, which would have made it easy for the police to survey, one would have thought. But perhaps it was deemed unthinkable in the general euphoria of his visit for such an atrocity to take place.

Our driver was of the opinion that only one person did the shooting and that he was hired. It was, he thought, a carefully-planned affair. The memorial erected in memory of that fearful day seemed somewhat peculiar. A partially enclosed square wall, a foot or so above the ground, roofless and with nothing inside.

21

PAINTING, POETRY AND PLAYERS

May was a particularly crowded month in Washington: interminable Sunday lunches; ESU events; a British Chamber of Commerce luncheon in New York and a special ballet première; Commonwealth Wives Tea at the Embassy; the Goodwill Industries Tour (another marathon like the one for the Incurables); a large Red Cross meeting plus the usual dinners and lunches. The Residence was also a hotel for passing British officials of one kind or another, whom we were always glad to see as they brought news from home. Besides, it was enjoyable to talk and let off steam with one's own countrymen.

One of the unexpected pleasures of being wife of an Ambassador to the US was the arrival of inscribed books from authors, both American and English. They would appear at the average rate of one a month. Some of the authors would be known to me and others not at all.

We held a lunch party for the retiring head of MI6 and the newly appointed head of the FBI, Patrick Gray. The latter struck us as a sensible and agreeable person, but as an appointee of Nixon's his confirmation in the Senate was in doubt. He told me that, on taking up his new job, he was dismayed to learn that drug-taking was on the increase and had become a widespread problem. He was greatly concerned because a friend of his, an American general who had been taken prisoner many years previously in Korea had, before his release, been told by his Chinese psychiatric interrogators, that it was intended to destroy an entire generation of young Americans by slipping them drugs. Since then, however, no agency had been able to discover any definite proof of Chinese participation.

A small item in the Washington press said that Lady Cromer, a secret artist, was planning to send a painting to an exhibition at White Plains in Virginia. This was the first that I had heard of it, nor had I done any painting. But this erroneous piece started an activity which gave some pleasure and meant a great deal of labour for the best part of the following year. An english artist, whom I barely knew, called me up on the telephone. He had read the piece in the newspaper and offered to take my painting with his to the exhibition in White Plains. I replied that there was no painting and that I was wholly in ignorance of the matter. The artist, however, insisted that as he knew the organisers of the exhibition he would investigate. This he apparently did, but could find no-one who could explain the origin of the newspaper report. He went on to say that the organisers would be glad if I did submit a painting, and he accentuated the fact that it was a serious exhibition and would be judged by professional artists and critics. With his encouragement I found the time to complete a small still life in oils which, to my utter amazement, won third prize. No joy from the press; instead was a piece describing me as being as unapproachable as Jackie Kennedy Onassis after I was seen at a lunch in the Senate.

The President and his administration had little reason to know from the Washington press of the swell of sympathy from the silent majority. Each morning criticism was piled on criticism for everything that he said and did. But by the early summer there was no doubt on our part that the President's tide of popularity was on the increase in the country at large. Even a Democratic Member of Congress whispered to me that he would like to vote for Nixon in the coming autumn Presidential election. Abusive mail poured in to the White House from various malcontents and it was fast becoming an embattled fortress against an invisible enemy.

On June 1st we were invited to a large dinner given by Senator Birch Bayh who had been running in the Primary Election as a Democratic candidate and had been doing very well until forced to retire due to his wife's poor health. The dinner guests were notable and all worthy Democrats, including Kay Graham, Perle Mesta and some leading political columnists. By chance, that evening coincided with President Nixon's triumphant return from Moscow, where a very successful meeting had taken place. The President decided to rush straight to the Capitol on landing at Andrews Air Force Base in order to address both houses of Congress. Rowley and those active politicians who were present left immediately after dinner to be present at the Capitol, while the rest of the company settled around the television screen to watch. I managed to find a place where I was able to see both the television and the faces of the guests.

The President received a standing ovation before and after his speech, but the audience of dinner party guests remained unresponsive and glum. The President received a rapturous welcome from Congress which he certainly deserved, but among the company I was in, there was none who shared in this acclaim. Instead, a vigorous discussion followed on any likely loss of votes to their party caused by the President's success at the summit. Snide remarks were made on Nixon's cunning in repairing to Congress the moment after his return. Certainly no-one was prepared to give the President any credit for what he had accomplished on behalf of America and, for that matter, the world.

The picture that I painted for the exhibition in Virginia had unexpected repercussions. Whilst being framed, it was seen by an American artist, a lady of compelling powers who, I discovered later, owned a share in the framing shop. She also took an active part in the Washington Arts Club where she asked me to put on a one-woman exhibition. At that time it seemed a good idea, especially as my newspaper-publishing brother had advised me to do something to attract, if possible, some harmless publicity to distract from the bad press which I received shortly after our arrival and which, he explained, would have been filed in all newspaper offices in the world and would be dug out time and again, being the last news item they had.

After agreeing to hold a one-woman exhibition, a date in October was chosen, and I was then told to complete at least forty pictures, a quite impossible order. Our son Vivian had been studying photography and was, by then, most accomplished, so the happy idea of sharing the exhibition and my work-load was born. Time is, as every busy person knows, elastic. With an earlier start in the mornings, more time given at weekends and with the summer leave, twenty-five pictures were finished, framed and ready to be hung by October. Vivian had taken some outstanding pictures. We received quite good publicity and, on the whole, it all went rather well. Many good friends supported us by buying most of the pictures. And one in particular was bought by a group of friends, a private club called 'The Tuesdays,' to which I had belonged since my first visit, and which met every Tuesday. They placed a plaque on the picture and presented it, most touchingly, to the Embassy where it hangs to this day. The Vernissage had gone off successfully, and somehow it all seemed worth the hours of labour that had gone into it. Many people told me that they thought 'it was great' that I should have done something on my own instead of being 'just an appendage.' San Francisco and Princeton asked for the exhibition to be sent to them, but I felt that those invitations were, possibly, more due to position than talent, so declined.

The start of my second Washington summer began with a large ladies' luncheon given by Perle Mesta in honour of the Vice-President's wife, Judy Agnew. Mrs Mesta, although a renowned hostess for the Democratic Party, sat between Mrs Agnew and Mrs Mamie Eisenhower. The seating was pure protocol but a surprise nonetheless. Mrs Eisenhower wore a huge gold medallion of her husband hanging from a chain round her neck. Music was played throughout the meal with the bandleader improvising on well-known songs which he dedicated to a selection of the guests. Madame de Paris was sung to the French Ambassadress, A Spanish Fandango for the Spanish, Arrivederci Roma for the Italian; specially-composed ones for Mrs Agnew and Mrs Eisenhower of a highly complimentary nature and, lastly me, which to my amazement was a ditty sung about Lady Cromer being the most elegant lady in town. If Mrs Mesta had carefully observed seating protocol with her neighbours, she did not with lesser mortals. Diplomatic seating presents no problems as they take their seniority simply from their length of stay, but Mrs Mesta wished to have the French Ambassadress at her top table, and as she was a new arrival, this gave great offence to the Belgian and Israeli Ambassadresses who said later that they had barely restrained themselves from walking out. It seemed rather odd since Mrs Mesta had been an Ambassador herself, to Luxembourg, and had inspired the musical 'Call me Madam.'

The next ladies' gathering was an even larger luncheon at the Cosmos Club. This was the Poetry Luncheon held by Mrs Arthur Burns, the wife of the chairman of the Federal Reserve. About ninety ladies sat at round tables, and after lunching listened to some of the other guests reading or reciting poems. To my utter dismay I was asked by my hostess to read a poem which I had not been shown in advance. It was a poem called 'Our City' and was about New York. Realising that grave offence would be given if I refused, I rose to my feet, shaking with nerves. It was, anyway, a difficult poem to read, serious and sad. After the first few lines my knees began to wobble and my voice to quiver. This condition gradually became worse. The last lines, 'Oh God,' emerged as a real cry for help, then 'unutterable pity, to be dead, and never again to behold my beloved city.' These last words were uttered with a sob of relief, and I only just managed to stagger to my seat, which was happily close by. My hostess was kind and said: 'I know

283

how you felt. For you it was London.' The audience, fortunately, on the whole seemed convinced that my trembling voice had been nothing more than emotion caused by the pathos of the poem. Unlike the English, Americans are sensibly brought up to overcome shyness, and to perform in front of friends and relations from an early age. My colleagues, however, were not taken in. The Italian and Belgian Ambassadresses knew precisely how I felt, and the latter whispered: 'The Europeans always take fright at speaking in public. The Americans are indeed lucky.'

By the following year I knew what to expect. I was given 'Camberley' by John Betjeman. More at ease, with a much easier poem to read, and one that only an english person could do justice to. When the words 'Poona Punker Park' were reached, they brought the house down which, curiously, gave me much encouragement. One of the guests that year was 'Dear Abbie,' an American agony column aunt, who had flown all the way from California to read an excerpt from Shakespeare as it had never been read before.

The social peak of that summer was, surprisingly, one of our own parties, which really hit the town and took Washington by storm. An amateur dramatic society had been formed within the Embassy, which was composed of seventy-five Britons and twenty-five Americans. Once a year they put on a week-long show of Olde Time Music Hall in the Chancery, during which the audience would sip beer while watching the turns and joining in the singing. The previous summer they had invited us to watch, and we were astonished and impressed by the sheer professionalism of the production and quality of the performance. It was also utterly amazing that no-one that we knew in Washington had ever heard of them. Therefore it seemed a God-given opportunity to give a party with a difference, and one that seemed certain to amuse.

John Palmer, a junior member of the staff, was the able producer, and he luckily greeted the idea of a special performance with enthusiasm: 'Like a Royal Command Performance,' he said, so arrangements for the following summer were put in train. I decided that it should be an evening similar to the old 'Players Theatre' in London, only better. A stage was built in the Chancery rotunda, a round, modern, cheerless meeting room, and this was totally transformed with wit and ingenuity into a most charming small Victorian theatre. The theme was Queen Victoria's Diamond Jubilee and the scene painters and decorators did a marvellous job. Patriotic placards and crimson cloth covered the walls with black and white blow-ups of Queen Victoria, Big Ben and St Paul's. There was no shortage of bunting either.

Nineteen round tables of six were placed in every available space, each covered with a red-checked table-cloth with the centre made up of a fat red candle surrounded with shiny green leaves. The effect was cheerful and harmonious and, we hoped, gave a flavour of Victorian England. A time when people were certain and confident of themselves, an escape from those troublesome early nineteen-seventies in America.

In order to surprise, we said little in advance of the party, and on the invitation cards simply wrote 'Music Hall' in the right hand corner. Most were puzzled, and many thought that it must mean a rather boring evening, possibly with Rowley or myself either playing a piano or singing, which would not be to the taste of Washington sophisticates nor busy officials, so declined to come. Others were simply curious and some, with more confidence in us (as they knew us better), were happy to take a chance. But the one person who was really aware of the significance of the invitation was the venerable and distinguished Mrs Nicholas Longworth. She knew what to expect and sang all the songs without referring to the programme. She told us that she was thirteen years old in 1897 and remembered all the words clearly from that date.

Amateur musicians made up a lively five-piece orchestra, and pretty young secretaries dressed in turn-of-the-century clothes, and sporting saucy straw boaters served a three course dinner during the intervals of the show.

Among our one-hundred-and-fourteen guests were some ambassadors, senior members of the administration, Congressmen, some english journalists and the more friendly Washington social writers. It was important that the room was full, and therefore new invitations were despatched as soon as a refusal came in, right up to the last-moment drop-outs, which meant constantly rearranging the table plan.

In order to keep up the element of surprise the guests were first given drinks in an unadorned stark lobby of the Chancery, made more cheerless without the embellishment of a single flower. Then when the curtains were drawn back by two charmingly-dressed young women, to reveal the ravishing little theatre, the astonishment was truly great, and with exclamations of pleasure and surprise the guests were shown to their tables. One excited lady remarked: 'It is the Moulin Rouge.'

The show went with a zip, and was compared to Broadway by one woman journalist. The sketches were delightful and funny, the singing good and the dances snappy. No-one made a slip or sang a false note. One fat and burly middle-aged security guard dressed himself up in a tutu with little wings, and sang: 'No-one loves a fairy when she's forty,' which was a riot. For a finale the entire company sang 'Soldiers of the Queen' followed by a robust rendering of 'Rule Britannia,' which brought the entire audience to their feet, clapping and cheering.

This party did us good, and our image as well, for which we were thankful. A nice letter arrived from one of the better social writers saying that it was the best party in Washington's diplomatic history. That might have been overstating it, but the Italian Ambassador was heard to say that other embassies were now ruined, and even a young man from the French Embassy, on hearing about the evening, said: 'Now we will have to send over the Folies Bergère.' Praise was heaped on the evening from all sides and adrenalin leaped through our veins. Perhaps, at last, the hostile writers would put away their pens.

The following summer we repeated the party to a different theme, with different songs. No longer a surprise, on that occasion we received one hundred per cent acceptances to the first batch of invitations sent out, whereas before it had only been fifty per cent. Senator Hugh Scott of Pennsylvania had even mentioned the evening in the Senate and was reported in the Congressional Record (equivalent to Hansard) as saying: 'What better example could be found of the Anglo-American "natural relationship" than members of both Houses of Congress, officials of the US Administration, and others from many walks of life joining together under the roof of the British Embassy to sing with equal fervour Yankee Doodle Dandy, and Land of Hope and Glory?' He went on to say much else, all of a laudable nature. And when our successors, the Ramsbothams, eventually took over, they told us that for months people, on meeting them for the first time, would implore them to go on with the Music Hall. They did, and we heard that Sir Peter Ramsbotham even took part himself, and sang a solo.

For some time the *Washington Post* had been running a campaign against bugging and telephone tapping by the authorities. They had also been busy investigating as much else as they could and had been pretty successful so far. The Pentagon Papers; the FBI, with the unfortunate Patrick Gray who had not been confirmed as Head, and Kleindienst who also failed to be confirmed as Attorney General, and others.

On June 19th at a dinner given by Henry Brandon where almost all the guests were Democrats, there was a sorry and depressing atmosphere, which was unusual in Henry's house. The Primaries were proving good auguries for the Democrats and some of the guests seemed to be much involved with the election from the stand-point of that party. There was also an odd and distinct undercurrent of excitement over a matter that seemed extremely important to them, but when described, seemed trivial to me; there had during the previous weekend been a break-in at the Democratic Headquarters in the Watergate Building, and five men were discovered installing a bugging system. It was assumed that these men were under orders from the Republican Party, as a telephone number found on one of them was that of an adviser in the White House. I asked my neighbour at dinner what purpose there could have been in bugging the place that could be of any consequence to the other side? (At that time it was fairly obvious to an outside observer that the Republicans were so far ahead that there could be no conceivable advantage in dealing in any jinks of that kind). It was laughable, but no-one was laughing. Besides, one had always understood that such activities were part of the rough and tumble of American politics.

After a summer spent in England and France we returned to the customary welcome in Washington. This time it was letter bombs, and one poor unfortunate secretary in the Chancery sustained the force of the explosion and had her hand blown off. From then on all our mail had to be examined closely.

On September 26th Rowley and I called on the President and Mrs Nixon to present him with a gold medallion and an enamel box on behalf of St Paul's Cathedral. Both the President and Mrs Nixon looked cheerful and well and were, as usual, charming and friendly. They left immediately afterwards to continue their election campaign.

At the Embassy the guest rooms were full for, once again, the World Bank meeting was upon us. John Connally had now been replaced at the Treasury by George Shultz, who had been Director of the Budget. An extremely able man, not a politician, but an ex-professor of immense charm and thoughtful wisdom whom we already knew and liked. Our Chancellor of the Exchequer, Tony Barber, on the other hand, seemed changed. Before he had been enthusiastic and wanting to please, but now his manner seemed uncertain and diffident. What had changed him, we wondered? Was it the cares of office or something else?

George Shultz sent his big speech for the forthcoming meeting to Rowley to read and to show to the Chancellor. This was a most friendly and complimentary gesture and Rowley was surprised when the Chancellor barely acknowledged the favour, and even neglected to thank George for his thought. Nor did he send a copy of his own speech in return, which really courtesy demanded. Neither did Rowley have sight of it, which is customary for the speaker's ambassador in a foreign country. Tony, when asked, simply murmured that his speech was not quite ready.

There had been some trouble over appointing a new head of the IMF. The Americans did not wish Pierre-Paul Schweitzer to continue, and they handled the matter rather clumsily. The meeting was opened by the President, who received reasonable applause for an appropriate speech. And then it was Pierre-Paul's turn and he, on rising to speak, received a standing ovation from all the world bankers and financial officials, which caused some embarrassment to the Americans. On the following day Tony Barber thought it fitting to praise and laud Schweitzer, and his words again produced a hearty burst of applause. But, unhappily, his speech came just before the new Secretary of the Treasury's, George Shultz. And, moreover, Tony Barber included some questionable technical points which, according to Rowley, were not in America's favour. George was not pleased. A good friend of Britain's, he minded deeply, particularly after previously showing his own speech to us and, therefore, displaying his friendship and trust.

Rowley's carefully cultivated and sincere relations with the Administration received a wound which took a long time to heal, and all for apparently no good reason. It was Rowley, in the first place, who had recommended to Ted that Tony, in his opinion, should be appointed to the Exchequer. We had known him and his family for some time, and had on one occasion invited him to dine with us in London.

That autumn saw many visits from prominent people. Alec and Elizabeth Douglas-Home were the first. Elizabeth, her happy and ebullient self, with a wonderfully easy manner, seemed genuinely touched when I met her off the train from New York. She told me of a New York restaurant that proclaimed: 'All the fish you eat here today slept last night in Chesapeake Bay.' She told me that she felt like a cannibal.

Peter Walker followed as our next guest, then Lord Gladwyn. The latter's first words to Rowley were: 'I have brought you a present and there is a photograph of myself on both sides of the cover.' It was his autobiography. My social secretary, Torie, remarked that 'he was the sort of person that started revolutions,' after he had treated her with hauteur and abruptness. Before his arrival he sent us a list of people he wished to see, but due to the passing of years they were sadly either dying, immobile or had left the world stage and lived elsewhere. A friend told us that Gladwyn, on his previous visit, was asked by a couple of ladies if he had noticed any changes in Washington since his previous visit. He replied: 'None, with the exception of you both, who look much older.' He had been one of our more eminent Ambassadors, popular with his staff and subordinates, if not always with his political superiors.

The Duke and Duchess of Kent were our next visitors. We went to New York to receive them and to accompany them to a film première, before returning with them to Washington. The Kent jinx is known to them, and they smilingly seemed to accept any unexpected set-backs. At a reception given by Mrs Lew Douglas in her apartment on the tenth floor the elevators broke down, and all the guests, including the Kents, had to make their exits via the kitchen and walk down the back stairs. The film which followed took place simultaneously in two cinemas, one above and one below ground. The Duke and Duchess were expected to divide their time between the two, and the last part of the film found us all in the underground cinema where, at the finish, we discovered that the cinema's elevators had broken down as well. This time we had to climb a very long flight of stairs to ground level. The evening's mishaps were not yet over.

After the film a dinner-dance was held at the Plaza Hotel. The chief guests were seated at four tables in alcoves raised from the dance floor. In the centre of each of the tables was placed an ornamental arrangement of fruit, sheaves of corn and three small candles. The Duke, Mrs Douglas, Richard Attenborough and I sat together at one of the small tables and had barely eaten a mouthful when the table centre suddenly and inexplicably burst into flames. It was the extraordinary presence of mind of Mrs Douglas that saved what could have become an ugly situation. She grasped with great firmness the flaming sheaves of corn and managed to quell the fire without the faintest damage to herself. The film was 'The Young Winston,' which Rowley and I were to sit through again a week later at another première in Washington.

In Washington, while the Duke and Duchess were being shown around the coin collection in the Smithsonian Museum, we were all suddenly surprised by a bevy of armed police who rushed in with the mistaken idea that a robbery was being committed. The burglar alarm had mysteriously gone off.

In October, another British Fortnight took place, this time at Gimbel's store in Pittsburg. In the past Pittsburg was regarded, as its name suggests, the pits. Thirty years earlier a visit to Pittsburg was something that only husbands did on business — a place which the reluctant visitor was commiserated upon when he returned. Smelly, ugly and an unthinkable place to visit, one was told by all and sundry. Now, to the enormous surprise of both of us, a magical transformation had taken place. Its position at the conjunction of two great rivers must always have been impressive, at least until the smoke and grime of the huge steel mills started obscuring the view. The greyness had gone, the pollution vanquished. The sun shone on tall, shining buildings, immaculately clean, soaring upwards between the two rivers, and now called 'The Golden Triangle,' with every justification. One could say, without any doubt, that it has a genuine claim to be one of the most beautiful cities in America.

While Rowley busied himself meeting various city dignitaries, I was given over to the Police Department. There had been some Irish demonstrations and it was thought I would be safest in their hands. This proved to be a very pleasant experience for me, escorted round the city in a police car and shown the sights by two armed Irish police officers who possessed all the charm and gaiety of their race and who gave me a most amusing morning. At the end we lunched together in the coffee shop of our hotel, and before departing they insisted on buying me a doll dressed as a British soldier which they shyly presented me with, and which emblem, given their Irish accents and ancestry was, I thought, wonderfully incongruous. No-one in the coffee shop thought it the slightest bit odd that an english women should be eating so merrily with two heavily-armed policemen.

The day ended with a formal Ball. It was rather unusual, in that after the dancing had been in progress for some time, an announcer suddenly informed the guests that the British Ambassador and his lady would now open the Ball, which involved our dancing alone under a spotlight. The Ball included a fashion show during which the commentator announced: 'Now we will show you some British knits.' 'You said it,' shouted a loud voice with an Irish accent.

The President of the Ball, a venerable gentleman, sat next to me at dinner. He opened the conversation by telling me that when he had visited Düsseldorf, he had been taken to see the largest brothel in the world, with three hundred and sixty-two rooms. Each room was ten foot by six and had a panic button installed. He continued by saying that his visit had been made out of pure curiosity, and that he was able to gain admittance and be shown round because he possessed an honorary police badge which, he said, he found very useful when travelling. After this fascinating revelation the elderly gentleman shut up and was not heard to utter another word.

On our return to Washington we were recommended by Rowley's advisers in the Chancery to hold a party with the Academy of Arts and Sciences to mark the fiftieth anniversary of the BBC. It was decided that we should hold a buffet dinner in the Residence to be followed by speeches and a film about the institution. We were not able to obtain a list of the guests invited by the Academy until the day of the party. We then discovered that 'democracy' had intervened as with the party for the LSO, and it was thought that the most democratic method of inviting the guests was to send all the invitations out at once and then to allow only those who accepted early enough to come. In my experience, it is usually the case that those who accept promptly are those with the least commitments and, possibly, those least in demand. One hundred and thirty people arrived at the party and among them I found one who looked more prepossessing than the others, and engaged him in conversation. He asked me why I bothered to talk to him, and if I knew the truth I would not. This immediately aroused my curiosity, and I persuaded him reluctantly to tell me. 'I have been on the wanted list three times,' he replied gloomily. Wondering what on earth he had done, but not liking to ask, and wishing to introduce a lighter note, I replied, 'How nice to be wanted.' From then on he silently and disconcertingly followed me about all evening, and not one of the other guests seemed to know or be acquainted with him.

The head of the BBC branch in the USA told us in his introductory speech that the highlight of the film that we were about to be shown was the singing dogs which, of course, we were all eager to hear. Unfortunately, however, the projectionist, who was also chairman of the Academy, managed to cut it out, to the disappointment of all. Besides the sound-track was out of sync. But in spite of everything the mixture of guests were out to enjoy themselves and did so.

There had recently been a strange lack of comment at social gatherings of both parties over the election and almost no discussion. Democratic friends said little except to shake their hands over their own candidate, McGovern. Hardly any paper stickers were to be seen although some had been surreptitiously stuck on a few embassy cars, unknown to the drivers. As for a Nixon sticker, we never saw any.

When President Nixon won the election with a landslide in November his overwhelming majority caused no surprise in diplomatic circles, and it came as a great relief to all the ambassadors as, with the possible exception of Ireland, they thought any other result would have been disastrous for America and, more precisely, her policies overseas.

Mrs Longworth decided to hold an election night dinner-party at her ancient sedate house full of a bygone atmosphere, and where one felt the furniture required respect and gentle treatment due to its fragility. Our hostess, on the other hand, was as spritely as ever and hugely enjoyed her own party, at the age of eighty-eight. Kay Graham, the publisher of the *Washington Post*, was among the guests. She issued rather more than her usual series of deep sighs, one supposed over the results of the election, which was all over by nine o'clock. After all, her newspaper had continued daily and for months its support for the Democrat candidate, and moreover, had mounted a strong campaign against President Nixon. The dinner-party broke up rather early, as is the custom in Washington. In fact it has often been said that if the senior guest has not made his or her departure by eleven o'clock then no-one is in a hurry to ask him again.

A new young social secretary was found by Torie Legge-Bourke who wished to return to England, so once again the social ropes and pitfalls had to be learned — also the intricacies and diplomatic niceties, which started with a Courtesy Call from the new Austrian Ambassadress who had been unfortunately mistaken for a stranger wishing to sign the Book. No warning reached me and her arrival was totally unexpected. By sheer luck I was at home and was able to smooth over any ruffled feelings. She proved to be half-Scots and half-Siamese, and was much placated when she discovered that I had a Thai daughter-in-law.

Thanksgiving came round once again, and this time we spent it in the Virginia countryside with an American widow who was an old friend. Being above all a family occasion, her grandchildren were there as well as her daughter and son-in-law. The latter was then the editor of the editorial page of the *Washington Post*, Phil Geyelin. His children, in their late teens, were trendy and affected a casual air. Interested in their views, I asked them to define a Fascist. 'Anyone in uniform,' they replied. Then it transpired that a Communist was a Fascist too, the only difference being, they told me, a Fascist was also a Capitalist. Both young men looked intelligent and both were proud that although the family owned five cars between them none were American-made. These young people were refreshing for their frankness, and yet seemed depressed and despairing of life.

Charles Bartlett, a newspaper man, spoke of the child of a friend of his who had just been expelled from school. The reason, he said, was because the child had defecated during a class as a demonstration against authoritarianism in school. One wondered what kind of world we were entering into.

The Ghanaian Ambassadress, a tall and imposing woman, came to call because she wanted to know why the Commonwealth Teas had been temporarily discontinued. I explained as best I could that as I was now thirteenth in seniority among the Commonwealth diplomatic wives, there was really nothing that I could do, and that any questions should be addressed to Canada, and to Madame Cadieux in particular, since she was the most senior. In any case, it would be presumptuous of me to take over since we were all equal within the Commonwealth. (This fact had been well rubbed in on my arrival).

It was the Afro-Caribbean Commonwealth that enjoyed the

teas most, and she was therefore most disappointed that I was unable to help. I asked her if the black African countries had themselves tried to form a group to meet monthly in a similar fashion, and she replied that they had tried, but that they could never agree on who should run it or be president. Neither by seniority or by rota had either system commended itself. She told me before she left, to my great surprise, that she had extracted a promise from her husband that, should either of them fall ill, the other would see that they were immediately flown back to Ghana for she did not trust the nursing in American hospitals.

Herman Wouk, the author, who resided in Washington, was writing his epic 'Winds of War.' 'It will be a modern historical novel such as Sir Walter Scott wrote in his time,' he told me at a dinner-party.

With the close of the year came the death of President Truman. A man of no great pretention but one of the best nonetheless. To represent the Government at the State Funeral, Lord Hailsham, the Lord Chancellor, was despatched to Washington. A great admirer of America and, indeed, half American himself, he was to become very disenchanted with the funeral arrangements. After waiting an interminable time at the State Department for the official bus to take him and Rowley to the cathedral, he became despondent, and when the bus finally arrived and proved to both dirty and smelly, even more so. All, it seemed, was chaos, and after the service was over, he walked the fair distance back to the Embassy in preference to the bus, and said afterwards that he had felt humiliated on behalf of his revered American mother.

22

THE PRIME MINISTER'S VISIT

At the beginning of January 1973 the Americans began a devastating bombing of North Vietnam. A new form of bomb had been invented called the smart bomb. Its precision was extraordinary. It could destroy a generator in a power station and yet leave the walls intact. It was, however, a secret weapon, and that, politically, was a pity. For the public remained unaware that civilians were safe and not being indiscriminately killed. All they knew was that the bombing was taking place and they therefore believed that innocent people were being killed and maimed. By January 14th the bombing was halted, amid general relief, possibly because the Inauguration was about to commence.

The inaugural balls and festivities are held primarily in recognition of all the time and trouble that supporters of the winning candidate had put into his election, and these supporters poured into the capital in their thousands hoping for a glimpse of the victors.

The first event was a reception given by the newly-elected Vice-President and Mrs Agnew, to be held at the Smithsonian Institution. We did not know what to expect, and did not know that anyone could go to this party for the payment of ten dollars. After all, we had received a grand engraved and embossed invitation card. The roads surrounding the Smithsonian were blocked, so our progress was slow, and became somewhat slower when we discovered that people were struggling to enter an already-overcrowded building. Inside the entrance a line of be-ribboned women greeted us with 'Glad to see you, and have fun!' They represented a kind of welcoming committee solely to greet newcomers. If we were to ask a question, such as: 'What do we do now?' they would look vague, as these did then. Fortunately another ambassador turned up, so clutching each other, and with the help of a uniformed aide, we endeavoured to pass through the crowds and finally reached a dismal room where we found a discontented group of diplomats cordoned-off on one side. 'I feel like a penned animal,' one ambassador said. Two others stepped over a rope and were quickly ordered to get back. Later a loudspeaker announced that the Vice-President was among us, as he started to shake hands as best he could in the small space available. Why we were all pushed into a small part of an otherwise not-so-full room remained a mystery, as indeed did the matter of why the Diplomatic Corps were invited at all.

We fared, however, better than some others, for those who had not been shown to the 'pen' found themselves suffocated by the enormous crowd, packed like pilchards. They literally had to fight their way out. Some unsuspecting ambassadresses had worn their most formal attire due to the grandness of the invitation card. Another had her ostrich-feathered dress completely ruined.

The following day we gave the next reception a miss. The Kuwaiti Ambassador, however, bravely made the attempt. Not allowed near the front-door, and in the pouring rain, he and his wife went home after enduring some three and a half hours in their car in a traffic jam.

Our next festivity was the Inaugural Concert at the Kennedy Center. The wear was formal evening dress. We dined pleasantly and quietly with the Secretary of Health, Education and Welfare in his charming small house. Cap Weinberger and his wife, Jane, were wonderful hosts and extremely kind to us. The other guests were Ronald and Nancy Reagan. It was a happy and relaxed dinner. The excellent food was prepared by Jane, and the Governor Reagan was in good and jokey form, with his pretty wife smiling and pleasant. From there we all continued to the Kennedy Center where in the lobby, called the Hall of Nations, a five-piece orchestra dressed in eighteenth century costume played God Save the King continuously. Although it is an American anthem as well, the vocalists sang loudly all the verses. The Weinbergers and the Reagans were amused as, indeed, we were. A photographer grabbed Rowley and me and insisted that we pose before this quaint orchestra, which caused much merriment to the Reagans and the Weinbergers. The King, of course, was George III.

We had good seats. My neighbour was the Archbishop of the Greek Orthodox Church in the USA. Four rows in front Henry Kissinger was happily autographing people's programmes. A number of the Administration were there, all friendly and nice. We felt a general warmth of feeling as if we were one of them; as if we belonged.

In the concert the Philadelphia Orchestra went through the same repertoire always used for these occasions. The first piece was 'The Fanfare for the Common Man,' short and rousing; followed by Beethoven's Fifth Symphony. During the first interval, trumpets heralded the Presidential party's arrival. A spotlight shone on the President's box and the audience rose to face it while one by one the First Family and Mrs Eisenhower entered. Each was given a brisk welcome. The next half of the programme began with Van Cliburn playing Grieg's Concerto in A Minor. Then Charlton Heston strode onto the stage and recited the Declaration of Independence, directly after which Rowley told me to stop applauding immediately. The concert ended with Tchaikovsky's 1812 Overture.

Bob Hope and Sammy Davis Junior were entertaining in the Eisenhower Theater while Soul and Rock music were being performed in the Opera House to capacity audiences.

The following morning, January 20th, was the day of the

299

swearing-in of the President and the Vice-President of the United States outside the Capitol. The Diplomatic Corps was instructed to gather at the State Department where they would embark in buses for Capitol Hill. Rowley, after the depressing experience of the Truman Memorial arrangements, would have none of it. He decided instead to take his own official car, and told the less-than enthusiastic State Department what he intended to do.

We set off in the Rolls with the Union Jack flying. On arrival, however, we found that it was no easy matter to gain entry to the enclosed area in spite of our pass and tickets. After two vain attempts at the first and second gates, a friendly Irish policeman allowed us in at the third gate. We heard later that the Diplomatic Corps buses encountered the same difficulty. We both walked over to the Senate building where various ambassadors were joining a long queue before gaining admittance. I was told to join the ambassadresses in their bus although they were waiting to disembark. After ten minutes we were shown to our seats which appeared to be successive rows of wooden planks set as far away as possible from the scene of events. They were not sheltered. The cold wind blew with an icy blast and we huddled together for warmth for well over an hour. Some ambassadresses had dressed up for the occasion. Others, clad in moderately thin material, were shivering with cold. A couple of hats blew off, faces became grey and pinched, yet the proceedings had not yet begun. Our husbands, fortunately, were seated behind the Cabinet members on a stand built out from the Capitol wall so were, happily, in a sheltered position. Various anthems were played; a deafening twenty-one gun salute; prayers, Episcopalian, Catholic and Jewish, were read, followed by the swearing-in and the Presidential Address.

At the end of these proceedings a man behind us yelled: 'All you wives will wait until the bus arrives.' It was the last straw for some of the ambassadresses. They shot me some very envious glances as I quietly and as unobtrusively as possible walked towards the warmth and comfort of the Rolls-Royce which stood only a few yards away.

Rowley and I were extremely fortunate in having been given an invitation for luncheon by George Shultz. He also most kindly invited us to watch the Great Parade from the Treasury building which commanded a splendid view of the processional route. Besides, our car could be parked alongside, and could take us home whenever we wished. It was a most thoughtful gesture. Watching the parade from the windows, our companions proved to be the two most powerful Union leaders in America, with their wives. Mrs George Meany made loud remarks in a strong Bronx accent and was referred to as Queen Mary by the others. George and Obie Shultz left us to take part in the parade, but not before telling us that we could use the Secretary's office in which to relax if we wished.

No country in the world knows better than America how to put on a parade. It was magnificent and lasted about four hours. Floats from each State, endless drum majorettes, and military, school children, police and, finally, the newly-elected President, his Cabinet and their wives, all waving vigorously to the crowds from their open cars. The President's car was hemmed in by walking policemen who, poor fellows, suffered from the occasional rotten egg or squashed tomato.

Meanwhile at the Washington Monument, a demonstration by thousands of dirty and bedraggled youngsters milled around carrying their national flag upside down before putting a match to it.

Ten days later our Prime Minister made his second official visit to President Nixon.

Ted and Alec arrived with Denis Greenhill, Burke Trend and an entourage of officials. Alec looked frail as he had been suffering from food poisoning. We all gathered in the library of the Embassy for a drink and chat soon after their arrival. Ted Kennedy, wasting no time, had sent a message to say he wished to see the Prime Minister. Alec was not much taken with the idea, but Denis Greenhill thought that he should see him in view of the fact that he might become President in the following election. I told them that we had not yet invited Kennedy to the Embassy and did not intend to do so. No more was heard of the idea.

The Prime Minister, neither wearied by the journey nor the lateness of the hour, insisted on dining with Henry Brandon (*The Sunday Times* correspondent). It seemed rather a strange thing to do as Henry, although undoubtedly the most influential of the British journalists was, like most of his confrères, in the Democratic camp. After leaving this party we were told that Senator Stennis had been shot by two young men outside his house in the most respectable neighbourhood.

The next day we sat down twenty-six for luncheon, all male except myself. Rowley had wanted a special cold buffet, which did not meet with approval from the butler, who when told that it would make the occasion more informal, said with a sniff, 'You mean, like an Army Mess.' The chef decorated individual pieces of chicken chaud-froid with slivers of truffles to represent sad and happy faces. The sad faces were perfect likenesses to Harold Macmillan.

Dr Warren, the PM's doctor, told me that Ted got a big kick out of these visits, but was not looking forward to the Commonwealth meeting in Ottawa in August as it was taking place during his yachting season. Ted told me of the wonders of decoration he was carrying out at Chequers. He had, evidently, employed John Fowler (at that time London's best and most expensive decorator). He had changed the housekeeper from Wilson's. Tony Lambton had found a Wing-Commander from the Women's Royal Air Corps who was proving most competent. She, in turn, had found an excellent Air Force cook. New roses bloomed in the garden and now, Ted imparted, he really enjoyed some happy weekends. Concerts in the great hall and Sunday lunch parties. Ted, as I came to realise later, is a perfectionist as a host, and in his habitations, as his house in Salisbury bears witness. Alec talked of farming. His beef prices were good and he now grew acres of

peas and beans when before it had been cabbages and potatoes. Beans and peas had become popular due to the wide
availability of household freezers.

The following day saw the official arrival at the White
House. The day was raw and chilly and Rowley advised me
to wrap up warmly; to wear, in fact, my ancient mink coat,
which hung like an old dressing gown, whereas I had wished
to don my new outfit. 'You will not be noticed in the throng,'
he said. No hat, because Pat Nixon was almost never seen in
one. At 9.30 am promptly, Alec, Denis, Burke and Richard
Sykes, the Minister (later to be tragically assassinated), Rowley and I climbed into cars with various members of the
Protocol Department and were driven to the White House via
the Diplomatic entrance and shown to the downstairs lobby.
There we found the Mayor and other leading dignitaries. I
had travelled with Mrs Smoak, wife of the Chief of Protocol.
She had thoughtfully warned me that I would be standing
alone and in front of the rest with Mrs Nixon. How I wished
I had not heeded Rowley's kind advice about the mink coat,
which seemed to me ever more out-of-date as we neared our
destination.

In the lobby the Annenbergs appeared. Unaware that I had
been briefed by Mrs Smoak, Lee Annenberg said: 'Come, you
must go and stand in the line next to Rowley.' She was a little
non-plussed as I lingered behind, then taking my arm she was
about to propel me along, when Walter intervened. 'Leave her
be. She has not got where she is by being headless,' he
chuckled.

When everyone had departed, and after a few moments,
Mrs Smoak led the way inside. She stationed herself behind
me as we both stood in front of everyone else and waited
silently for about ten minutes. It was cold, but I would sooner
have shivered than enjoy the warmth of my baggy old coat in
the face of some sixty news photographers. Finally the President and Mrs Nixon arrived and were shortly joined by the
Prime Minister. A nineteen-gun salute went off, followed by

the national anthems. The Prime Minister reviewed a detachment of soldiers followed by a welcoming speech by the President and a response by the Prime Minister written by Rowley's new secretary, Charles Powell. During the speeches the President and Prime Minister turned their backs on us in order to face the press. After a welcome cup of coffee in the White House we all dispersed.

That evening the State Banquet was held. Our contingent drove to the White House with an escort from the Chief of Police. On arrival the more senior members of our party were escorted to the private apartments on the top floor. From the lift we entered a long wide passage with half-moon windows at each end. The walls were painted a brilliant clear yellow and the effect was one of cheerful sunlight. We were led into the oval sitting-room where good antique furniture, exquisitely arranged flowers, two magnificent Cézannes and a brilliant burning fire created an extremely elegant effect.

A happy atmosphere was ensured, I felt, by Patricia Nixon and her family. Pat Nixon seemed to me to be a much under-rated woman. Neatly dressed and well groomed, very fine of feature and always sweet and charming. The suffering that she was to endure without complaint was still to come. After some refreshments we were escorted to the ballroom where the other one hundred and ten guests were assembled. Among them a familiar face stood out: that of Cary Grant. There was, however, no time to chat. We had mistakenly been announced as Ambassador and Mrs Annenberg, and no sooner had we joined the throng than a flourish of trumpets sounded the arrival of the President, Mrs Nixon and the Prime Minister, who immediately took up their places in a receiving line to welcome the guests as they passed on their way into the dining-room, the line of guests being headed by Alec, Rowley and me.

A long table with chairs on one-side only faced a room full of round tables. I discovered my place to be between the President and the Secretary of State, much to my surprise and pleasure, for it was the first time an opportunity had arisen for a private chat with the President. I found a pair of shy, serious but friendly brown eyes turned towards me. Our conversation ranged from world affairs to the media; from Disraeli to Churchill, both evidently heroes to the President. He talked of his high admiration of the British, chiefly because of their firm stands in time of difficulty. For a shy man his easy manner came as a nice surprise, and resulted in no pauses in the conversation. He went on to say how despairing he was of the intellectuals. 'They always get it wrong,' he murmured, explaining how the necessity of the bombing of North Vietnam had been so misunderstood. And did I realise that, without it, the Americans would never have obtained the cease-fire and peace agreements.

The President poured out his disgust of the media in general and of several individual columnists in particular, all of whom for years had been preaching in their columns and on television the benefits of a sudden withdrawal from Vietnam, and castigating the President's policy of peace and withdrawal with some semblance of honour. Yet when the cease-fire and peace agreement were achieved, they immediately fell to criticising those. The poor President was truly trying to be a statesman and he had, in fact, succeeded in the eyes of the world, but not in the eyes of his own countrymen. Not possibly for the first time in history, but brutally unfair nonetheless; but then so is life.

I asked the Secretary of State, Bill Rogers, who was in a very jovial mood, what the President's favourite subject of conversation was, and he replied 'sex.' We laughed and I had to confess that I had failed to bring topic A up. My conversation with him from then on remained on a frivolous level. We plotted an outing in disguise to see the 'Last Tango in Paris,' considered to be very daring and celebrated for its pornography, although probably quite mild, for the fashion in such films had barely begun.

The President, who seemed to be finding Ted Heath not

305

the easiest of neighbours, turned my way again. In answer to my question on destiny, the President replied that he had never felt a sense of destiny, but was nevertheless a fatalist. I felt somehow relieved. Turning the conversation another way, I told him how excited our French chef was at the prospect of the President lunching with us the following day. 'But I must tell you that I shall not eat anything,' he said. This remark must have settled into my subconsciousness for I woke up in the middle of the night after a short but worrying dream. I had dreamt that all the other guests, noticing that the President had not allowed a morsel of food to pass his lips, had with one accord shouted: 'Our food is poisoned,' and pointed an accusing finger at me. Early next morning I contacted the White House to find out what, if anything, the President wished to eat. The reply that came back was to the effect that the President was only joking, and that he was, in fact, looking forward to eating an excellent lunch. But the President had not been entirely joking, for when I asked Henry Kissinger, he replied that the President never ate much for lunch, only a little cottage cheese.

The White House banquet continued with the customary speeches. The Air Force Strings played and we rose to drink the health of both the Queen and the President. At one stage I laughingly mentioned to the President that I had thoroughly enjoyed being 'Mrs Heath,' having been elevated in rank to the senior British spouse, since Ted had no wife and Lady Douglas-Home had stayed at home. Nixon enjoyed this and wrote on his place card 'To Mrs Heath, with Best Wishes, Richard Nixon.' He showed it to Ted who did not look amused. But the Secretary of State and I laughed heartily.

After the banquet it was arranged for a famous singer by the name of Mary Costa to entertain us, but unfortunately that very morning she had fallen downstairs and sustained a broken leg. Instead the Army Choir was brought in. This was a rare treat, for apart from the Red Army Choir, there is nothing in the world to compare them with. They were quite marvellous. We had 'The Road to Mandalay' sung with great vigour, soloists popped up and down, and many other well-known tunes were played and sung.

Before the entertainment began and people were being settled in their seats, the chief guests were taken upstairs to the private apartment. In one room stood a piano, and as we passed it, Nixon invited Ted to join him in playing a duet. It seemed to me a splendid idea, but Ted would have none of it, and fairly brusquely declined.

When we finally left the party, Alec beckoned to me to go first, but fully realising that I had gone well above my station, and as it was nearly midnight, I told him that my car must have turned into a pumpkin and insisted that he left first.

Our luncheon for the President was not without anguish. The Prime Minister wished to send engraved invitations out in his own name from the Embassy. This, however, was contrary to custom. In a foreign country only the Head of State or her Ambassador can send invitations out from an Embassy. Ted, presumably unaware of this protocol, was none too pleased, but Rowley stood firm as the Queen's representative in the Embassy.

Some time before Lee Annenberg got in touch with me, and when I told her that we were thinking of inviting the President for lunch she advised me that it would be a waste of time, as the President never attended a function at an embassy unless it was given by a Head of State, for if he did he would have to attend them all. There was logic in what she said, but I had a feeling that President Nixon would make an exception for Britain.

The guest list and table plan presented problems. Should the President and Prime Minister once again sit next to each other? After an enquiry, the State Department advised us that it was not necessary so long as we sat at round tables, which we were intending to do anyway. The dining-room sat a rather limited number, just four tables of twelve, and as quite a large contingent of White House and Administration officials were coming, plus our own side, that only left four from outside. We selected Minority Leader of the House of Representatives, Gerald Ford and his wife Betty, as two of them.

The flower arrangements I did myself, placing large bowls of red rose buds, blue irises and white freesias in the middle of each table. It was only when I had finished that the Secret Serviceman appeared. They all wore S for secret as a pin on their lapels, and each flower arrangement was peered at and parted with the petals closely examined for bugs or other devices.

The Prime Minister arrived in the nick of time to be with us as the President and Mrs Nixon's car drew up. Cameras clicked, television whirled. I took the President upstairs and around the assembled guests, and not for the first time was I grateful for my experience as a member of the Queen's Household. We had allocated each guest a number to correspond with the table that he would be seated at; since most knew each other it did not seem necessary to have a large table plan on display, although the Prime Minister was supposed to have been sent one. I took the President into the dining-room where, for what seemed a long time, we chatted in front of television cameras while we waited for the Prime Minister and Mrs Nixon to join us. When they eventually did, Ted could not find his place, which was slightly embarrassing.

On the other side of the President I had placed Mrs Ford, for it seemed likely that as he must see the White House and Administration wives quite often, a change might be pleasant. I did not expect, however, that it would turn out to be the first time that they had met, other than for a brief handshake, and I was surprised when Mrs Ford trembled with nerves and seemed quite alarmed when I indicated that she should sit next to the President.

I had known Betty Ford ten years earlier when we had both been members of International Group II. She had been a vital, enthusiastic, pretty young woman, full of excitement and the exhilaration of coming fresh to Washington. Not a bit shy, she had been most friendly and likable. But now she appeared to be quite changed, withdrawn, silent and nervy. To break the awkwardness I related to President Nixon that all those years before we had belonged to the same monthly ladies' luncheon club. Since that time, it had become well-known for the number of members' husbands who had either become President, or nearly done so as Presidential candidates. They included Lyndon Johnson, Eugene McCarthy and various others. One could have almost called it, I told him, 'a nursery for Presidents' wives.' Little did I think at that time that Betty Ford would succeed Pat Nixon, and I am certain that it was very far from any thought of Betty's either. The President proved as easy to talk to as the evening before. He informed me that he never took much exercise, except swimming. He therefore ate little. Besides, he said, the more one exercised the more one ate. Our first course was Sole à la Edouard VII which gave further cause for chat, King Edward having been renowned for his prodigious appetite. President Nixon then speculated on the fact that english people ate rather more than Americans, and yet remained slim. We agreed that it must have something to do with the climate. Our talk then turned to other topics and then to Black Africa. He thought that it might not be a bad idea to give aid only to those countries that practised democratic government, then added, perhaps more realistically, that it was not really a questions of forms of government, but where the interests of the United States lay. He then asked me why it was that the media criticised America's aid to right-wing, if non-democratic governments while approving any aid to left-wing ones which, if anything, were far more tyrannical. After this he gave me his views on the United Nations, which exactly matched Rowley's. Finally we reached the subject of sex. This came about through hearing that the redoubtable and venerable Mrs Longworth had been seen at a pornographic film in order, so she said, to keep abreast of the young. Judging by President Nixon's laugh, perhaps it was, after all, a subject that he enjoyed. It certainly caused hilarity to the Secretary of State on my other side. The Secretary, Bill Rogers and I, hardly had the time to exchange a word other than to speculate on what sort of disguises we would wear to see 'The Last Tango.'

Finally, at two-thirty, the Nixons made their departure, but not before asking if they could glimpse the portrait of Field Marshal Montgomery painted by President Eisenhower. Rowley had to nip up to the top floor to fetch it as there was no member of the staff around. The portrait, although wooden, is a good likeness and an excellent attempt for an amateur.

The President, Prime Minister, their entourage and Rowley all departed for Camp David that afternoon. When they returned Rowley told me that the President said, with a chuckle, that he had 'enjoyed Lady Cromer' and that he had found her even more radical than himself!

Henry Kissinger seemed rather piano throughout the Embassy lunch and did not seem at all himself. He told me that he had put on a great deal of weight, and one could see that he undoubtedly had. It must be the Chinese food? 'No,' he replied, 'the Russian — those everlasting, long and tedious speeches which have to be translated while I have nothing to do but eat.'

23

SOUTHERN HOSPITALITY

One of the benefits of being an ambassador's wife was that she has an almost unfair advantage, as hostess or privileged guest, over her husband, by being seated at dinners or lunches next to an important or interesting man. The ambassador's neighbour, more often than not, would be the celebrity's wife; sometimes a pleasure, but seldom as stimulating. (Three years later the tables were neatly turned when Rowley hosted a dinner for the American Ambassador to London, Anne Armstrong. On that occasion he sat between her and Margaret Thatcher, then Leader of the Opposition).

Caspar Weinberger told me how thrilled he was to meet, for the first time, the legendary Mrs Longworth, with whom he chatted after dinner in our Embassy. She had recently celebrated her eighty-ninth birthday and was in sparkling form. On arrival she ordered a very dry Martini. Cap opened their conversation by asking how her father, President Theodore Roosevelt, had taken the news of President McKinley's assassination. 'With sheer rapture,' she replied. Her merry mood lasted throughout dinner, and afterwards the ladies withdrew to the drawing-room where she teased a strict Roman Catholic friend with the words, 'to be absolutely pure you must have loads of children, but I am not pure at all as I believe in contraception and abortion.' The Roman Catholic rather sharply replied that it was all a matter of self-restraint. Mrs Longworth, having no wish for the talk to continue down such a banal path, said: 'when a woman conceives five or six

311

minnows after taking a fertility drug, how can they possibly have souls?' My Roman Catholic friend would not be drawn. 'Another thing,' Mrs Longworth continued, 'no-one over eighty should have a vote or legal ability to make a will.' I asked her who she had voted for in the last Presidential election. 'Certainly, I voted for Dick,' she replied, 'but I would never vote for Spiro Agnew, and if he should run against Teddy Kennedy, I would vote for the latter. But if John Connally would run then, above all, I would vote for him.' By which time I figured she would be ninety-three. Mrs Longworth did, in fact, last until her mid-nineties. One could see clearly the pretty face she once had peeping out through the years, as sometimes can be seen on the very old.

Cap Weinberger told me that there was a rumpus taking place about two black girls aged twelve and fourteen who had been sterilised with their mother's consent in Alabama. This had been taken up by the press to be used for political reasons. Cap also told me that at that time seven million people had been sterilised in the US. One million in only the last year.

At a dinner given by Mrs Ethel Garrett for Tom Gates, head of a big New York bank, he asked me why Rowley did not visit New York as often as he did when Rowley was living in London. I tried to explain that it was because he was kept extremely busy in Washington. 'But New York is where all the decisions are made,' he said. I did not like to counter that it might have been true some thirteen years earlier but that it was certainly no longer the case, although possibly New York preferred to think so.

On February 25th we attended the Mardi Gras Ball. Senator Russell Long, the son of Huey Long, a famous name in Louisiana, had invited us. The Chancery was surprised at our friendship with the Longs. He was the influential Chairman of the Senate Finance Committee and had been courted by various British Ambassadors. But we had an inside track in mutual close friends, the Wickcliffe Moores, who had known my family for years, and Wickcliffe had been an outstanding newsprint salesman for the family business. He was also an old and valued friend of Russell's.

Unhappily the day before the ball I had undergone an operation under local anaesthetic in the Washington Hospital and had emerged with seventeen stitches in my abdomen. Nevertheless we could not disappoint the Longs. They might well have misunderstood any excuse and been offended.

The ball took place in the huge ballroom of the Sheraton Park Hotel. This Washington event, we were told, had become more popular than the famous ones in New Orleans which had, through the years, declined into stiffness and too much formality. Therefore thousands of Louisianans travelled to Washington for this ball. When we arrived we found the Longs surrounded by eager constituents. The ballroom held over four thousand people and was crowded. Russell asked me to dance, and on the way to the floor presented me to the Chairman of the Ball, who had as his guests at his table George Shultz and Cap Weinberger, both of whom greeted me warmly and seemed amused to see me in the arms of Russell Long. In the course of the evening we discovered that, not only the Chairman of the New York Stock Exchange was present, but also the Chairman of the Federal Reserve, and their presence proved to be of some practical use to Rowley, for amidst the showers of simulated gold coins thrown at the guests, Rowley was able to discover that the rumour which had reached London about the huge sales of gold the Americans were about to make had absolutely no foundation in fact.

Russell declared that he would disappear at some stage as he was a leading member of the Krewe, which appeared to mean that he would be a prominent member of a numerous body of men dressed in strange costumes, and whose faces would be obscured by small silk masks with two holes for the eyes. They made their entrance with the Floats accompanied by French and Spanish dancers and strolling musicians. The

313

Krewe wore numerous bead necklaces on each arm, and carried large bags of coins. They trotted and jigged down the aisles throwing necklaces and coins with some force at the assembled company.

At around eleven o'clock a fanfare of trumpets sounded before an announcement was made to the effect that the evening was also honouring the Inter-American States, and therefore a parade would now commence of twenty-seven Ambassadors and their wives from these countries. Each was announced and slowly walked down the aisles following their national flag carried by an American Marine. Rowley and I, feeling thankful that for once we had been spared, were a bit taken aback when the announcer spoke up again to say: 'We have among us another important guest who is visiting an ex-colony.' Sure enough we both had to rise and take a bow.

Then the full military band marched in playing the American anthem, followed by other patriotic pieces, for each of which everyone stood. Next came the entrance of the King. A Louisiana gentleman dressed in gorgeous robes, shimmering in silver and gold, wearing a crown and carrying a sceptre and with his long train flowing behind him. He walked regally round the room, eventually coming to rest on a huge throne raised on a platform at the far end, from which time he appeared to have no other duties. The King was followed by twenty or so Queens, each being announced as they made their entrance. The Queen of the Tomato Industry, and other Louisiana interests. They were all clothed in magnificent robes with huge trains on which were embroidered emblems signifying which industries they represented. One was the Queen of the Fishnets and Oil Wells. She wore a gold mesh dress with little silver derricks sewn on.

Finally, after a big flourish of trumpets the Queen of the Ball was announced. Even more gloriously dressed, she slowly advanced down the centre aisle — surprisingly to the tune of Land of Hope and Glory, as the Secretary of Inter-American Affairs covered his face with his hands and George Shultz, glancing at Rowley, quietly shook with laughter.

After all these parades had finished the dancing began. It was the custom of members of the Krewe to shed their remaining beads and necklaces and ask any stranger to dance. Everyone by then was becoming very merry and pretty boisterous. Rowley told me that it was time for us to leave or I would be dragged away and, as he pointed out, I was really in no fit state to dance, which was indeed true, for my stitches nipped every time I moved. The *Washington Post* printed a piece the next day saying that the Mardi Gras Ball had been a great success and enjoyed by everyone except the British Ambassador and Lady Cromer who, they said, left early.

The raid on the Democratic headquarters was beginning to become the focus of journalistic attention although it had not yet become a topic of general interest. Another six weeks would make a great difference.

The Bahamas were looking forward to their Independence in July and Mr and Mrs Pindling decided to visit Washington before this was to take place, so we decided to give a luncheon in Prime Minister Pindling's honour. He was leader of the Progressive Liberal Party. We also invited the Jamaican Ambassador and his wife, Mrs Fletcher. In the course of lunch Mrs Fletcher bemoaned the fact that she had no official car and chauffeur, but had to borrow her husband's when the occasion warranted. Mrs Pindling, however, assured her that when the Bahamas had their Independence, their Ambassadors' wives as well as the Ambassadors would each have a car and driver, and said that their Ambassador in Washington had already been chosen. I had not realised until this lunch how much rivalry there was between the islands of the Caribbean. When the beautiful chocolate-skinned Mrs Pindling announced that her husband's father came from Jamaica, Mrs Fletcher sharply replied, 'Well, that is why your husband is Prime Minister.' Mrs Pindling ignored this remark and turning to me, said that she was giving a surprise present to her husband on his birthday. It was to be a new Rolls-Royce!

Senator McClellan attended one of our weekly dinners. He told me that at the age of seventy-seven he had run again for Congress in the election the previous October. Strangely, he had gained votes from the young in Arkansas but, at the same time, he had lost some long-standing support. This was evidently because the sixty- and seventy-year olds, having retired from active life to nurse the aches and pains of old age, did not favour an even older person, however active, running for re-election.

A Parliamentary Commission arrived in March to investigate the running of the British Embassy and Military Mission. It was the first time this had ever taken place. One member of the delegation managed to make himself thoroughly unpopular with everyone. Firstly he questioned the arrangements made for the visit, and was then ill-mannered as well. An invitation to a party given in the delegation's honour by the Minister's wife, Mrs (now Lady) Sykes (whose husband was later, as our Ambassador, assassinated in The Hague), who had sent him an engraved card, had it sharply returned with a large 'No' written across the front. At the meeting of the Chancery and Military Staff, he intervened in order to announce that he was scandalised that certain members of the Chancery were unable to pronounce the names of some American cities correctly. Rowley, who chaired the meeting, irritated him still further by asking if he was therefore in favour of special classes being given to newcomers in the American language?

If there was extravagance at the British Embassy it was in London that any investigation should have been made; an example being the day when, to the horror of all the members of the Embassy, a huge carpet, costing an enormous sum, was laid in the Rotunda, the reason for which was unknown. It was accompanied by an order saying that only on two occasions a year could it be taken up. As the Rotunda was used for dances, bazaars, by the Embassy Players, as well as in many other causes in which a carpet would have been a hindrance, we were all appalled. Even the cleaning, particularly after cocktail parties, would be a problem, whereas before, with a polished wooden floor, all the debris was simply swept up. No-one ever discovered who had been the instigator of the carpet, and on no-one in the Embassy had it ever dawned that such an impractical extravagance was necessary. To admonitions from the Department of Environment to spend any money on new soft-furnishings and wallpapers (when they made their periodical visits to Washington) I would reply with a polite reminder that I did not intend to spend any of the tax-payer's money.

The Labour members of the delegation also complained that the Embassy had not bothered sufficiently with 'The Hill' (Congress). One wondered which disgruntled left-wing member of the House of Representatives had conveyed this message. It was plainly impossible to invite all the hundreds of members to dine. And like the other ambassadors, we tended to ask the many important chairmen of committees. And like them we were in competition for the pleasure of their company. We had, however, asked the four most important Senators to meet this Commission, and they came. It was a relief, too, when they showed by the warmth of their greeting just how well they knew Rowley and me. After the Commission left, polite thank-you letters were received from all the Conservative members, and none at all from the Labour ones. The visit was, I suppose, an attempt at some party-political mileage. There was certainly little gain in the field of Anglo-American relations.

On April 10th we set out on a visit to some of the old Southern States. First to Charleston in South Carolina. We were accompanied by Rowley's secretary, Charles Powell and his pretty wife, Carla. Charles had been sent by the Foreign Office as a replacement, and Rowley had specified that he wished, particularly, for a secretary with an excellent sense of humour. When Charles first took up the post, he tended to find Rowley's remarks more amusing than Rowley expected, and this puzzled him, for not all his remarks were meant to be funny. He then remembered his special request. Charles proved to be the perfect secretary, and indeed, went on to become indispensable to Prime Minister Thatcher. If Charles was rather shy, his bubbly wife was certainly not. Charles and I shared the same birthday, and at a dinner party which was held to celebrate the joint occasion, Rowley toasted us by saying that Charles was the keeper of his conscience and that I was the keeper of his heart. Charles' wife, being Italian, found some American names very difficult to pronounce, and in Charleston, that of Mrs Quattlebaum quite impossible. Mrs Quattlebaum had been designated our guide and mentor. She met us at the airport, and wherever we went she was beside us. The more attempts that Carla made to say her name the funnier it became until we all became hysterical with laughter, with the exception Mrs Quattlebaum, who simply looked perplexed.

At a Charleston dinner-party we met General Mark Clark who had commanded an American army in World War II. I asked him the same question that I had asked Field-Marshal Earl Alexander of Tunis some years earlier: 'What makes a great man?' General Clark answered at length giving a list of qualities: loyalty, courage, integrity and many other virtues of a similar kind, whereas the Field-Marshal simply answered, 'A great man is a person who makes decisions and carries them out.' But their thoughts may more have been on qualities that make a great general.

Before we started on our trip I had specifically asked, indeed pleaded, that at no time would we find ourselves in a small propeller-driven aircraft, and I had been most definitely reassured that we would not. The details of our visit had been arranged by the Consul in Atlanta who had, we understood, told Charles Powell that any likelihood of that contingency was out of the question. However, none of us had reckoned, as we should have, on the Consul surrendering to the Governor of North Carolina when the latter generously offered to send his aeroplane to fetch us for luncheon. To my horror, and Charles' mortification, at the airfield one of the smallest types of propeller-driven aircraft was waiting for us. Furthermore there was a high wind.

There was really no other option open to us if we were to reach the Governor of North Carolina's mansion for lunch, other than to cancel and give offence. It was more than likely that the Governor had arranged a lunch party, although we had not been told. Also there was, and is, a certain rivalry between the two Carolinas. Therefore it was unthinkable to visit one and not the other. Steeling myself and hoping for the best we embarked and found the journey far worse than anything we had anticipated — earache, compounded by a turbulent half-hour, during which we were tossed about in a most terrifying manner. It was, however, poor Charles who succumbed. White as a ghost, he was taken terribly ill, and on arrival was quietly taken away to lie down.

Dazed, and feeling both sick and frightened, I pleaded with the pilot to put us down in the nearest field anywhere. It really no longer mattered. This he immediately did without saying a word, and to my bewilderment a large black limousine was drawn up beside a very deserted-looking landing place. A very important-looking man stood beside the car and told us he was the Governor. 'What a curious coincidence that you should be passing,' I muttered, feeling completely disorientated. He was somewhat surprised, as we had, in fact, reached our destination.

Food was the last thing that we needed, but at what proved to be, not unexpectedly, a large and formal lunch, we tried to do the best we could. General Westmoreland was seated beside me. He had just retired from commanding the American troops in Vietnam. We talked of the media, and the general remarked with some force, that the *New York Times* and *Washington Post's* coverage of the fighting in Vietnam was 'not the same war that I was associated with.'

The Governor was delighted by Rowley's story of an ancient ledger he had seen in the Bank of England which recorded the interest that Martha Washington had received at six-monthly intervals on her British Government bonds during the War of Independence.

The Governor told me that the southern states were very proud of their old buildings dating back some three hundred years, but when he came over to England he realised that by english standards they were not really very old. I replied that I quite understood how he must feel. Then, noticing that his face had fallen, added that, of course, we British feel the same way when we go to Rome. This remark so pleased him that towards the end of lunch, both Rowley's story and my remark was recounted to the whole table.

The Governor realised how bad our flight had been and knew that poor Charles was still laid out in one of the bedrooms, so he kindly decided to lend us one of his cars instead of his aeroplane for the next leg of our journey — the long drive to Atlanta, Georgia. This took almost four hours, and that evening we were scheduled to dine with the Governor of Georgia and his wife, Jimmy and Rosalynn Carter. Our dinners and lunches in other States in no way prepared us for this one. Governor Reagan's in California had been a simple, elegant affair, but this one in Atlanta was neither.

The Governor's mansion in Atlanta was comparatively new, Atlanta having been burned to the ground during the Civil War. A new classical and imposing building had been built in keeping with the old one. Rowley and I had been told to wear formal evening clothes and, accompanied by a motor-cycle escort we thus set out wearily from our hotel after a very hasty change of clothing.

At the door of the Governor's mansion two military policemen stood to attention. Inside we were greeted by two young women wearing evening clothes, and sporting long white gloves, who escorted us to the drawing-room where the rest of the large company were waiting. The room was rather startling for it was almost entirely upholstered in shiny red satin. After a certain time had elapsed, the Governor and his lady made their entrance and walked royally down the rows of guests.

The news of our uncomfortable flight had gone before us and there was clearly some satisfaction in the apparent discomfiture of a neighbouring Governor. Governor Carter lightly drew attention to the fact that his official aeroplanes were all jet-propelled. Surprisingly, everywhere that we went, people seemed to have heard of our rough flight, and yet we had never mentioned the experience ourselves in order not to embarrass the nice Governor of North Carolina.

Jimmy Carter appeared to bear a curious resemblance to Jack Kennedy, which he certainly took no pains to discourage. We sat down at an extremely long table in the dining-room, the Governor at one end and his wife in the far distance, at the other. In the course of dinner I learned from the Governor that he was not a Southern Democrat, but a Democrat from the South — a sharp distinction in American politics. Carter, a lively talker, also possessed and easy manner and a ready smile. He was a friendly person, but his eyes revealed, I thought, a calculating mind belied by a disturbing naïvety. We discussed the huge black vote which had largely put him in power. He was evidently keen to expand welfare for the poorer workers. 'We give a dollar a day to mothers with no husbands, and a dollar a day for each child. This,' he continued, 'is a scandal. It should instead be increased.' I pointed out that if it was, surely few fathers and mothers would bother to go through the formalities of marriage, an institution which, sadly, seemed to be disappearing anyway. I asked him if he thought an accent on welfare spending could lead to an auction between the political parties as it had in England, which meant, in the long run, an impoverishment of the Exchequer coupled with a devaluation of the currency. Jimmy Carter listened carefully and then replied: 'We can afford it as we are a rich country.' It occurred to me that here was a candidate to lead the Democrats into a successful election (although with time and chance nothing can be certain).

The next day Rowley called on the Mayor and State officials while I chose to visit the Yerkes Center. The Center is the leading primate centre in the United States and, possibly the world. On the edge of the University Campus and close by a select residential area lives a large collection of apes. The Director of the Institute, Professor Geoffrey Bourne, showed me around. He was clearly very proud of the research work, and fond of the numerous inmates, all of which he knew by name; gorillas, orangutans, chimpanzees and other monkeys. He shared my belief that oriental people were likely to have been descended from the orangutans and westerners from the African apes, the orangutans being reserved people by monkey standards, introverted, contemplative and quiet, while chimpanzees are quite the opposite. It was interesting to discover that food is the chief motivation in the ape world, coming well before sex or territorial possessions. Many medical experiments were carried out under anaesthetics, and the operating theatre would have been the pride of any human hospital. Also the food being carried from a spotless kitchen was quite as appetizing as in many a restaurant. One monkey worked a rather primitive computer, ordering the food it wished, or even a video for its television. The video was, of course, of itself or other monkeys. One ape had become addicted to cannabis cigarettes and, as we passed him, he favoured us with a world-weary glance as he flicked off the ash with a lazy yet sophisticated gesture.

The infant monkeys lay in cots wearing diapers. It was interesting to discover that although apes are the most intelligent of all animals and can be taught a great number of tricks there is no way in which they can be house-trained. Their low emotional and stress ceiling causes a lack of control. It was not a happy find to discover that the blood of apes is constituted the same as humans, or that they possess the same numbers of chromosomes, for with genetic engineering who knows what one day this may lead to?

24

THE MOUNTING CLAMOUR

On our arrival back in Washington I was dismayed to find that the talk was of nothing but the scandal of Watergate. The relentless investigations of the *Washington Post* filled the newspaper with columns of allegations. Our Democratic friends were, nevertheless, elated, although one or two did bring themselves to admit that the scandal would not do much good to America's image overseas.

The situation was ironical, for President Nixon had behaved with exemplary propriety when, after the election of 1960, and before he had conceded to Jack Kennedy (who won with a small margin) he had not brought up any voting scandals. There had been stories of massive vote frauds in Chicago and Texas. It was rumoured also that dead men's votes had been used in Cook County. Before being the chosen Republican candidate in that election he had been Vice-President and had the country's reputation at heart, and in particular its chief offices. Therefore he told those that urged him to question the election that he would not do so as the scandal would hurt the Office of Presidency. He did, undoubtedly, do what he thought was best for his country over Vietnam in the face of civil strife and furious opposition. That his downfall should in the end have been caused by a political caper, however underhand, did not seem altogether fair.

As the month of April wore on, and under unremitting attacks from the press, the situation became even more threatening. The affair had now been taken up by Congress,

which tried and succeeded in uncovering further misde-
meanours. Haldeman and Ehrlichman were dismissed. John
Ehrlichman had dined and lunched with us at the Embassy
and we had found him to be pro-British and agreeable.
Possibly he would have been more at home in the Sergeants'
Mess, but that was not to his disadvantage.

President Nixon appeared on television to try and explain.
He looked tired and rather frail and his manner was a bit
maudlin. By that time he must have begun to realise the
disloyalty of some of his staff. Also, what had been done in his
name, knowingly and unknowingly. The *Washington Post* was
baying for his blood, I wrote to a friend on April 30th 1973.
The day before we lunched with Senator Byrd of Virginia.
Most of our drive was down the Harry Flood Byrd Highway
from which we deduced that the name Byrd must be one of
great distinction in that State. My first meeting with Harry
Byrd had been at a cocktail party soon after we had first
arrived; a nice-looking man engaged me in conversation without an introduction. We enjoyed our chat, and he finally asked
me if my husband worked in the British Embassy. 'Oh yes,' I
replied. 'And what does he actually do?' he asked. My subsequent answer caused some embarrassment until he shot
back, 'Well, I am a Senator.' We both decided we were quits
and laughed heartily.

His luncheon in Virginia was attended by many people;
other Senators and some White House personalities were
among the guests. It was an occasion when the regional dish
of Virginia baked ham was served, and nowhere does it taste
as good. Peter Flanigan, one of the President's chief advisers,
was among the guests. He told me that bugging had been a
custom in the United States ever since its invention; that
Senator Goldwater's headquarters had been bugged by the
Democrats, and when the Senator had complained loudly to
the press, the incident was given no prominence and no-one
had taken any further notice. 'At least,' Peter added, 'since
the Democrats are now being so pious, they have obviously

cut off any chances that Teddy Kennedy may have had.'

That evening we dined with a British newspaper correspondent who disarmingly confessed that he paraphrased Rowley's speeches on lecture tours, for which he regularly got paid. Rowley was delighted to hear that his speeches, which got little coverage, should have a wider audience than he realised.

In a telephone call between Cap Weinberger and me about a fund-raising event at the Folger Library, Cap said that whenever he left the White House, outside which the press now continually gathered, or on any other occasions when they wished to talk to him, and to whom he had a great deal to tell on the subject of his work as Secretary of Health, Education and Welfare, all they were depressingly interested in was the affair of Watergate.

This miserable scandal fell unfairly and hard on those good, honest and able people who were loyally serving their country, and had done their best and who were proud to be members of the administration of President Nixon. It did, in fact, completely ruin a period which they should have been able to look back on with pride for the rest of their lives. It was with a happy feeling that justice was done in at least two cases, when George Shultz and Cap Weinberger returned to office under another President as Secretary of State and Secretary of Defense, and to eventually retire with honour and distinction.

One evening around that time we dined with the John Kauffmanns. He was the-then publisher of the Washington evening newspaper. A fairly large dinner, the talk kept throughout the evening to the all-engrossing subject of Watergate. This topic chased all others from everyone's minds, like an earthquake or a hurricane. Mr Kleindienst, who had become Attorney General after all, although not for long, bemoaned the fact that the White House had thought very poorly of Nixon's chances of being re-elected. Now, forlornly, they wished that they had contacted the embassies which, with their detached view, the White House realised, had a distinctly opposite opinion. 'I suppose you were all sending telegrams to your governments telling them of Nixon's certain re-election?' he asked me, and I replied that as far as I knew that was certainly the case. 'Then all we had to do was contact your embassy, and any other efforts would have been totally needless.' It was a sad fact, and one wondered whether there would then have been no Watergate; 'For the lack of a nail,' for the lack of one telephone call to an embassy, the House of Nixon might have remained standing.

The atmosphere in Washington was becoming very unpleasant. Watching the hounding of anyone is painful, and the character assassination of a Head of State infinitely more so. In their unrelenting vehemence and pitiless anger, one could not help reflecting on a deeper, possibly almost unconscious feeling. Could it be that some sections of society wished for revenge? That having had their idol, Kennedy, so rudely taken from them, followed by Kennedy's and Johnson's defeated policies in Vietnam, their frustrated feelings became focused on Nixon, their scapegoat. Surely, the intensity of feeling generated was more than just a pious rejoicing over the misdemeanours of some officials in one political party?

We attended a dance in May given by a select group of Washington socialites, 'The Fivers.' My first dancing partner told me that he was busy telling all the ambassadresses to tell their husbands to telegraph home that the President had only a fifty-fifty chance of retaining his position. My next partner, who was also a Democrat, said he longed for the impeachment of the President. I told him that the outside world thought that Nixon was the best President since Truman, owing to his statesmanlike foreign policies. It was, however, a waste of breath. (It seems that when countries periodically brandish their new-found virtue, all the dormant puritan principles come to the fore and, mixed with hysteria and political mileage-seeking, the result is formidable and not a little frightening).

327

Sunday's *Washington Post*, in a long article covering two pages, followed the history of American wholesale fraud in and out of government since the earliest settlers — in each case a story of greed and illegal means of acquiring riches. The paper then ended the article by declaring that Watergate was the worst of all, because of interference with the course of free democratic elections. Even some Republicans, seeing that the Ship of State might be beginning to founder, also began to call for a general cleansing. Rowland Evans, a rightward leaning columnist, was congratulated for giving first prize to two water bugs at the Kennedy pet show. He, at least, exhibited a sense of humour.

In lighter vein, my turn came to give the luncheon for International Group One. I hired a bagpiper to play Scottish tunes, which was a great success. The ladies were enthraled, if slightly mystified, and said they had never seen a sporran quite so close. I had some trouble explaining what it was for to the French Ambassadress. We held a Thé Dansant for the American Museum in Britain. The theme was The Twenties, and it was fully attended, mainly by the elderly, who danced the charleston with considerable vigour. Some said there was a long line of ambulances outside to take the revellers home. Most of the guests had come in genuine twenties costume which, they said, they had never had the heart to throw away.

In early May a fund-raising event was organised at the cathedral. The theme was Great Britain. It was to be a Flower Mart, and I was asked to open the event by cutting a ribbon on the steps of the cathedral. But, before doing so, the Bishop of Washington asked me to plant a Glastonbury Thorn in memory of the Duke of Windsor. He gave me a long preamble about the sanctity of the Thorn and how it blossomed on Christmas Day, while I could not but think that a dogwood would have been more appropriate.

Around the cathedral were small booths selling both flowers and other items. Barbara Bush was in charge of one which she described as a 'cloakroom for goldfish' (the fish had been bought or won from other stalls by children). Prizes were to be given 'for the most authentic booth,' the meaning of which I never discovered. Some stall-holders had volunteered to be judged, but most had not. One booth called itself 'The Uncommon Market' which, to my mind, deserved a prize, but it did not win anything. When it actually came to the prize-giving, instead of the winners coming to receive their prizes, it was for the Presenter (me) to find the winner at their stalls. This did not prove as easy as one might think, and I could only suppose this method was thought to be more democratic. Shown the prize-winning stall, I presented the first prize to a lady standing behind the counter whom I mistook for the stall-holder. It became plain quite quickly that she was instead a customer. It was, however, all taken in good heart. With the second prize I found the rightful winner, but as she had just stuffed a large marshmallow into her mouth she was quite unable to speak. There was a display of Scottish dancing which much intrigued the crowd, for many said they had never before seen men in kilts, pointing their toes. One item being sold which proved to be very popular was little stuffed mice dressed up as clergymen.

May 16th was the beginning of the first Senate Investigation of Watergate on television. Two clean-limbed young Americans, Odal and Keogli, gave evidence. One declared his total belief and admiration for the President and both appeared truthful and the best specimens of America. Describing that session the next day the *Washington Post* called it 'dull, dreary and disappointing.'

The next day we watched James W McCord Jr, the indicted Watergate man, who talked. He appeared a strikingly different type and took every opportunity to smear the President, until even the investigating Senators began to grow wary.

There was, not surprisingly, a run on the dollar, thought to have been caused by the lack of confidence produced by the Watergate Investigation and the uncertain consequences from it. That same evening Kay Graham, the publisher of the *Washington Post* received the Woman of the Year Award for Economics and Business.

At a dinner that week Bill Fulbright looked as if he had swallowed a bowl of cream. No longer talking about Vietnam, he was in bubbling form. But Joe Alsop, another guest, was far from complacent. He remarked how frightful it was to watch the Democrats gleefully making jokes and laughing over Watergate without a care or notion of the damage they were doing, not only to their country, but to the Western World. At this time it did not seem as if anything could actually be pinned on the President himself for all, so far, was rumour and hearsay.

On May 23rd the Congressional Club held their annual Breakfast honouring the First Lady. In reality it was a gala lunch attended by some eleven-hundred women. They included all the wives of the Supreme Court Justices and the Cabinet. Each of the wives of senior officials was escorted down a raised cat-walk by a Marine in full dress (the Marines always seemed to be the chosen ones for escort duty). As they made their way thus to the top table the assembled company either clapped or left their hands in their laps. The First Lady was the last to arrive, and in spite of the strains of Watergate, Pat Nixon wore a brave smile and jauntily walked along, her skirt swinging, and dressed, as always, as neat as a pin. She made a light and charming speech and received a standing ovation for her courage and dignity. There were some who were reluctant to stand at first but, in the end, they all did and not-a-few shed tears.

Rowley told me that an ambassador has to exercise more diplomacy with his own Government than the one he is accredited to. When ideas come from Whitehall which are blatantly idiotic, and are strongly rebutted by the man on the spot, he is ignored. But if the man in Whitehall's ideas are carefully praised, then carefully demolished, there is a good chance of winning the argument.

The following month we held a dinner party for Henry Kissinger. We invited the Wickcliffe Moores down from New York, still a most successful newsprint salesman for my family's business, and a one-time professional conjuror of great talent. He had no equal when it came to card tricks. We did, naturally, ask the Russell Longs who were his good friends, also George and Barbara Bush and Senator Talmadge (who was taking part in the Watergate inquiry), among others. It was lucky that we had Wick Moore to entertain us after dinner for an understandable gloom descended on those Washington parties which included members of the administration. For besides Henry the party also included two Secretaries: those of Commerce and HEW.

Rowley introduced Wick after dinner as the man who had performed in front of, and baffled Winston Churchill and President Wilson. 'No,' Wick's wife corrected, 'President Wilson of General Motors,' which raised a laugh. Wick singled Henry out to participate in the tricks, and he was totally mystified. One specific trick involved asking Henry to place the red and black cards face down as he was told, and was completely perplexed when the colours were shown to have been laid in separate piles. He told Wick: 'I think that I had better take you to Paris with me.' This was for his next round of negotiations. George Bush was fascinated by every trick and wanted to know how they were done, but Wick was giving no secrets away. One of the American guests asked us which country Wick came from. 'Kentucky,' Rowley replied.

During dinner Henry told me that Henry Brandon's telephone had been tapped by a previous administration. He also said that there would be a press release the next day to the effect that the Kennedy administration had gone in for bugging in a big way, but the Embassy failed to find this picked up in the newspapers.

Henry mentioned how extraordinary his career had been. One moment high as a mountain, the next plunged into an

331

abyss. The trough at that particular time was caused, under-standably, by Watergate, which was having a predictable and devastating effect on Kissinger's brilliant efforts in the foreign policy field. He murmured dismally that 'no really clever or distinguished man would want to enter Presidential adminis-trations after this.'

Meeting Bill Blair, the Director of the Kennedy Center, at a dinner party about this time, I was surprised at the inten-seness of his distaste for Nixon. Bill, a man of great personal charm, told me with a wry smile that on a recent visit to London people had said that 'of course you are all rallying round your President in his time of need.' But Bill must have sadly disappointed them. On that evening he was particularly angry over Nixon's words: 'Truth is the most important thing of all.'

Another guest was Congressman Bingham from New York State, a most upright soul. He told me that never had such behaviour been perpetrated before in American politics. I remained doubtful and said that perhaps they had been lucky in not having been found out. Bingham then turned to a shrewd-looking elderly man for support, and asked him if the Democratic Party had ever indulged in the kind of behaviour that we were now reading about. The elderly gentleman, a Mr Rowe, proved to have been President Truman's campaign manager. He replied with a laugh: 'Well, one of my Chicago friends would say to a prospective fund giver, "Do you want your donation registered or not?" He would then open two drawers on either side of his desk. "The right one is for registered money and the left one is not. Which do you want me to put yours in?"' Congressman Bingham was dumb-founded. Mr Rowe had not heard our previous conversation.

At about this time Burke Trend, the then Secretary of the British Cabinet, flew over. I took the opportunity to ask him if American deals and political tricks were practised at West-minster. He was horrified at the suggestion. He seemed to be much concerned over a very different matter: that leading servants of the State in America, such as Dean Rusk (ex-Secretary of State), who had played their parts with loyalty and patriotism, were, in the end, cast away without honour and certainly oblivion. Perhaps it would be the same in England. I pointed out... 'were it not for the House of Lords, a notable depository for the distinguished.'

On 6th June I received a Courtesy visit from a distraught new German Ambassadress. Chancellor Brandt was about to make a visit, and the new Ambassador and his wife had arrived only a few days before. Their flat in the Residence was empty of furniture as their own was still in transit. There were no domestic servants at all, with the exception of a Hungarian gardener, who had tried to reassure them by saying, 'I do everything.' But in fact his only contribution was hosing the terrace and, by mischance, the guests as well. When told heatedly to go further away, he had not returned for two days. No bottle openers could be found and, since it was very hot and everyone needed a drink, the six security guards in attendance were told to find some, with the result that, at intervals, each would arrive happily brandishing an opener.

The German Ambassador himself had rushed off to the White House to present his credentials before the arrival of the Chancellor, only to be mistaken for the Chancellor himself by being welcomed with a flourish of trumpets. The Chancellor arrived fifteen minutes later, so it was a pretty close-run thing. At the end of the Chancellor's visit, the von Stadens returned exhausted to their Embassy, only to discover that the removal men had just arrived with their furniture. This seemed to me to be an almost typical example of the perils, demands and comedies of diplomatic life.

Joy Billington, a social page reporter, wrote that week of the imperiousness of the French Embassy over food. When she was covering a party of the 'Tastevins' at the French Embassy before coming on to the Music Hall at the British Embassy, a member of the French Embassy told her that if she was going on to the British Embassy for dinner, she had better eat first. The printed piece was deadly serious and a highly-flustered French Ambassadress telephoned me in a state of much agitation to apologise. I reassured her that there was absolutely no cause to think that any offence had been taken. And, as a further comfort, pointed out that our chef was himself French.

The Commonwealth Wives monthly teas had recommenced, and Madame Cadieux, the Canadian Ambassadress had, by general consent, become the President of the group, and it was her turn to be At Home to the wives. Anita Cadieux, a French-Canadian possessing vitality and intelligence, agreed with Cable Television to do a piece on their Embassy and its entertaining. We were not, however, told that our tea party would be included in the programme, nor how public the party would become.

Liberal Canada, held strangely conflicting views which were certainly represented in Anita and they were made more perplexing by her dual language.

Anita took the wives to be possibly more sophisticated than they were. The Commonwealth wives had declared several times that we were all equal within the Commonwealth, and equal was how she wished to treat them. Gathering round after tea all listened to what she had to say with rising dismay. She took them to task, and stated that the meetings might as well lapse since none of the senior (in diplomatic terms) wives wished to be President, i.e. Cyprus, Mauritius or Singapore. She went on to remind them that as they were equal they must, therefore, take their turn. She was, in my view, completely right, and it was certainly logical. But the effect of her words appalled. As she continued I became aware of various Indian and other sari-clad ladies moving towards me, murmuring 'Mother Country,' and giving me supplicating looks. Being tall, I was able to look down and smile faintly. Worse, however, was to come. As the television cameras started to record, Anita announced to the world in general that this tea party was an example of one of her Embassy's 'second class parties.'

It is possible that in French it may sound a great deal better, and we knew what she was trying to say, but unfortunately the vast majority of the guests took grave offence. With a rustle of Indian silks and African cottons, shocked, they sought my intervention. 'You must do something,' they cried. But I politely told them that as one of equals, and as I had not been invited to be President, there was really nothing that I could do, and reassured them as best I could that Madame Cadieux's words, I felt sure, were not intended to be in any way offensive. Fortunately at that moment a television interviewer grasped my hand and pulled me on to the terrace. Glad to have been extracted from one difficult situation I found only that I had been presented with another, and without any preparation.

In general the Americans look on the British Commonwealth as a humorous oddity, and when the interviewer asked me to define it, all I could think of saying was: 'Well, we speak the same language, and we all enjoy drinking tea.' Quickly escaping, I discovered on my return to the party that a lady from Swaziland wrapped in a toga of coloured cottons, was holding forth and getting very excited. Anita had evidently said that if the meetings went on at all they should not be tea parties. She had, unfortunately, left out the word 'necessarily.' The Swazi lady, by this time incensed and completely misunderstanding poor Anita, kept repeating loudly: 'She should not have invited us to tea and then say she does not want to give it to us.' Not making matters any better, the lady that poured the tea only spoke French.

25

THE BEGINNING OF THE END

'The best lack all conviction, while the worst are full of passionate intensity.'

Yeats.

The Chairman of the Senate Investigation Committee on Watergate was Senator Ervin. Hard of hearing, his bushy eyebrows shot up and down like railway signals when he became excited. He was fond of making unusual remarks to encourage the young men who came before the Committee, and to help them spill the beans, such as: 'We are all fellow travellers on the way to the tomb.' It was, we were told, not so much that he played to the gallery as to his constituents in North Carolina. He was, apparently, in danger of losing his seat and needed the publicity, so it was said. There was certainly no doubt that he was relishing the inquisition. He loved to quote freely from Shakespeare, but usually not correctly. Almost every day a member of the Committee murmured that 'something is rotten in the State of Denmark,' to a point when the Danish Ambassador began to think of making a complaint. Judge Sirica of the Grand Jury was, we were told, a Democrat, in spite of newspapers calling him a Republican. It was his severe sentence of twenty years which had, it was said, caused the conspirator McCord to say as much as he did.

William Rees-Mogg, the then-editor of *The Times* in London, made a speech at the National Press Club in Washington.

He had recently published a searing leader in *The Times* called 'Due Process of Law' criticising the American system of trying people three times over: the Grand Jury (abolished in England years ago) and which was meant to be held in camera (but whose business was leaked to the press), criminal courts and Senatorial investigations and, not least, trial by the press. His editorial was printed in the *Washington Post* accompanied by what I thought was a poorly-argued riposte.

When William Rees-Mogg arrived in Washington he found that, to his astonishment, he had stirred up a hornet's nest. I hoped he would have the courage to warn the American newspaper publishers of the dangers of their present journalistic ethics, and this he certainly did. He bravely said that 'the press in the United States has a duty to be fair to their President,' and that the nation's press, taken together, were not discharging that duty. That they had not given Nixon any credit for his major contribution in foreign affairs, and that their press was biased, and not willing to give credit where credit was due.' He really took them to task, and added for good measure that 'It is impossible to have a free press unless it is a fair press.' The next day the Embassy could find no reference of any kind to Rees-Mogg's speech in the *Washington Post*, and only a small piece on the back page of the *New York Times*. William told me that, in his view, where there is a plurality of newspapers, passionate views could be expressed at will, but where there was only one serious national paper, as in Washington, then it must present its views in a balanced and fair manner.

I was glad that someone with as liberal views, as I knew Rees-Mogg to hold, should comprehend this lack of balance. For it is possible that the most serious matter in America at that time was the abuse of the freedom of the press. The *Washington Post* seemed to be after President Nixon with the determination of a lean and hungry panther.

The third week in June saw the arrival of Mr Brezhnev on an official visit to poor beleaguered President Nixon. Due to the Russian visit, the Senate decided to postpone the Watergate hearings until after his departure.

Towards the end of June we lunched on *HMS Rothesay*, which was making a Courtesy visit. Mayor and Mrs Walter Washington were the chief guests with an American admiral and his wife. The Mayor made a small speech in which he disarmingly told of his first visit to a British naval vessel. This had taken place during the bad rioting in Washington after the death of Martin Luther King. He had felt safer away from the fires in the city. 'I guess,' he said, 'that no-one would fire that ship without a big struggle, so I am really glad to be back on one of Her Majesty's ships.'

It was generally acknowledged that the most zinging parties in Washington were held at the Iranian Embassy since the arrival of Ardeshir Zahedi, the Iranian Ambassador. He was then a bachelor, having earlier been married to the eldest daughter of the Shah. It was his second tour of duty as Ambassador in Washington and, in the interval, he had presided at the Embassy in London where he had been considered dashing and popular as well. On June 23rd he held a party to celebrate the Secretary of State's birthday but, as always a hazard in diplomatic life, the honoured guest was called away by the President who was in California. Nevertheless the party went ahead without him.

About sixty people sat at one long table. The first course was, as hoped, perfect Persian caviare, accompanied by champagne. The Ardeshir did his Cardinal Puff act with various guests, which had the desired effect of causing people to relax. After the second course we were told to clap our hands three times with those opposite and then kiss each of our neighbours. This was all right for me as my dinner partners were arguably the best-looking men in Washington. But Rowley did not fare so well, and therefore did not think much of this diversion. For the dessert we were told to put our arms through those of our neighbours and sway from side to side chanting, 'Oushka Moushka' followed by a loud 'Yad' and a quick sip of champagne then another kiss for each neighbour. This ritual was repeated three or four times. As my partners were Senator Percy and Elliot Richardson it was no hardship.

Ardeshir made a speech referring to the days when he washed up dishes as a university student, and ended by telling us of the entertainment to come after dinner, by which time everyone was anticipating at least a belly-dancer. We were ushered into a traditional room and seated on cushions placed on the floor, but we were to be disappointed for the entertainment proved to be that of an elderly gentleman playing a comanche, an instrument described by Rowley as looking like an overgrown onion attached to a emasculated violin. He began by playing eastern music and ended with a minuet by Schubert. After the concert a dance band played, beginning with a series of Paul Joneses, which proved popular, but which had long gone out of fashion. The main dish at dinner was called 'youngest sister-in-law' because, the Ambassador told me, it was a dish of rice concealing tender tit-bits.

This party was, with hindsight, another sad twilight, like Nixon's — soon to be gone. In this case all the fun, gaiety and extravagance was to be replaced by unremitting austerity. On looking back, perhaps there was a certain desperation in the liveliness of the hospitality, almost as if they knew that time was running out.

Charles Bartlett invited Rowley to play the part of George III in a spoof with Art Buchwald at Mount Vernon on Independence Day. Needless to say, he refused. But we did attend, at Charles' invitation, a gathering elsewhere to celebrate the occasion. Art Buchwald read the Declaration of Independence in full. He asked the audience to boo every time George III's name was mentioned, and to cheer whenever the word revolution or freedom was spoken. The result was that Rowley and I cheered when the audience booed. One wife of a Cabinet official said, 'I cannot think why they are celebrating as we are now putting up with far more than we ever did under George III.' Some people were rather embarrassed that we were there and yet, at the same time, clearly delighted.

The autumn of 1973 witnessed the Yom Kippur war. Early in October the Middle East erupted, with the Egyptians staging an attack on Israel on their sacred Day of Atonement. The State Department and the Foreign Office were equally caught napping by this act of belligerence, as neither had listened to reports from the field.

Henry Kissinger had just been appointed Secretary of State, ironically himself a Jew. He was extremely worried that this small but vicious war could easily escalate to include both Russia and America. He turned for advice to Britain, as being so well-versed in Middle Eastern problems, and in particular to Rowley, which caused his telephone to ring night and day almost continually for a week. The Americans had no representation in Egypt at that time, and therefore Rowley was used as a conduit between the United States and the Egyptians, while righteous and ineffectual noises issued forth from the United Nations. Rowley's advice to Henry was to wait for at least three days, in order to see which course the war would take. Henry's response was to ask Rowley if he was suggesting that he should sit back and allow the Egyptians to drive the Israelis into the sea. Rowley replied that 'only someone who is wholly unfamiliar with the history of the Egyptian Army could ask such a question.' Within ten days it had become, instead, a question of how to stop the Israelis from entering Cairo!

When some reporters asked Henry how he felt, since within his first week of becoming Secretary of State a war had broken out, he replied: 'I like to start with a bang!'

There were many changes in personnel in the State Department which for the diplomats meant getting to know the new incumbents. Watergate was causing such turmoil that Henry said that it was becoming impossible to keep his files abreast of the frequent changes in the Nixon administration. As it was he was now making his own announcements of new appointments, when they were customarily made by the President.

That same week of the Yom Kippur war the Vice-President resigned. His resignation had nothing to do with Watergate and everything to do with being Governor of Maryland. It was a different scandal and a fairly commonplace one in the political history of America. Spiro Agnew had publicly said that he was innocent of any wrong-doing and was believed; therefore his resignation came as another shock. The hounds of purity were on the scent of all political misdeeds, and he was yet another ninepin to fall.

In the meantime Rowley and I had to leave the Embassy for the redecoration which we had put off for so long. It fell to the Public Service Administration to find us other accommodation. A spacious apartment in the Watergate building was, in all seriousness, offered, but Rowley pointed out that he did not think that the British Ambassador would profit from such an address. So instead we acquired an apartment which the discredited Agnews were just vacating. Asked what kind of atmosphere they left behind them, I could truthfully say that it was a pleasant one.

The announcement on October 20th that Kissinger was to visit Moscow in order to discuss a settlement of the Israeli war came as a great relief. Rowley, at a fairly emotional meeting at the State Department, was asked by Henry if he was right to go, and he replied: 'Yes, since the Israelis look as if they are winning.' Both exchanged a meaningful handshake, and then Kissinger quipped: 'I find that my Israeli brothers are not dissimilar to the North Vietnamese,' (i.e. impossible to negotiate with). (In early November Kissinger had become quite exhausted after a five-hour discussion with Golda Meir who did not give an inch, and was wholly intransigent. Without extracting from Golda some counter to play with, it was evidently difficult for Henry to visit the Arab capitals and negotiate with their leaders).

During the Middle East crisis US troops were on Medium Alert. The situation within the country because of Watergate had become so uncertain that Kissinger had to publicly deny that the Alert had anything to do with domestic reasons. Also, that the President had no other choice than to follow the advice of his top advisers.

A fire broke out in our apartment just before the arrival of Solly Zuckerman for luncheon. Fortunately it was put out without ruining either our rooms or the food. Solly had come over to visit his friend, Admiral Rickover. He was full of news and opinions. He told us that he advised Gordon Richardson when he became Governor of the Bank of England that if he should prove to be a popular Governor he would not be a good one. He then warmed to the subject of Kissinger, whom he liked and had known for years. He did not evidently think him as clever as others thought. 'His great conceptual thinking may mean he is good at strategy, but his tactics are poor. He would lose a troop of boy scouts between Parliament Square and Waterloo Station.' I wondered, with all due respect, whether Winston Churchill would have done any better.

The Iranian Ambassador told me that it was a pity that America was so obtuse in her relations with the Arabs. 'They do not understand them,' he said. Chou en Lai told Marquis Childs, when the latter was visiting China as a syndicated columnist, that he could not understand what the Watergate fuss was all about, since surely American politics had always been the same. It did seem strange to all foreigners that America should rejoice in demonstrating its prudishness to the world over any moral lapses in its government. Also, unhappily, few Americans seemed to be aware, or apparently care, how Watergate had crippled the President in making any statesmanlike decisions.

While Kissinger was in Moscow trying to bargain for a cease-fire in the Middle East, Elliot Richardson, who had succeeded Mr Kleindienst as Attorney General and was regarded as Mr Clean, gave in his resignation. Archibald Cox, the Justice Department Prosecutor in the Watergate Cover-Up had been appointed by Elliot. Both were New Englanders, and both were of a liberal persuasion. Cox, on television, showed a puckish personality, his sense of humour and of mischief shone brightly from his countenance. He giggled and made oblique remarks against the President.

President Nixon made a deal with Senators Ervin, Stennis and Baker that for the sake of maintaining executive privilege, a summary of the President's tapes would suffice and, therefore, the dignity of the office of President be preserved. Elliot agreed to this but Cox not, although ordered to by the President, who then dismissed him from his post as Prosecutor. It was then that Elliot chose to resign, which action was regarded as a stab in the back by White House officials who considered that he had been in a position to persuade Cox to agree to the summary. Also that he might have warned the President of his own impending resignation.

Elliot had, knowingly or unknowingly, gained a reputation of being the image of respectability by both Democrats and Republicans. He was a consensus politician, being a liberal Republican. One of his close friends described him as being 'half enlightened and half a stuffed shirt.' At Elliot's press conference he did try to defend Nixon, who had, after all, appointed him to high office, and by his silence condemned him. My Democratic friends said at the time that if Elliot decided to run for President they would all vote for him. He was fast becoming famous. Also his 'doodles,' which were clever, were becoming valuable and people clamoured to own them.

General Haig, at that time one of the chief assistants to the President, told the Senators that Richardson had lied when he said that he did not approve of the President trying to limit Cox's investigation and that, in fact, he had agreed that Cox had gone too far. Elliot then stated publicly that he had not told a lie since the age of twelve years old. He was certainly honest enough when he later arrived in London as United States Ambassador, and publicly said that he would be spending his time while in Britain writing a book.

The dreaded word impeachment was now becoming common currency. Professor Goodhart of Oxford University announced that the President was legally entitled to withhold his tapes on the basis of the national interest, but that this would not preclude impeachment by Congress.

We held a dinner party primarily for Julian Amory (a right-wing Conservative) who, however, had to cancel. Instead we found that Joe Grimond (ex-Leader of the Liberal Party) was to be in Washington so we invited him, much to the surprise and amusement of our other guests. The White House Flanigans were there, both intensely and emotionally loyal to the President, and both very intelligent and agreeable. Senator Pell (a liberal Democrat) and Senator Mathias (a liberal Republican and an outstandingly nice person) were also present, and were vigourous in their censoriousness of the President. Stewart Alsop was also among the guests and he related to me a touching story.

Stewart had gone on a journalistic visit to Nixon's mother in 1959 when Nixon was Vice-President. On driving away he suffered the unpleasant experience of his sun-glasses blowing up due to the heat in the car. He returned to old Mrs Nixon, who carefully and kindly removed the small pieces of glass from Stewart's eye. He told me that she resembled Nixon in looks and possessed enormous charm. During her ministrations she told Stewart about the Teapot Dome scandal which had rocked America when Nixon was a boy. She said that her son had followed the story carefully in the newspapers, and remarked to her that one day he would go to Washington and clean up the place and help make politics and politicians honest.

Rowley always maintained that had Nixon been taken up by the WASP establishment in New York when he first practised law there none of the scandals would have occurred.

By this time the newspapers were saying that Nixon was emotionally unbalanced, but at his press conference on television he handled himself fairly well, even if his voice sounded rather choked with emotion. He put forward some of his administration's successes, including the-then present Middle East position. But when his questioners asked him if he was angry with certain newscasters he retorted with some force: 'I am only angry with those that I respect.'

If President Nixon was, by that time, physically and mentally worn out, lesser men would have collapsed earlier. The burden of taking unpleasant decisions such as the Haiphong bombing; of trying to extricate America with some vestige of honour from a war not of his own making (while the media appeared not to understand, vilifying him instead, and as the younger elements rioted in the streets and burned him in effigy); to find himself a figure in a remorseless Greek tragedy with no positive ray of relief, pilloried for misdeeds, which he knew better than anyone had been committed by former administrations with and without the knowledge of their Presidents; to see friends and colleagues blamed, even imprisoned; to witness the distress of his family and disloyalty of those he had trusted, would surely have crushed any ordinary mortal.

When I deplored the disloyalty of some of Nixon's White House officials to Sir Isaiah Berlin, he replied that 'you cannot expect the rats to line up with the captain on the bridge when the ship is sinking.'

We dined one evening with Peter and Brigid Flanigan and Leonard Garment, also a White House Adviser, was present. He lamented over the shockingly bad language the tapes revealed that the President frequently used. Trying to find some words of comfort I suggested that, at least, they would show that they had not been doctored, but even that gave no solace.

Dinner parties were now fraught with difficulties. One could not be certain that an honoured guest would not be publicly discredited or disgraced before the dinner took place.

Shortly after the Flanigan evening we dined with the Deputy Secretary of the Treasury, Bill Simon, and his wife. This occasion coincided with the President's television and radio press conference, which became known as the 'I am not a crook' appearance. Unquestionably our hosts must have wished that they had not asked us on that very evening in view of this broadcast, but no-one wanted to miss it.

On our way to the Simons' house we both listened to the car radio, for the press conference had begun. It was compelling, and we were reluctant to miss any of it, but could not delay our arrival. As we drew up at the front door I glimpsed a group of people in the side room watching the television, and wondered if they could be staff or offspring and if there would be an opportunity to join them. On our arrival we were shown into the drawing-room where, to our disappointment, there was no television, or for that matter, any other guests. The warm welcome the Simons gave us belied a certain uneasiness. Unable to resist, I said that we had been listening to the President in the car, and could we go on doing so since no other guests had arrived? 'But they have,' Bill Simon admitted. 'They are all watching it on the television and there are no more available seats.' There seemed to be a curious reluctance to let us join them, possibly because we were foreigners, even an embarrassment over the situation: it was hard to guess. I stated that it was important that Rowley should see it because of his job, and that we would be quite happy to sit on the floor. The other guests proved to be George and Obie Shultz, Ken Rush, the Deputy Secretary of State, and many others, all American, and all insiders.

We all sat glued to the box, and watched a gripping and yet shocking scene. 'The stag at bay,' the cornered fox being bitten by snarling hounds, or was it a bear being baited? One thing was certain, it was a most tragic and unsporting display. Moreover, it was the public humiliation of an American President and, at that time, the leader of the Western World.

The President fended off the questions with some skill, although he made one unfortunate slip of the tongue when he mistakenly said that 'all were guilty unless proved not guilty.' The questions were barbarous and included personal ones, as well as on Watergate. It was, nevertheless, an heroic performance and was well received by those in the room.

At dinner I sat between Bill Simon and Ken Rush. Ken told me how for the past few months it had been impossible to communicate with the President as he had shut himself off like a wounded animal, whereas before Ken had rarely been able to complete a round of golf without being interrupted by a call from the President. Ken went on to say that one of the saddest elements in the tragedy of Watergate was Nixon's admiration and self-identification with General de Gaulle. When Nixon was out of office the General had always gone out of his way to see him, and had always treated Nixon with the greatest respect, and made it clear that he thought that Nixon would be President one day, and an outstanding one at that. Nixon, on his side, had studied de Gaulle and like him, wished to dedicate himself heart and soul to his country. But where General de Gaulle controlled his Assembly and enjoyed a good press, President Nixon had neither, which, in the end, was his undoing. Ken continued that the President tended to leave small things to others, and of course it was frequently the small things that killed you, such as tripping over a stone.

At another evening that week, Cap Weinberger was my neighbour at dinner. He was very despondent and worried about his future career and his present job. He told me that he could make some of the decisions in the Department himself, but the larger ones had to go to the President, but now no reply came from that quarter, nor any help. 'A kind of non-Government exists,' he said.

Some Cabinet members now became embarrassed to go out socially, which meant having to listen to attacks and mockery of their President and his administration. Even Republican Senators like Senator Dominick from Colorado were in distress over their prospects in the following year's Senatorial election. He explained that most of his State's newspapers were strongly democratic in their views and poured out as much vitriol as in Washington. I asked Peter Dominick why he did not find out some wrong-doings in the Democratic camp, and he answered that it would be an easy thing to do, but those newspapers that were influential in his State would not print them. We spent another Sunday in the country with our old friend, Celia Bolin, whose son-in-law was Phil Geyelin, the editor of the editorial page of the *Washington Post*. It was also the tenth anniversary of the assassination of Jack Kennedy, and this was very much in the mind of Phil Geyelin, whose idol he had apparently been. I sat between him and Ambassador Ellsworth Bunker at lunch, and Phil inveighed against President Nixon. He was not prepared to acknowledge Nixon's successful foreign policy and, what confused me, said that he had simply carried out that of Kennedy. I asked him if he thought the war would have taken place if Kennedy had lived. He judged not. But it was known that President Kennedy had sent, no doubt for the best of reasons at the time, 16,000 American troops to act as combat 'advisers' to the regular South Vietnam units. It was interesting to discover that many were certain that Kennedy would have had the answers to all the problems. And again I wondered whether Richard Nixon was taking the unconscious blame for the death of Jack Kennedy. There was so much passion, and some could not bring themselves to give credit to Nixon for anything. Even the appointment of Gerald Ford as Vice-President was criticised, although one journalist reluctantly conceded that swift confirmation by the Senate was vital, and there were no obvious candidates.

Ellsworth Bunker, my other neighbour at lunch, was a model of quiet rational thought. Ambassador Bunker was one of those extraordinary Americans of advanced years who continued in harness until late in life, and yet managed to keep the vigour of their intellect intact, with the added benefit of a mature wisdom built on long years of experience. At the age of eighty he had only very recently retired from being Ambassador to South Vietnam, which must, at the very least, have been a hardship post. He disclosed that it was only at the end of the war that a super bunker had been built for his safety. Before that he had had to make do with only a makeshift one. Pot shots had been fired at regular intervals into his sitting-room from a Catholic graveyard. But when he requested that the local police should protect that area, nothing would induce them to do so, for they said that they would be far too scared at the thought of meeting a Roman Catholic ghost. Ambassador Bunker went on to say that on returning to Washington after so many years away he had found it a 'cultural shock.'

Rowley decided by early 1974 his tour of duty as Ambassador should end. Three years, he said, was enough. There was also the consideration of the British general election which was due, and what we thought was the almost certain outcome of a Labour win. 'I will not give Harold Wilson the satisfaction of sacking me,' he said. Therefore he gave the British Government notice of his retirement, and in November the announcement of his successor, Sir Peter Ramsbotham, was made. Our friends hastened to tell us how sad they were, and total strangers wrote to say how sorry they were. One even went as far as to say: 'You added an extra touch of zing to my life.' How I managed that, is beyond me.

To our surprise the elegant and extremely poised Lorraine Cooper asked if she could call on a very important matter, and we were even more surprised when we found out the reason. John Sherman Cooper had retired from his long and distinguished career in the Senate, and now in his late seventies, was still available for Government appointment. Old age was certainly not a bar from obtaining a responsible job, and after all there was David Bruce who had only recently been sent to China; and there was also Ellsworth Bunker who had only just retired.

Washington is a city almost exclusively centred on Government. After any new Presidential election or shake-up, speculation on who gets what and where is the absorbing and general topic. Little else is talked about. Now, with the 'fall-out' of Watergate, and with people losing their jobs or being re-allocated, conjecture was again rife. To retire and be a back-number in Washington was only for those who had other interests and a philosophical turn of mind. We heard that there had been an embarrassing evening at Averell Harriman's when Averell had twice toasted John Cooper as 'our future Vice-President, and if not that, then America's coming Ambassador to Moscow.' There was evidently some disappointment when that latter post had gone to someone else, and Lorraine felt this most deeply.

There in the sitting-room of our apartment sat this most poised, sophisticated, exotic and beautifully dressed woman, supplicating Rowley with tears falling from her eyes, to do her a favour and ask Henry Kissinger to give John the ambassadorship of Egypt, Bonn or NATO, in that order. 'I know how close to Henry you are,' she said. Rowley tried to tell her that it was really beyond his brief to interfere in any American appointments, but if the opportunity arose, he would certainly put in a good word for John. There was, understandably, an atmosphere of embarrassment after Lorraine made her plea, and she apologised. To ease the discomfort, I told her that she could not have paid us a greater compliment in coming to Rowley to ask for his help.

Some time later John was offered, and accepted, the post of Ambassador to East Germany. It seemed a paradox that the most sophisticated lady in Washington should preside over a bleak embassy in a country of Communist austerity. Nevertheless, Lorraine professed to be delighted. She took, as butler, our first footman, who remained with them for years and was devoted to her. She was, I always understood, a great success, and for her part, she always maintained how much she had enjoyed her time there. A woman of distinction, intelligent, kind and thoughtful, she was much liked by the young, and yet was the personification of an age which ended with World War II.

Henry Kissinger, as Secretary of State, decided that it was time to give his first formal Diplomatic Reception at the State Department. This was the first we had been invited to. Possibly because of Watergate, it was in place of hospitality at the White House. The entire Corps of Ambassadors and their wives attended, and we stood in line for some forty minutes before being ushered into what Rowley termed the Presence Chamber. Henry stood in front of two flags and faced a velvet rope which penned in the press corps. After being received we all filed into the Franklin Room where surprisingly I was introduced to Audrey Hepburn, the film star. She was quiet and polite and by no means conspicuous, so few noticed her presence. The Franklin Room was dominated by a raised desk from which Henry proceeded to address us. In his rolling phrases and with a faintly guttural accent he treated us to a fairly lengthy speech. We all laughed when he joked that 'a practice common to both Diplomats and Congressmen is that they will both report home, with the difference that the Congressmen will say that the Diplomats were drinking openly and talking secretly, while the Diplomats will say that the Congressmen were talking openly and drinking secretly.' He concluded by saying that 'We are in one of those rare moments in history where it is possible to bring about a new international order. The goal will be to move from a peace based on security to a peace based on community.' He ended by saying that 'the magnitude of what we strove for will move the world over a new threshold and into an era of stability and peace.' Standing in the front row, Henry came towards me as he finished. Realising that I was expected to murmur something, I told him, with truth, that it had been a pleasure to have listened to such magnificent english. He replied, 'That is the greatest compliment that you could have given me,' before going on to receive many tributes.

George Shultz came up to us to tell us, most touchingly, how sorry he was that we were leaving. He told us that at the Finance Ministers' meeting he mentioned to Tony Barber that we were irreplaceable and greatly loved. On hearing this we felt that our three-years in Washington had, after all, been worthwhile. Someone knocked the end off my cigarette which, I am afraid, burned a hole in the carpet right under the eyes of the Chief of Protocol. 'Help, I have set the State Department alight.' 'It does not matter one bit,' he replied.

Occasionally in my life I have been asked who of those that I have been fortunate enough to meet and talk to did I think were the greatest. Without hesitation, then as now: Winston Churchill, Henry Kissinger and Margaret Thatcher. When asked why, I would reply because all three had or have a grasp of global matters, not only in their own season but for the time to come. That does not mean that they were perfect; they had faults like anyone else.

Willis Armstrong, who was about to leave his job at the State Department and was a good friend of Britain's, told us that the State Department affairs were chaotic. That in spite of Henry's brilliant and many qualities, he was no administrator. 'He is a one-man band, who plays every instrument in turn.' Willis continued that, in his eyes, Henry was not an American, and therefore did not understand Americans, and that this was a danger. In fact, of course, it was for that very reason that Henry was so successful with other nations, for he had the wisdom of the old world about him. There was also, doubtless, some jealousy over Henry's spectacular career.

Senator Saxbe of Ohio was nominated as Attorney General. He was the fourth Attorney General in a year. He told me that the only difference he detected in the President was his speech. He had begun to talk unnaturally fast.

On December 6th Rowley went to the swearing-in of the new Vice-President, Gerald Ford. There was the, by now expected, confusion. After waiting half an hour in an unfurnished room, the ambassadors were called in by the Chief of Protocol in order of precedence. To Rowley's discomfiture, he found that he had been overlooked, although he was now thirty-six in seniority out of one hundred and thirteen. He discovered, after lodging a complaint, that he was not on the list. After that had been sorted out the ambassadors trooped on to the House floor to applause, only to find that their reserved seats had been already taken. The unfortunate occupiers were then turned out.

Gerald Ford, to everyone's surprise, made a good speech, which under the circumstances, could not have been easy. His remark that 'I am a Ford, not a Lincoln' met with great approval from the audience.

From our arrival in February 1971 to our departure at the end of January 1974 there seemed to be a continuous swell against the establishment, an undercurrent of discontent. Now, after three years, those who wished for the downfall of President Nixon were soon to obtain their goal. The sands were fast running out, and it would have been indeed sad to have stayed on and witnessed his final humiliation.

When it became known that we were leaving, kind friends and acquaintances immediately asked for a date to give us a Farewell Party. They also asked us to give them a list of people that we would like them to ask. There were a great many parties, and in order that the same people were not to be continually present at each one, I worked out a system of listing different names in coloured ink, so that few friends went to a Cromer party more than twice. Another consideration was that Rowley always had to make a short farewell speech, and there were not too many variations.

One memorable dinner was given by the Flanigans. Although for few in number, it was headed by Henry Kissinger and his future wife. George and Obie Shultz, Bill and Carol Simon and Cap and Jane Weinberger were there. It was a happy evening, although I missed the Kissinger quips, since he talked in the group that contained Rowley. One was: 'Opportunities cannot be hoarded. Once past, they are usually irretrievable.' Only as we were leaving I heard him say jokingly that he did not mind the British Ambassador leaving before him, but that he would not wait for the German Ambassador. Bill Simon explained to me how impossible it was to make the liberals understand about 'risk.' They only thought about riches that had been made, never about those fortunes that had been lost. 'Why,' he said, 'I must have invested in over five hundred dry wells before I struck a good one.' George and Cap had been arguing most of the day. George, as Secretary of the Treasury, had been trying to curb the demands from HEW, one of the great spending Departments, which Cap was in charge of. I said to George: 'As Cap was previously Director of the Budget, he must know all the difficulties of overspending?' 'That is just it. He knows too much,' replied George with a smile.

The proudest evening was the party that the Weinbergers kindly gave us at Blair House. This is a building where visiting Heads of State stay, as the White House is too small. Situated opposite, it is an elegant eighteenth-century house, and we were astonished to find, in pride of place, an oil painting hanging on the wall of a member of Rowley's family, the first Lord Ashburton. This made the venue welcoming, and certainly it was a very good party and enjoyed by all who came.

On January 17th Rowley took his leave of President Nixon in the White House. Their interview lasted fifty minutes during which, Rowley told me, the President spoke almost continuously. From what he said, he appeared to be much more friendly to Europe than Henry had indicated. Naturally his own problems were not spoken of. He was extremely cordial, and he jokingly said that he wished he could have made me head of the women's campaign for his re-election; and then, touchingly, asked him to give me one of his pins of the Presidential seal. Forty television cameras were wheeled in latterly for a three-minute scene.

The week before we made our final departure a presentation party was held by Virginia Bacon, one of the last remaining of the Washington Hostesses, then aged eighty-four. The presentation speech was delivered by Justice of the Supreme Court, Potter Stewart, who had become a close friend, with his delightful wife, Andy. The gift, chosen by Rowley, was a piece of Steuben glass shaped like an obelisk resting on four golden griffins. The griffin, being the mythical offspring of the lion and the eagle, appealed to Rowley for its symbolism and its suitability. There were other presents. One, a small antique enamel Bilton box, had a touching message inscribed on the lid: 'May Briton's sons forever be a conquering people loved and free.' Paradoxically the giver, Bernice Maguire Smith, was very proud of her Irish ancestry, as is her distinguished husband, Gerard. Our friendship had been a long-standing one from our first tour of duty.

We were much moved by a farewell dinner at the Italian Embassy where Egidio Ortona had gone to the trouble of finding and playing Beethoven's little-known variations on God Save The Queen and Rule Britannia.

We finally left with heavy hearts. We had lived among kind and warm-hearted people for three years. Their interests had become ours. Their lives and events a source of continuing interest to us. The horrors of Watergate had brought us close to the Administration. They had felt us to be sympathetic, which we were, and if we showed partisanship, it was inevitable. To be close to Government was, after all, Rowley's brief. Now, no doubt, the time had come for a professional diplomat to take over. By the nature of things, and by his training, he would, presumably, be less close and more detached.

Our departure from the Embassy, as our arrival, was made between lines of domestic staff. May, the head housemaid, gave me a deep curtsy; Peter, the second footman, bowed low and kissed my hand, while Eade, my chauffeur, blinked back tears. We left by train, and were seen off by a group of friends and a platoon of Chancery personnel, headed by the Minister and Admiral Easton who, as Head of British Defence Staff, was attired in full dress uniform.

As our train slid out of the station our thoughts moved ahead; the green and pleasant land beckoned. The future would be less exciting, but given good health and luck, that elusive pursuit of happiness might still be in our reach.

26

POSTSCRIPT

Rowley most sadly died quite suddenly in the early hours of March 16th 1991. On the last day of his life he re-read some of the typescript of this book with evident enjoyment. From the first he gave me great encouragement, relating episodes, giving facts, and passing on remarks that I would otherwise not have known, besides being in complete agreement with all the views and opinions stated in this book.

INDEX

33rd Guards Brigade, 8.

A
Acheson, Dean, 231.
Adair, Sir Allan, 11.
Agnew, Mrs Judy, 282, 283, 297.
Agnew, Spiro, 273, 274, 312, 341.
Aldington, Lady Araminta, 243.
Alexander, Field-Marshal Earl, 318.
Alexandra, HRH Princess, 230.
Alsop, Joe, 88, 194, 232, 330.
Alsop, Stewart, 344.
Amies, Hardy, 187, 228.
Amory, Julian, 344.
Anne, HRH The Princess, 230.
Annenberg, (later Hon) Lee, 303, 304, 307.
Annenberg, Ambassador Walter, 184, 258, 260.
Arden, Elizabeth, 92.
Armstrong, Hon Anne, 311.
Armstrong, Willis, 352.
Ashton, Sir Frederick, 115.
Astor, Lady, 28.
Astor, Lord, 20.
Athelhampton, 31, 32.
Attenborough, (later Sir) Richard, 291.

B
Bahawalpur, Nawab of, 130.
Baker, Mrs George, 43.
Baker, Senator, 343.
Balsan, Madame Jacques, 43.
Bangkok World, 198.
Barber, Anthony (later Lord), 76, 242, 244, 288, 289, 352.
Baring, Evelyn Bingham, 47, 101.

Baring, Hon Evelyn, 46.
Baring, Sir Evelyn (later 1st Lord Howick), 70.
Barings, 37, 47, 182.
Bartlett, Charles, 295, 339.
Bax, Sir Arnold, 21.
Bayh, Senator Birch, 281.
Beaumarchais, Monsieur, 252.
Berlin, Sir Isaiah, 211, 345.
Betjeman, John, 284.
Billington, Joy, 333.
Bingham, Congressman, 332.
Black, Eugene, 70, 76.
Blair, Bill, 224, 245, 332.
Blundell, Sir Denis, 188.
Bolin, Celia, 348.
Bondi, Professor, 236.
Braithwaite, Warwick, 21.
Brandon, Henry, 75, 287, 302, 331.
Brandt, Chancellor, 333.
Brezhnev, 337.
Brown, George, 167, 168.
Bruce, Hon David, 349.
Buchanan, Hon Wiley, 232.
Buchwald, Art, 339.
Bunker, Ambassador Ellsworth, 348, 349.
Burger, Chief Justice Warren, 273.
Burnet, (later Sir) Alastair, 115.
Burns, Arthur, 195.
Burns, Mrs Arthur, 283.
Bush, (later President) George, 253, 331.
Bush, Barbara, 253, 328, 331.
Bush, Mrs Prescott, 253.
Bush, Senator Prescott, 88.
Butler, (later Lord) Rab, 115.
Byrd, Senator Harry, 325.

C

Cabot, Ambassador, 72.

Cabot, Mrs, 73.

Caccia, Lady, 87.

Caccia, Sir (later Lord) Harold, 86.

Cadieux, Madame Anita, 204, 295, 334, 335.

Caesar's Palace, 262, 265.

Callaghan, James (later Lord), 106, 167, 169, 175.

Carr, (later Lord) Robert, 224.

Carter, (later President) Jimmy, 321.

Carter, Rosalynn, 320.

Carusi, Gene, 238.

Castle, (later Baroness) Barbara, 115.

Castro, 85.

Cayley, Lady, 18.

Cayley, Sir Kenhelm, 16.

Cecil, Lord David, 230.

Charles, HRH Prince, 236.

Chataway, Christopher, 188.

Chiang Kai-Chek, 73.

Child-Villiers, Arthur, 47.

Childs, Marquis, 342.

Childs, Mrs Marquis, 201, 223.

Chou en Lai, 238, 342.

Church, Senator Frank, 201.

Churchill, Arabella, 216.

Churchill, Lady, 49, 51, 56, 57, 58.

Churchill, Sir Winston, 48, 50, 54, 172, 331, 342.

Clark, General Mark, 318.

Clarke, Colonel Frank, 39.

Cliburn, Van, 299.

Clifford, Clark, 238, 239.

Cobbold, Lord Kim, 93, 100, 101, 104.

Congressional Record, 287.

Connally, John, 195, 220, 240, 242, 243, 244, 254, 255, 288, 312.

Connally, Nellie, 254, 273.

Coombs, Nugget, 112.

Cooper, John Sherman, 43, 201, 349.

Cooper, Lorraine Sherman, 126, 191, 193, 200, 248, 349.

Cooper-Church Amendment, 201.

Cooper-Key, (later Sir) Neil, 13.

Cornwallis, Lord, 187.

Costa, Mary, 306.

Cox, Archibald, 343.

Cromwell, Oliver, 58.

Crosby, Bing, 93.

Crowe, Sir Colin, 253.

Crowther, (later Lord) Geoffrey, 46.

D

Darwin, Sir Robin, 172.

Davis, Sammy Jr, 299.

Day, Sir Robin, 183.

Dayan, General, 204.

De L'Isle, 1st Viscount, VC, 187.

Desborough, Lady, 104.

Dewey, Thomas, 267.

Dillons, Doug, 126.

Dobrynin, Anatoliy, 205, 248, 264.

Dobrynin, Mrs, 232.

Dominick, Senator, 347.

Douglas, Mrs Lew, 290, 291.

Douglas-Home, Elizabeth, 173, 290, 306.

Douglas-Home, Sir Alec (later Lord Home), 173, 183, 200.

Dudley, Lord, 45.

Dulles, John Foster, 70, 85.

E

Easton, Admiral, 356.

Eden, Sir Anthony, 61.

Edinburgh, HRH The Duke of, 230.

Ehrlichman, John, 270, 325.
Eisenhower, Mamie (Mrs Dwight), 89, 92, 224, 282.
Eisenhower, President, 85, 221, 310.
Elizabeth, HRH Princess, 44.
Elliott, W H, 5.
Ellis, Dr Osian, 230.
Ellsberg, Daniel, 231.
Errington, Viscount, 3.
Ervin, Senator, 336, 343.
Evans, Rowland, 328.

F

Fianna Fail, 116.
Fine Gael, 116.
Flanigan, Brigid, 345.
Flanigan, Peter, 243, 270, 325, 344, 346, 353.
Fleming, Ian, 48.
Fletcher, Ambassador, 315.
Folger, 272, 273, 326.
Ford, (later President) Gerald, 308, 348, 352.
Ford, Betty, 308, 309.
Fowler, John, 302.
Freeman, Catherine, 188.
Freeman, John, 182, 189, 190, 191, 193, 272.
Fulbright, Senator Bill, 251, 274, 330.

G

Garment, Leonard, 345.
Garrett, Mrs Ethel, 312.
Gates, Tom, 312.
Gaulle, General de, 347.
George V, King, 52.
George VI, King, 52.
Geyelin, Phil, 90, 295, 348.
Gilligan, Governor, 246, 247.
Gladwyn, Lord, 290.
Goldwater, Senator, 325.
Goodhart, Professor, 344.

Gow, Mr, 101.
Graham, Kay, 210, 281, 294, 330.
Grant, Cary, 304.
Gray, Patrick, 279, 287.
Greenhill, Denis (later Lord), 301.
Grenadier Guards, 61.
Grey, Lady Jane, 56.
Grierson, Ronnie (later Sir), 250.
Grimond, Jo (later Lord), 344.
Guards Armoured Division, 11, 15, 32.
Guest, Mrs Polk (Lily), 194, 213.

H

Haig, General Alexander, 343.
Hailsham, Lord, 296.
Haldeman, 270, 325.
Halifax, Earl of, 192.
Harcourt, Lady, 74.
Harcourt, Lord, 73.
Harding, Gilbert, 190.
Harmsworth, Esmond (later 2nd Viscount Rothermere), 5.
Harmsworth, Sir Leicester, 272.
Harmsworth, Vere (later 3rd Viscount Rothermere), 39, 106.
Harriman, Averell, 236, 350.
Hartwell, Lady, 184.
Hasnie, Governor, 127, 129, 130, 131, 133, 136, 137, 138, 140, 141, 144.
Hasnie, Mrs Ismat, 133, 140.
Hatch End, 8, 12.
Heath, Edward, 115, 173, 174, 176, 183, 188, 225, 258, 267, 305.
Heathcoat-Amory, Derick (later Viscount Amory), 67.
Hepburn, Audrey, 351.
Hepworth, Barbara, 193, 222.
Heston, Charlton, 299.
Higgins, Terence, 243.
Hildegarde, 92.
HMS Rothesay, 338.

Hood, Lord, 86, 87.
Hope, Bob, 299.
Howe, Betty Deering, 42.
Humphrey, Hubert (later Vice-President), 88, 224.
Hussey, Captain Thomas, 22.

I

International Monetary Fund, 67, 76, 78, 86, 93, 107, 242, 243, 289.
Iveagh, Lord, 119.

J

Jacobson, Per, 76, 93, 107.
Jaeger, 266.
Jefferson, Brigadier Julian, 10, 11.
Johnson, Lyndon (later President), 88, 174, 239, 259, 309.

K

Kauffmann, John, 326.
Kemsley, Viscount, 23.
Kennedy Center, 221, 224, 245, 267, 269, 270, 298, 299, 332.
Kennedy, Edward, 215, 245, 260, 301, 312, 326.
Kennedy, Mrs Rose, 214, 223.
Kennedy, President, 88, 90, 99, 120, 125, 126, 181, 196, 215, 222, 242, 277, 321, 324, 327, 331, 348.
Kent, Duchess of, 87, 290.
Keogli, 329.
Khan of Kalabagh, Nawab, 144.
Khan, President Ayub, 134.
Khan, Sardar Barket, 135.
King, Cecil, 115, 170.
King, Martin Luther, 338.
Kissinger, Henry, 207, 223, 224, 232, 235, 237, 248, 250, 267, 299, 306, 310, 331, 332, 340,
341, 342, 350, 351, 352, 353.
Kleindienst, Richard G, 229, 287, 326, 342.
Kline, Ray, 237.
Korovushkin, Mr, 122.
Kritsky, Mrs, 146.
Krock, Arthur, 94.
Kudryavtsev, 152, 157, 159.

L

Lambert, Constant, 21.
Lambton, Tony, 302.
Legge-Bourke, Torie, 218, 227, 236, 259, 290, 294.
Lenin, 152, 153.
Lippmann, Walter, 90.
Lloyd, Selwyn, 91, 108, 114.
Long, Huey, 312.
Long, Russell, 331.
Long, Senator Russell, 312, 313.
Longworth, Mrs Nicholas, 120, 266, 267, 285, 294, 309, 311, 312.
Lucet, Monsieur, 252.
Ludmilla, 150, 153, 157, 159, 160.
Lutyens, 194.

M

Macauley, Mrs Edward, 201.
Macmillan, Harold, 59, 100, 101, 107, 114, 173.
Macmillan, Lady Dorothy, 59.
Makins, Dwight, 62.
Makins, Sir Roger (later Lord Sherfield), 62.
Malton, 16.
Margaret, HRH Princess, 230.
Marlborough, Duchess of, 43.
Marriott, Sir John, 23.
Martin, Hon William McChesney Jr, 121.
Mary, HM Queen, 20, 21.
Mathias, Senator, 344.

Matyenka, Mrs, 148, 149, 150.
Maudling, Reginald, 114, 126, 164, 170, 173.
Maxwell, John, 37.
McCarthy, Senator Eugene, 88, 229, 309.
McClellan, Senator, 316.
McCone, Mrs John, 92.
McCord, James W Jr, 329.
McGovern, Senator, 294.
McGrory, Mary, 199.
McKinley, President, 311.
McNamara, Bob, 232.
Meany, George, 229.
Meany, Mrs George, 301.
Meir, Golda, 341.
Menuhin, Yehudi, 268.
Menzies, Michael, 15.
Menzies, Robert, 50.
Mesta, Perle, 281, 282, 283.
Meyer, Lady Barbadee, 23, 24.
Millard, Sir Guy, 192.
Mills, Mrs Ogden, 45.
Minto, Lord, 140.
Mobutu, President, 208.
Moiseiwitsch, 20.
Monroney, Senator Mike, 238.
Montgomery, Field Marshal Viscount, 54, 310.
Moore, Henry, 115.
Moore, Wickcliffe, 312, 313, 331.
Morgan, J P, 41.
Morgan, John P II, 259.
Morgan, Junius, 41.
Mountbatten, Philip, 44.
Moynihan, Dr, 116, 117.
Munnings, Lady, 51.
Mwila, Madame, 259.
Myddelton, Fiona (later Lady Aird), 87.

N
Nash, Paul, 115.
New York Times, 198, 231.

Nixon, 280.
Nixon, Mrs, 344.
Nixon, Mrs Richard, 92, 196, 200, 206, 288, 303, 304, 308, 309, 330.
Nixon, President, 90, 182, 195, 196, 199, 202, 219, 224, 237, 238, 252, 258, 281, 294, 301, 306, 307, 309, 310, 324, 325, 326, 327, 332, 337, 339, 341, 343, 344, 345, 347, 348, 353, 354.
Northcliffe, Lord, 5, 20.

O
O'Brien, Leslie (later Lord), 257, 258.
O'Kelly, Sean, 119.
Odal, 329.
Onassis, Jackie Kennedy, 224, 280.
Ormsby-Gore, Sissy (later Lady Harlech), 111, 120, 125.
Ortona, Egidio, 355.
Ortona, Julia, 203.

P
Palmer, John, 284.
Pan Am, 191.
Parker, Lady, 55.
Peacock, Sir Edward, 38.
Pell, Senator Claiborne, 344.
Pentagon Papers, 231, 232, 287.
Percy, Senator, 339.
Perleman, Mr, 263, 264, 265.
Perry, Lord, 39.
Persia, Shah of, 172.
Pickup, Mr, 19.
Pindling, Mr, 315.
Pompidou, President, 253.
Poskonov, Alexei, 145, 146, 147, 150, 151, 153, 155, 159, 160, 161, 162, 163.
Poskonov, Maya, 146, 148, 160,

162.
Powell, Charles, 304, 317.
Powell, Enoch, 115.
Previn, André, 267, 268, 269.
Profumo, Jack, 246.

Q
Queen, HM The, 184, 198, 229, 232.

R
Ramsbotham, Sir Peter, 272, 287, 349.
Rasch, Richard (later Sir), 4.
Rasminsky, Lou, 163.
Reagan, Governor Ronald (later President), 260, 299, 320.
Reagan, Nancy, 261, 298.
Rees-Mogg, William (later Lord), 336, 337.
Reston, Sally, 274.
Reston, Scottie, 274.
Revelstoke, Lord, 175.
Reynolds, Alan, 115.
Richardson, Gordon (later Lord), 105, 342.
Richardson, Hon Elliot, 208, 339, 342.
Rickett, Sir Denis, 76.
Rickover, Admiral, 342.
Rippon, Geoffrey (later Lord), 216.
Rippon, Sarah, 217.
Robens, Lord, 171.
Rockefeller, Laurance, 223.
Rogers, Bill, 237, 305.
Rolls-Royce, 192.
Roosevelt, President Theodore, 267, 311.
Rootham, Jasper, 123, 151, 155.
Rose, Mr, 142.
Rowe, Mr, 332.
Rush, Ken, 346.
Rusk, Dean, 333.

Russell, Hon Edward, 271.
Ryan, Dr, 119.

S
Safire, Bill (William), 252.
Salisbury, 5th Marquess of, 61.
Sandys, Duncan (later Lord), 50.
Sargent, Sir Malcolm, 20.
Saxbe, Senator, 352.
Scarborough, 16, 19.
Schlesinger, Arthur, 125.
Schweitzer, Pierre-Paul, 242, 289.
Scott, Colonel Dave, 276.
Scott, Senator Hugh, 287.
Sevilla-Sacasa, Dr Guillermo, 203.
Shultz, George, 288, 289, 301, 313, 314, 326, 352.
Shultz, Obie, 301, 346, 353.
Simon, Bill, 346.
Simon, Carol, 353.
Simonds, Lady, 56.
Simonds, Lord, 59.
Sinatra, Frank, 235.
Sirica, Judge, 336.
Smith, Hon Gerard, 355.
Smith, Mrs Gerard, 201.
Smith, Mrs McCain, 216.
Smoak, Mrs, 303.
Soames, Christopher (later Lord), 49, 50, 58.
Soames, Emma, 216.
Soraya, Queen, 85.
St John Nursing Brigade, 8.
Stadens, von, 333.
Staff College, 13.
Stammers, Kay, 15.
Star, The, 212.
Stennis, Senator, 302, 343.
Stevens, John, 122.
Stiebel, Victor, 4.
Suggia, Guilhermina, 21.
Swat, The Wali of, 137, 138, 139.
Swinley Golf Club, 38.
Sykes, Lady, 316.

Sykes, Richard, 303.

T

Talmadge, Senator, 331.
Teapot Dome, 344.
Thatcher, Margaret, 311, 318, 352.
The Sunday Times, 218.
Thorold, Guy (later Sir), 68, 69.
Thorold, Mrs (later Lady), 74.
Times, 245.
Townsend, E Reginald, 113.
Toye, Colonel, 192.
Treasury, 32.
Trend, Burke (later Lord), 301, 332.
Trevelyan, Humphrey (later Lord), 115, 159.
Trevelyan, Lady, 146.
Tristar Airbus, 219.
Truman, President, 296, 327.
Tubman, President, 113.
Turner, Eva, 20.

V

Valera, President Eamon de, 117, 118, 119.
Vivian, 257, 258, 282.
Volcker, Paul, 274.

W

Walker, Peter, 224, 225, 290.
Ward, Hon Peter, 45.
Washington Post, 199, 207, 210, 231, 315.
Washington, Mayor Walter, 228, 338.
Weinberger, Hon Caspar, 298, 299, 311, 312, 313, 326, 347, 353, 354.
Weinberger, Jane, 353.
Westerham, 50.
Westmoreland, General, 319.

Wheeler, Charles, 188, 189.
Whilhelmina, Queen, 232.
White, Justice Byron, 231.
Williams, Ralph Vaughan, 21.
Wilson, Harold (later Lord), 111, 165, 170, 174, 176, 184, 185, 219, 239.
Wilson, Mary, 218.
Wilson, President of General Motors, 331.
Wilson, President Woodrow, 91.
Windsor, Duchess of, 44, 45.
Windsor, Duke of, 228, 328.
Wise, Mayor Wes, 277.
World Bank, 67, 70, 76, 78, 86, 89, 91, 111, 115, 243, 244, 288.
Worsley, Kate (later HRH Duchess of Kent), 87.
Wouk, Herman, 296.
Wright, Lady (Oliver), 272.

Y

Yom Kippur, 340.

Z

Zahedi, Ardeshir, 338.
Zuckerman, Solly (later Lord), 236, 342.